NEW YORK CITY BASEBALL

BOOKS BY HARVEY FROMMER

New York City Baseball: 1947–57 (1980)

The Great American Soccer Book (1980)

Sports Roots (1979)

Sports Lingo (1979)

The Martial Arts: Judo and Karate (1978)

A Sailing Primer (with Ron Weinmann) (1978)

A Baseball Century (1976)

New York

By HARVEY FROMMER

City Baseball

THE LAST

GOLDEN AGE:

1947–1957

Macmillan Publishing Co., Inc.

New York

Macmillan Publishing Co., Inc.
866 Third Avenue, New York, N.Y. 10022
Collier Macmillan Canada, Ltd.

Library of Congress Cataloging in Publication Data
Frommer, Harvey
    New York City baseball.
    1. Baseball—New York (City)—History. I. Title.
GV863.N72N483   796.357'64'097471   79-27628
ISBN 0-02-541700-2

First Printing 1980

Designed by Jack Meserole

Printed in the United States of America

Statistics on pp. 203–219 reprinted with permission from the Macmillan Baseball Encyclopedia, Third Revised Edition, edited by Joseph Reichler. Copyright © 1969, 1974, 1976, 1979 by Macmillan Publishing Co., Inc.

For the girl who became my wife,

who went with me to Ebbets Field

to see Danny McDevitt pitch in the

last year of the Brooklyn Dodgers

CONTENTS

ACKNOWLEDGMENTS

For listening, editing, shaping, criticizing, inspiring, rooting, tolerating—my wife, Myrna, with this, as with all my efforts, ranks first.

Old Dodger fans Trudy Mason and Ron Gabriel provided insights, time, and resources, and a large debt is owed to them.

Additionally, many thanks to those who kindly shared time and memories: Cal Abrams, Richie Ashburn, Red Barber, Buzzy Bavasi, Joel Berger, Roz Boyle, 'Willie' Brandt, Don Carney, Jack Carney, Jerry Coleman, Marvin Doblin, Jimmy Esposito, Joe Flynn, Sid Frigand, Carl Furillo, Jim Gilliam, Howard Golden, Tommy Holmes, Monte Irvin, Jack Lang, Tom LaSorda, Eddie Logan, Stan Lomax, Eddie Lopat, Sal Maglie, Jerry Martin, Johnny Mize, Mickey Morabito, Lou Napoli, Peter O'Malley, Walter O'Malley, Joe Pignatano, Pee Wee Reese, Arthur Richman, Rachel Robinson, Irving Rudd, Garry Schumacher, Jack Schwarz, Lee Scott, Dick Sisler, Duke Snider, Lou Soriano, Horace Stoneham, Valeda Stoneham, Jim Thomson, Bob Turley, Robert F. Wagner, Wes Westrum.

Office of the Borough President of Brooklyn, WPIX-TV, WOR-TV, New York Mets, New York Yankees, Los Angeles Dodgers, San Francisco Giants, Association of Professional Ball Players of America, Office of the Baseball Commissioner.

The team on the bench—who heard the words and listened lovingly—Jennifer, Freddy, and Ian.

And Bill Griffin of Macmillan, who adroitly managed the entire project from start to finish.

NEW YORK CITY BASEBALL

In those days we thought the three teams would go
on forever.   *— Former New York
City mayor,*
ROBERT F. WAGNER

The Move

On the fifth day of August, 1955, with the Brooklyn Dodgers in first place, fourteen games in the lead and driving to their third pennant in five years, their first world championship, a *New York Times* front-page story noted that the National League had granted permission for the scheduling of eight Dodger games for 1956 in Jersey City, New Jersey. Ticket prices at Roosevelt Stadium would be the same as at Ebbets Field: box seats, $3.00 and $2.50; reserved seats, $2.00; general admission, $1.25. The Dodgers charged 75¢ for an Ebbets Field bleacher seat, but there were no bleachers at Roosevelt Stadium.

Brooklyn Dodger president Walter O'Malley indicated that he had wanted a new playing site for the team since 1948. With six million dollars of his own available for the building of a stadium, he said he wanted New York City's aid to facilitate the acquisition of a site.

Abe Stark, president of the New York City Council, said, "I am quite perturbed about the O'Malley announcement. I would prefer to see all the Dodger games in Brooklyn where they have their natural roots and where they have done so well over the years." Dodger fans were less formal in their reaction. Some brought signs to Ebbets Field protesting the plan. "Leave us not go to Joisey," said one.

The Jersey City plan was to be followed by many months of bureaucratic committee meetings, grandiose blueprints, mistaken intentions, political pronouncements, rumors, threats, schemes, insults . . . and the move of the Dodgers of Brooklyn and the Giants of New York to California. The move was painful to many, but it was not without precedents.

1

In the years before World War II, Bill Veeck's St. Louis Browns planned to relocate in Los Angeles. The war intervened. When it ended, Veeck had moved on to Cleveland. The Browns remained temporarily in St. Louis. On March 18, 1953, in the first major league baseball franchise shift since 1900, the Braves of Boston became the Braves of Milwaukee. Boston was left without National League baseball for the first time since 1876—breaking the pattern of sixteen major league teams that had existed for fifty years. After thirteen home dates, the Milwaukee Braves drew more fans than the Boston Braves had attracted during the entire 1952 season. In 1954, the Browns finally moved from St. Louis, becoming the Baltimore Orioles. In 1955, the Athletics transferred from Philadelphia to Kansas City.

"Part of the impetus for the move of the Dodgers and the Giants was the transfer of these teams, especially Milwaukee, and the money they were making," notes former Brooklyn Dodgers publicist Irving Rudd. In 1955 and 1956, the Dodgers won the pennant. In both years the Braves outdrew the Dodgers by almost a million in home attendance. O'Malley feared that the Braves were stockpiling money for talent and that the Dodgers would be priced out of the market.

Another factor, Rudd believes, originated one balmy summer night in the early 1950s:

"O'Malley was leaving Ebbets Field after a night game," said Rudd. "He was in his chauffeur-driven Buick. He gets stuck in a traffic jam around what is now the site of the Meadowbrook Parkway. He's going east, and he sees a tremendous amount of cars going west. 'What's that?' he asks his chauffeur. 'That's all the people coming home from the trots, Mr. O'Malley.' Suddenly, O'Malley's ears perked. His eyes perked. He recognized this was a counterattraction. Harness racing had yet to reach its peak, its real peak. Bingo! Smack! Click! O'Malley was a shrewd man. He already saw the demographics. Hey, what were those 20,000 people doing there and not going to a ball game at Ebbets Field?"

Other interpretations were offered by O'Malley:

"The Dodgers had earned their nickname in the early days at Ebbets Field when the fans dodged trolleys to get to the ball park," said the man who smoked twenty expensive cigars a day. "We didn't have a real parking lot; there was only room for seven hundred cars. Now the public was on wheels. Each year we got mounting complaints because of the vandalism to automobiles. I was very much concerned about the future when my mother-in-law and my wife wouldn't go to Ebbets Field unescorted because of the hoodlums and purse snatchers. I began to become concerned about a location where women, who at the time made up thirty percent of the audience, were afraid to go to the ball park. Studies informed me that Ebbets Field would soon be an unsuitable place for night games. . . . The ball park was in need of repair. We'd patch something up and something else would need our attention. The cost was high and never ending."

"The scene at Ebbets Field," according to Stan Lomax, who covered many games there for the *Journal-American*, "was one of riding on the crest of a volcano. If they didn't get a new park, they would have had a riot or some terrible disturbance. Especially at the midweek games—there was too darn much drinking. There were narrow aisles, the seats were too close and you had a rough, tough bunch there. If somebody threw a bottle or stabbed someone—that's all that was needed—the dynamite was there . . . with too many people in too small an area."

Despite the problems, O'Malley claimed he thought something could be done "to drastically improve or replace the ball park on the same site. I went to Norman Bel Geddes, the famed architect, and he told me that such a new stadium would be a financial impossibility. Ebbets Field occupied a city block—to extend it in any direction was virtually impossible."

On October 4, 1955, what many thought was a baseball impossibility took place. Southpaw Johnny Podres won the final game of the World Series, and the Dodgers, after five frustrating attempts, finally defeated the New York Yankees to become world champions. "They must never leave Brooklyn," announced John Cashmore, Brooklyn borough president.

On October 6, after one of the most riotous celebrations in Brooklyn history, O'Malley said, "Certainly, the matter is out of our hands, but I don't see how anyone could want the Dodgers to leave Brooklyn . . . we don't ever want to go anywhere else. I am now more confident than ever that something will turn up that will enable us to build a new home befitting world champions."

Mayor Wagner had many meetings with O'Malley seeking ways to keep the Dodgers in Brooklyn. Wagner's life had been a political one and also one deeply involved with baseball. "My father was a United States senator," said Wagner, "and a great ball fan. He used to lecture me about reading the sports pages. 'Why don't you read the editorial pages, they're much better,' he would say. He knew the pitching and batting averages better than I did. 'How do you happen to know all the averages?' I asked him. 'Well,' he said, 'I just peruse the papers a little bit.' But he was a dyed-in-the-wool baseball fan. That made me the same. So there was a fan's interest at work in my dealing with O'Malley. . . . Walter was an amusing fellow. He was bright. He was a good story teller, but shrewd as could be. We had some pleasant times together, but he was never going to give up anything. He was tough."

"The O'Malley," as he was called, was born on October 9, 1903, in New York City. A 1926 graduate of the University of Pennsylvania (he was a fraternity brother of Stan Lomax), he received a law degree from Fordham in 1930. "I got involved with the Dodgers when I discovered it was pleasant and good business to bring clients to the park." A director and stockholder of the Dodgers in 1932, legal representative in 1943, part owner in 1944, and then president and principal owner in 1950, O'Malley grew more and more restive as politicians procrastinated.

O'Malley knew what he wanted but didn't know if he would be able to get it. He had a vision for the first domed stadium on twenty-three acres of land in Brooklyn's downtown commercial center at the terminus of the Long Island Railroad. "It was at the intersection of Atlantic and Flatbush Avenues," he said, "the only site in the city where the three subway lines converged. It would have solved two problems—the molesting of women and the parking situation."

Stan Lomax, in addition to reporting, was a popular baseball radio voice of the time. He said, "Down deep inside I've always been a

Brooklyn Dodger fan. I remember when I was a kid sitting for twenty-five cents near the left field foul line at Ebbets Field and watching Zack Wheat play in front of me. He was God in Brooklyn. I had to love the damn Dodgers. On a clear day with the wind blowing from where I lived on Lenox Road, I could hear the cheering at Ebbets Field.

"The Atlantic Avenue site was an ideal spot for them. All of Brooklyn and Long Island could have come in by train. It could've been done and done well, and Brooklyn could've been the damndest sports town in the world which it was and isn't any more, but I don't think the politicians were ready for it."

In January 1956, the office of the borough president of Brooklyn announced that a Site Selection Committee designated to deal with the problems of the Dodgers had not yet had an official meeting. "The committee has six months in which to act," the announcement continued. "Results will be available in early summer."

A Sports Center Authority Bill was put before the state legislature by Mayor Wagner in February 1956. Aimed at implementing the acquisition of the Atlantic Avenue site by the Dodgers, the plan became a political football. Upstate legislators argued against it claiming it would not benefit the whole state, only Brooklyn. New York City lawmakers engaged in spirited debate on the merits of the bill.

Early summer of 1956 was tinged with all types of ironies, and the feeling that there was no sense of urgency to do anything about the finding of a new home for the Dodgers. The "Joisey Bums" played eight games in Roosevelt Stadium, selling out the twenty-five-thousand-seat ball park each time. In the autumn of 1950, the Jersey City Giants had played their final game in Roosevelt Stadium. The former number-one farm team of the New York Giants had drawn just 69,000 fans for the entire 1950 season. In 1941, the Jersey City Giants had recorded an Opening Day crowd of 61,164 to set a minor league attendance record. Now O'Malley's "road show" had placed the Dodgers in the former ball park of the former top minor league team of Brooklyn's arch rivals, the Giants. And the use of the Roosevelt Stadium facility would become the launching pad for the move of the Giants and the Dodgers to California. Another ironic touch was that

Brooklyn won each of its Roosevelt Stadium games except one. That one loss was to the Giants. A Willie Mays home run enabled Johnny Antonelli to edge Don Newcombe, 1–0.

In midsummer 1956, the New York State Legislature created a Brooklyn Sports Authority to deal with the problems of a new playing site for the Dodgers. "We are at a standstill," said Charles J. Mylod, head of the group. "We know what we want to do, but the budget for the authority has not been approved."

In October of 1956, the Dodgers announced the sale of Ebbets Field to a Brooklyn real estate developer. "We will be able to play at Ebbets Field through 1959 if it is desired," a Dodger spokesman said. "The lease insures us of a home until a new stadium can be built." The Montreal Royals ball park, the home of the top farm team of the Dodgers, was also sold.

The sale of Ebbets Field was followed by the sale of the player who symbolized the power and verve of the Dodgers. New York City baseball fans—especially Brooklyn fans—had come to expect almost anything. But the sale of Jackie Robinson on December 13, 1956, to the hated "enemy" New York Giants was just too bizarre to be comprehended. For on May 15, 1956, Sal Maglie had been picked up on waivers from Cleveland after pitching impressively in an exhibition game against the Dodgers at Roosevelt Stadium. The former "most hated opposition pitcher" won thirteen games and helped the Dodgers win the 1956 pennant. Maglie in a Brooklyn Dodger uniform pitching to Jackie Robinson in a New York Giant uniform evoked an image bordering on the absurd.

The image never registered. Pitcher Dick Littlefield and the $35,000 ticketed for the Dodgers for Robinson remained with the Giants. Robinson waited until January, and in an exclusive article in *Look* magazine announced his retirement from baseball. "My legs are gone and I know it. The ball club needs rebuilding. It needs youth. It doesn't need me. It would be unfair to the Giant owners to take their money."

Rachel Robinson placed Jackie's decision in perspective. "My husband was a person of extreme loyalty, of devotion to family and to team. A person like that can't make changes very easily. He had already made up his mind that he would not play for any other team but the Dodgers. He just knew that. That was coupled with the fact that he had been trying to find his way out of baseball for two years before he was traded. The last couple of years, he had trouble getting ready for spring training, getting in shape . . . it could just never have been."

Giant owner Horace Stoneham wrote to Robinson: "All of us wish you well, success and happiness, but I can't help thinking it would've been nice to have had you on our side for a year or two."

Stoneham's feelings were motivated by emotions and a generous dash of financial considerations. Robinson's legs may have been gone, but he was still a drawing card. Placing one of Brooklyn's living legends in a New York Giants' uniform—even for a year or two—would have been a financial windfall for Stoneham, a further boost to the rabid rivalry of the Dodgers and Giants. Just how significant a factor the rivalry of the two teams was to the Giants is reflected in this attendance statistic from July 10, 1955: After their twenty-fourth Polo Grounds date, the Giants had drawn 513,476. Seven of those dates had been with the Dodgers accounting for an attendance of 220,739.

During the early months of 1957, O'Malley visited Los Angeles for talks with Mayor Norris Paulson and County Supervisor Kenneth Hahn. The talks focused on the feasibility of the Dodgers moving to California. Reporters noted that the Dodger owner had acquired a forty-four passenger plane. "It would prove very useful," he said, "if the team decided to leave Brooklyn."

"It was quite obvious at that point in time that if the Dodgers would go," recalls Mayor Wagner, "the Giants would go too."

A reporter asked Horace Stoneham, "What will happen if the Dodgers move to California?"

"We will have to move too," was the Giant owner's reply.

"What about the kids?" the reporter asked.

"I've seen a lot of the kids," said Stoneham, "but I haven't seen too many of their fathers at the Polo Grounds lately."

Accounts of that time depict Stoneham as being verbally sandbagged by O'Malley into considering the move to California. "I explained to Horace," O'Malley is quoted as saying, "that there were four million people living in the nine counties around San Francisco, and that if we took our rivalry to California, it would flourish as never before."

Stoneham was not pushed. He jumped. Even with the rivalry, the Giants were suffering at the box office, playing in a rapidly deteriorating neighborhood. Attendance at the Polo Grounds in 1956 was 629,179. Three years before it had been double that amount. By 1957, what had been a lucrative and constant source of revenue—season boxholders—had decreased considerably, to about 600. The portly Giant owner reported his team had made a profit in only two of the past eight seasons.

By the spring of 1957, O'Malley and Stoneham had spent much time negotiating with New York state, city, and borough officials. "We have done our part," the Dodger owner said. "We would like to remain in Brooklyn: There is a short time before we could be forced to an irrevocable step to commit the Dodgers elsewhere." Stoneham insisted that "the maintenance of our rivalry with the Dodgers is of prime importance in anything we do."

A fantastic vision for a new home for the Giants was developed by Hulan Jack, borough president of Manhattan. His office introduced a plan for a park to be built on stilts near the railroad yards in midtown Manhattan along the Hudson River. The proposed stadium would seat 110,000, garage 20,000 automobiles, and accommodate a thirty-story office building.

Parks Commissioner Robert Moses suggested sites for a new park for the Dodgers. "He wanted us to consider a location near the Brooklyn Battery Tunnel," recalled O'Malley. "I told him that's a good spot for you. Everyone has to pay you a toll—but with a cemetery on one side and the bay on the other, it's not too good a site for us. It's even worse than Ebbets Field."

O'Malley was equally unreceptive to the Moses suggestion of a site in Flushing Meadows, Queens—the present location of Shea Stadium. "Going there," O'Malley snapped, "was no different, in a sense, than going to Jersey City or L.A. You would not be the Brooklyn Dodgers if you were not in Brooklyn. I told him that if I were going to move from Brooklyn to Queens, I might just as well move to the West Coast. It wouldn't be the Brooklyn Dodgers in Queens."

By April of 1957, the park on stilts for the Giants, the tug of war over the Atlantic Avenue site for the Dodgers, rumors that the Giants were headed to Minneapolis, to St. Paul, to Houston, the placing and receiving of hundreds of transcontinental phone calls by O'Malley and Stoneham, the vituperative remarks of New York City politicians aimed at Mayor Norris Paulson of Los Angeles and Mayor George Christopher of San Francisco escalated the inevitable. Photographs of "The O'Malley" touring the city of Angels in a helicopter prompted one Brooklyn wit to remark, "Maybe that bum's lookin' for a ball park in the sky?" As things would turn out, the comment was not that far off.

"I was very good friends with Norris Paulson," said Mayor Wagner, "and he was telling me a little more than Walter knew he was telling me. Walter was protesting he wanted to stay in Brooklyn. Norris said he had him just about signed up out there."

In May of 1957, at a special meeting of the National League in Chicago, the vote was in the affirmative to grant permission for the Dodgers and the Giants to move if they wished to. "Previously they were unable to make any definite commitments," said National League president Warren Giles. "Now they are free to make a decision one way or the other."

The National League vote did not surprise Wagner. "Walter had the cards right from the start," he said of the Dodger owner, who was also part owner of the Brooklyn Borough Gas Company, the New York Subway Advertising Company, and the Long Island Railroad. "He had the ball club. He had the influence in the league. I'm sure he knew well that there would be no opposition from them to his moving the Dodgers out of Brooklyn."

In June of 1957, O'Malley guaranteed a playing site for the Dodgers in Los Angeles. He purchased the Pacific Coast League franchise of the Chicago Cubs and their Wrigley Field Stadium in Los Angeles. Allegedly the transaction was agreed upon at the annual New York Baseball Writer's Dinner. O'Malley, it was reported, passed a note to Cub owner P.K. Wrigley, seated next to him on the dais.

"How much do you want for Los Angeles with the ball park?"

"One million," Wrigley wrote back.

"Sold!"

In July it was Horace Stoneham who was 'sold' on moving out of New York City. "I will recommend to the board of directors of the New York Giants," he announced, "that we leave and go to San Francisco after this season." In all his public statements, O'Malley kept insisting that his roots were in Brooklyn and that he desired to remain in Brooklyn. One columnist wrote, "The O'Malley has the longest roots known to man."

The owner of the Dodgers and the owner of the Giants presented radically different public images. O'Malley came across as a political wheeler-dealer, a smoker of big, long cigars, a man who had greased the way for the exile of Branch Rickey to Pittsburgh. A roly-poly type, his thick eyebrows and accentuated speech pattern suggested the kind of person who would foreclose mortgage payments on a widow and four children. Stoneham was quieter, gentler. He looked like an out of uniform Santa Claus. O'Malley was the calculating initiator of the scheme to move two New York City traditions; Stoneham was a naive follower. Giant fans generally were resigned to the move. Dodger fans fought it. "The O'Malley" was their rallying point.

Thousands wore blue and white buttons that said, "Keep the Dodgers in Brooklyn." Rallies at Brooklyn's Borough Hall became a weekly event. Pickets would march in front of Ebbets Field and 215 Montague Street, the main office of the Dodgers. O'Malley had once called them "the most loyal fans in the world." Always vocal, always unrestrained, the fans of the Dodgers were showing the world their loyalty.

Kids dressed in baseball uniforms and carried printed signs produced by adults. "Mr. Moses, Don't You Dare Take Our Dodgers Out Of Brooklyn." "Our Answer To Queens and To L.A. Is NO! They Stay in Brooklyn." "Bob Moses: Our Answer To Your Queens Site is NO!" "Commissioner Moses: 3 Million People Of Brooklyn Say NO! (To Queens (Or L.A.) Or Anywhere Else!)" "Brooklyn Is The Dodgers. The Dodgers ARE Brooklyn."

They marched in what is now Cadman Plaza Park in front of Brooklyn's Borough Hall just a few blocks from the main headquarters of the Dodgers. The uniforms the youth wore were baggy; "Cadets" and "Eagles" and "Panthers" were written across their shirt fronts. Most of the kids wore blue Dodger caps with the letter "B" in white centered on the front.

Adults smiled in support as they watched the procession from behind police barricades. Many of the men in the crowd wore gray fedoras and print ties. And in the lapels of their wide suits, some had the blue and white button: "Keep the Dodgers In Brooklyn."

The noise level of the rallies carried into the municipal buildings that flanked one side of Court Street and into the office buildings on the other side. Windows were opened just as they had been from time to time over the years to watch the pennant-winning Dodgers parade.

There was no violence. Blue uniformed New York City policemen with white gloves were positioned at the perimeters of the crowd, smiling and sympathizing with the demonstrators.

"I remember the songs, the rallies, the petitions, the furor in Brooklyn," said Ron Gabriel, back then a rabid young Dodger fan and today the president of the Brooklyn Dodgers' fan club. "There was one rally on the steps of Brooklyn's Borough Hall that stands out. A lot of politicians and movie stars were there. People wore blue and white pins that said, 'Keep the Dodgers in Brooklyn.' Borough President John Cashmore did most of the talking. Each of the speakers ended with the lines: 'That's baseball, that's the Dodgers, that's Brooklyn.'

"It was time of petitions. The real fans used to put in time getting signatures on these long sheets of paper that were white with blue lines. There was room on each petition for about a hundred signatures. If you just stood at a subway station during the rush hours you could get a couple of dozen sheets filled out. My parents objected to my staying out late getting the signatures. . . . I had to lose my allowance, but it was worth it."

Newspaper and magazine articles provided sports fans with in-depth examinations of the off-the-field scrambling to keep the Dodgers and Giants in New York City. On July 22, 1957, Parks Commissioner Robert Moses published an article in *Sports Illustrated* that further revved up the political debate. The article was entitled: "Robert Moses and the Battle of Brooklyn."

". . . For years, Walter and his chums have kept us dizzy and confused. First everything was geared to rapid transit customers, then it was all for the carriage trade. On one day they pictured a vast modern arena, putting Rome to shame, with tier on tier of seats and seas of eager, downturned faces. The next day they conjured up an outdoor studio occupying little space, without stands, bleachers, parking fields or people, and with the players lightly doffing their hats to an unseen audience that is far away from weather, oafs, oaths, hecklers and bottle throwers, buoyed up on home cushions, chewing chocolate nuts, drawing cigarette smoke lazily through a million filters or lapping up somebody's dry beer and rising only to feed a meter or turn a closed-circuit gadget. . . . meanwhile, having hypnotized New York, these gentlemen continue mysterious negotiations with other less goofy cities.

"It is claimed that Brooklyn would not be Brooklyn without the beloved Bums. The same thing was said about the *Brooklyn Eagle*, which nevertheless folded. That was a damn shame, and so, in some respects, would be the departure of the Dodgers, although a new location elsewhere on Long Island could hardly be classed a tragedy. I shall leave it to people closer to politics and public opinion to prove what proportion of the three million and more residents of Brooklyn really care a great deal in view of the slim attendance at Ebbets Field, the convenience of television, etc. Certainly the political retina will be less clouded after Election Day. Unfortunately it looks as if the decision will have to be made before then . . ."

On September 12, the old Dodger, Harry (Cookie) Lavagetto, signed a one-year contract extension to manage the Washington Senators. Cookie had succeeded another old Dodger, Charlie Dressen, in May of 1956 as manager of the Senators. While Lavagetto was rejoicing over his new contract, financier Nelson A. Rockefeller announced his interest in attempting to keep the Dodgers in Brooklyn.

On September 14, the New York Yankees increased their American League lead to six games with a victory over the second place Chicago White Sox. Mickey Mantle hammered a homer and a triple. That day New York City Corporation counsel Peter Campbell Brown ruled that the city had the right to condemn the Flatbush Avenue site for a new home for the Dodgers, provided the area was part of a general slum clearance program. Brown's ruling intensified the political debate.

Queens Borough President James A. Lundy said, "It would be like building a baseball stadium in Times Square." Lundy argued in favor of the Flushing Meadow Park site in Queens. The city owned the land, he said, and there would not be a need for condemnation or the sale of the property at a markdown to private business.

City Controller Lawrence Gerosa and City Council President Abe Stark also opposed Brown's ruling. "Why should the city suffer a financial loss by condemning private property and then selling it to the Dodgers?" Stark argued.

The Giants made their decision before Election Day. Less than a month after the Moses article, the Board of Directors of the team voted to move the Giants to San Francisco. The one dissenting vote was cast by M. Donald Grant. The iconoclastic stockbroker would persist in his efforts to sustain National League baseball in New York City and would become the controversial chairman of the board of the New York Mets.

On the field, the Dodgers and the Giants played listless baseball, the inevitable result of all the threats, the anger, the aborted plans, mistaken turns, and fantastic schemes that had made New York City National League baseball a roller coaster ride of hope and frustration for everyone concerned.

"I was coming to the end of my career in 1957," recalls Pee Wee Reese, "and so were others on the team. Our club was in pretty bad shape and some of us had picked up injuries. There was talk, of course, among the players about the move, but I thought they'd build the stadium. I even made a small bet with Don Zimmer which I lost. I never thought New York City would let the Dodgers and Giants go; why in Brooklyn, in that little ball park, we drew a million every year. The move completely surprised me and most of the other players."

September 1957 was a painful time for Dodger and Giant fans and players. Each day brought the end of the New York Giants and the Brooklyn Dodgers just a little closer.

On September 1, the last game the two teams ever played against each other at Ebbets Field took place. The Giants won. A week later, in a half-empty Polo Grounds, the Giants nipped the Dodgers, 3–2, in the last game the two teams ever played against each other in the big park under the shadow of Coogan's Bluff.

On September 16, a day Mayor Wagner moved New York City and New Jersey closer together by giving general approval to the concept of a rapid transit link between the two areas, the schism between Los Angeles and New York City widened.

The City Council of Los Angeles voted 11–3 to open official negotiations with the Dodgers. "We are at the crossroads," Mayor Norris Paulson shouted during the City Council debates. "Are we going to be a bush league town or are we going to be major league in everything? If we delay this, it goes out to the world that the city of Los Angeles has lost its guts."

Mayor Wagner huddled with Nelson Rockefeller at City Hall, attempting to block official moves by Los Angeles to get the Dodgers. In the City of Angels, the Board of Supervisors voted unanimously the sum of $2,740,000 to provide access roads to the site of Chavez Ravine. That same day the United Press reported, "There is nothing settled on the move of the Giants to San Francisco." Dodger fans received faint hope from another UP report that claimed the Cleveland Indians were interested in moving to Los Angeles.

On September 17, at a Gracie Mansion meeting, a new Rockefeller plan to keep the Dodgers in Brooklyn was submitted to Walter O'Malley. No information as to what the plan consisted of was revealed. One bit of conjecture was that O'Malley was willing to pay $10 million toward purchasing the Atlantic Avenue site and constructing a new ball park, that the city was to sell the site for much less than the condemnation price, that the Dodgers, the Long Island Railroad, and Nelson Rockefeller would pick up the difference. Another variation was that the site would be sold to the Dodgers at the condemnation price and Rockefeller would lend the Dodgers the difference between the price and what O'Malley considered "a reasonable figure."

On September 18, O'Malley said, "The offer has merit," but explained that he would defer action only until October 1—the date by which he said he had to notify the National League if the Dodgers were going to move to the West Coast. "I can't wait too much longer," he emphasized, "since what is needed is nine votes of the Board of Estimate and we haven't seen them yet."

Wagner feels "that O'Malley was playing it both ways. He wanted to stay. His roots were in Brooklyn. Walter liked the land in the Atlantic Avenue area because he looked at the suburbs as a great source of fans. So many of the Dodger fans lived on the Island. He thought they'd come right in on the train to a new stadium . . . but the temptation in California was so great, he couldn't resist it."

Harold McClellan, a major negotiator to bring the Dodgers to California, underscored the temptation. "There will be no hard feelings," he said on September 19, "if the Dodgers decided it would be good business to stay in Brooklyn, but sound business judgment will persuade Mr. O'Malley that the Los Angeles offer is more attractive."

On September 21, a front-page *New York Times* headline said: "Rockefeller Bid To Help Dodgers Ends in Failure." The story explained that Rockefeller had made a new proposal in which he expressed a willingness to pay up to $3 million for the Atlantic Avenue area land. O'Malley's response was that any proposal involving $3 million "priced the Dodgers out."

Wagner's view of Rockefeller's efforts is that "they were a little more talk than anything else. His offers were little more than a drop in the bucket. You not only had to clear the land, you had to move the markets that were there, settle litigation, and then build."

There was a rally on September 21, and another rally on September 22, the day the last home run was hit at Ebbets Field; it was one of a pair recorded by Duke Snider in a 7–3 win over Philadelphia. There were no major negotiations among the politicians. The inevitable had arrived.

"Had it all happened five years later," Wagner observed, "the outcome would probably have been different. The idea of municipalities building stadiums or helping in the building of stadiums was not really politically possible in New York City in 1957. History moves in strange ways. It cuts into the routine, the very routine of things." The changing demographics and the invention of the jet had cut into the very routine of the history of the Dodgers of Brooklyn and the Giants of New York.

On September 24, 1957, in the forty-fourth season of Ebbets Field, the Dodgers played their final game in the little ball park. Only 6,702 attended. The Brooklyn Dodger theme song was piped over the public address system:

> *Oh, follow the Dodgers*
> *Follow the Dodgers around*
> *The infield, the outfield,*
> *The catcher and that fellow on the mound*
>
> *Oh, the fans will come a running*
> *When the Dodgers go a gunning*
> *For the pennant that we're fighting for today.*
>
> *The Dodgers keep swinging*
> *And the fans will keep singing*
> *Follow the Dodgers, hooray.*
>
> *There's a ball club in Brooklyn*
> *The team they call 'Dem Bums,'*
> *But keep your eyes right on them*
> *And watch for hits and runs . . .*

Pee Wee Reese paused at the top of the dugout steps, waved his right arm, and nine white- and blue-clad Dodgers with the letter "B" on their blue caps trotted out to their positions on the real green grass. The crowd roared.

The final Brooklyn Dodger lineup at Ebbets Field was makeshift. Gino Cimoli was the center fielder, flanked by Elmer Valo in right field and Sandy Amoros in left. Gil Hodges played part of the game at first base and part of the game at third, alternating with Pee Wee Reese, who played third base, and Jim Gentile who got in a few innings at first base. Don Zimmer was the shortstop. Jim Gilliam played second base. Roy Campanella caught most of the game. Joe Pignatano relieved him with a couple of innings left. Danny McDevitt was the Brooklyn pitcher. The game lasted two hours and three minutes as the Dodgers nipped the Pirates, 3–0. Gil Hodges, the last Dodger to bat in Ebbets Field, struck out. Gladys Gooding played dozens of old sentimental songs on the organ. But the theme song of the day seemed to be that old favorite, "Say It Isn't So."

Public address announcer Tex Rickards was formal to the end. "Please do not go on the playing field at the end of the game," he announced in his resonant voice as he had done thousands of times before. "Use any exit that leads to the street."

When the final out was recorded, Gladys Gooding began to play "May The Good Lord Bless You And Keep You." She was interrupted by the recording of the Dodger theme song: "Follow The Dodgers." When the record was completed, she switched to "Auld Lang Syne." It was the last music heard at Ebbets Field.

"Then the fans tore up the place," recalls groundskeeper Jimmy Esposito. "They grabbed pieces of grass, home plate. There was no way of controlling them. We just let them go."

Jack Carney remembers the final post-game TV show. "All those who had been associated with televising the games were there, and they were crying." Happy Felton, the rotund host of the "Talk To The Stars" program, presented his Dodger uniform to Carney. "I went to the back," says Carney. "I put on the uniform. The camera panned down to my feet. I didn't have any shoes or socks on. I didn't have a team anymore. And I was crying."

The grounds crew later raked the infield smooth, covered up the mound and home plate.

Ebbets Field would linger on until the morning of February 23, 1960, when a two-ton ball would cave in the roof of the visiting dugout, readying the ground for a housing project.

The Dodgers moved on to Philadelphia for their last road trip. "That whole last week was slow death," said Jack Lang, who covered the end of the team. "All those players who had been so brilliant were now getting old, barely managing to win. They had won the pennant in 1956 in what was the last great gasp of the Brooklyn Dodgers and the guy that won it for them was Sal Maglie."

Seventeen days earlier, the old Giant, the former Dodger, Sal Maglie, hurled the New York Yankees to a three-hit, 5–0 triumph over the Cleveland Indians. It was his twenty-fifth career shutout, his first in the American League, his first Yankee Stadium start since October 8, 1956—a day he pitched brilliantly for the Dodgers only to lose to Don Larsen, who pitched a perfect game.

By September 29, the Yankees had clinched another pennant. The

Dodgers had clinched third place and were in Philadelphia in Connie Mack Stadium for their last game of the season, the last game the Dodgers of Brooklyn would ever play. Less than ten thousand watched the Dodgers defeat the Phillies, 2–1, in a game that lasted one hour and fifty-eight minutes. That final Dodger batting order consisted of: Gilliam 2b, Cimoli cf, Furillo rf, Hodges 1b, Kennedy lf, Jackson 3b, Zimmer ss, Pignatano c, Craig p. Roy Campanella was an unsuccessful pinch hitter and Sandy Koufax, who won five of nine decisions in 1957, pitched one scoreless inning of relief.

Sunday, September 29, was also the date of the last game of the New York Giants. Before the game ex-Yankee Tommy Henrich, who had been a Giant coach in 1957, resigned. "I don't think it would be fair to my family to uproot them," he said.

On that day, twenty bands performed and 150,000 paraded as the Milwaukee Braves prepared to fly to New York City to meet the Yankees in the World Series. Casey Stengel's team had won its eighth pennant in nine years. Milwaukee had recorded its first National League pennant.

At the Polo Grounds, the home of the Giants since 1891, some of the 11,606 fans brought banners. One banner proclaimed: "Stay Team, Stay. Go Horace, Go." Horace Stoneham had seen his first major league game on Decoration Day, 1912. "The pitcher was Christy Mathewson," he said, "and the catcher was Chief Meyers. We drove up the dirt speedway used by people with sulkies to the entrance behind home plate." Horace Stoneham viewed the last game of the Giants from the dressing room in the center field clubhouse.

Manager Bill Rigney had nervously wandered about the dressing room before the start of the game singing a popular song of the day, "Bon Voyage." He listed in the starting lineup as many of the players from the 1951 and 1954 Giant pennant-winning team as were available: O'Connel 2b, Mueller rf, Mays cf, Rhodes lf, Thomson 3b, Lockman 1b, Spencer ss, Westrum c, Antonelli p.

The final home run—and the last run scored at the Polo Grounds —was recorded in the top of the ninth inning by Johnny Powers, a rookie Pirates' outfielder.

When Dusty Rhodes dribbled the ball to short for the final New

York Giant out, the clock atop the old clubhouse in center field read 4:35. The game was over. The Giants lost to the Pirates, 9–1, and New York City lost its oldest baseball institution.

"When the last out was made," Westrum recalls, "there was an uproar. People grabbed sod, seats; they were all over the place grabbing for souvenirs." A few scavengers made off with the awning over the right field bull pen. A youngster stole second base; others dug up home plate. "I thought I'd never return to the Polo Grounds," said Westrum, whose playing career ended in that last game of the New York Giants, "but I did when the Mets came along." In 1962 and 1963, the San Francisco Giants played eighteen games against the New York Mets at the Polo Grounds. It was the interim home of the new National League team, before they moved to the site in Flushing Meadows, Queens, suggested to Walter O'Malley as a playing area for the Dodgers.

This last day, a band of former Giant rooters gathered under the clubhouse in center field. Set to the music of "Farmer In The Dell," they sang over and over:

> *We hate to see you go.*
> *We hate to see you go.*
> *We hope to hell you never come back.*
> *We hate to see you go . . .*

Old Giants Frankie Frisch, Jack Doyle, Moose McCormick, Rube Marquard, Sid Gordon, Sal Maglie, and Monte Irvin tarried a while after the game and then, grudgingly and misty eyed, left the Polo Grounds. Mrs. John McGraw, widow of the legendary former Giant manager, had watched the last game of the New York Giants with the team's former heroes. "It would have broken John's heart," she said, holding the bouquet of American Beauty roses given to her in the pre-game ceremonies. "I prefer to regard this as just the end of another season."

Three musicians gathered in the visiting team's bull pen when the Polo Grounds was virtually empty. One had a trumpet. The others carried trombones. They played and sang "The Giant Victory March." The tune was composed in 1946 and originated from Horace Stoneham's desire for musical competition with the organ playing of

Gladys Gooding of the Dodgers. The song was played over the Polo Grounds loudspeaker after each New York Giants victory:

> *We're calling all fans*
> *All you Giant ball fans*
> *Come watch the home team*
> *Going places 'round those bases*
> *Cheer for your favorites*
> *Out at Coogan's Bluff*
> *Come Watch those Polo*
>   *Grounders*
> *Do their stuff*

While the trio performed for the dozen or so spectators who formed their sad audience, a group of workmen began to dig up sixty pounds of Polo Grounds turf. Nine inches deep and two feet square, the sod was presented the next day to San Francisco Mayor George Christopher; it was to be retained and ultimately planted in the outfield of the new ball park of the Giants in San Francisco.

New York Giants publicist Garry Schumacher helped select the area for the transplanting of the Polo Grounds turf. "If all the people who claimed they were there for the final game of the New York Giants were actually there," he said, "we wouldn't have moved in the first place."

The Milwaukee Braves—the team that had moved from Boston in the first major league franchise shift since 1900—battled the New York Yankees in the World Series on October 7. On that date, the Los Angeles City Council voted 10–4 to allow the Brooklyn Dodgers to move to their city. The Dodgers were given the major part of a tract of land called Chavez Ravine. About a mile from Los Angeles City Hall, close by Chinatown, Chavez Ravine was a hillside of tangled weeds and old houses at the main juncture of the city's radial freeways. The city of Los Angeles was to allocate $2 million for preliminary grading; the county would pay $3 million for access roads to the new stadium the Dodgers would build that would cost $10 million, seat fifty thousand, and have parking for twenty-four thousand cars. The days of the trolley Dodgers belonged to another time. Wrigley Field, the twenty-two-thousand-seat PCL park, was given to the city of Los Angeles by the Dodgers. Oil revenues—if any—were to be placed in a trust fund to be supervised by the Dodgers and the city for youth recreation. "If I'm going to be a carpetbagger," quipped O'Malley, "then I might as well carry the satchel."

At 4:00 P.M. on October 8, 1957, the official end of the Dodgers of Brooklyn was announced. The site of the announcement was ironic. In the World Series press room of the posh Waldorf-Astoria Hotel in Manhattan, publicity representatives of the Dodgers and the National League read prepared statements. Dodger President Walter O'Malley and National League Commissioner Warren Giles were not present.

The statement read for Warren Giles was upbeat and personal:

"The National League has again demonstrated it is a professional organization. The transfer of the Giants and the Dodgers means that two great municipalities are to have major league baseball without depriving another city of that privilege. The National League and I personally will miss New York, but it is human nature to want to reach new horizons. We look forward to 1958 when National League baseball will be played on the West Coast."

The Dodger statement was terse and businesslike:

"In view of the action of the Los Angeles City Council yesterday and in accordance with the resolution of the National League made October 1, the stockholders and directors of the Brooklyn baseball club have today met and unanimously agreed that necessary steps be taken to draft the Los Angeles territory."

Underscoring the changing times and the changing demographics was the release on that October day of figures from a special census of the population of New York City. The report noted a population decline of 96,486 from 1950. New York City's population was now 7,795,471—down 1.2 percent from 1950. Loss in state aid would be just one of the implications of the census for New York City.

Mayor Robert F. Wagner, who had invested much official and unofficial time struggling to keep the Dodgers and Giants from moving, responded to a question at a press conference regarding O'Malley's "good faith" in the negotiations: "I can only say that in my conversations with him he said he had no commitments, and I have to take the man's word."

Dodger fans did not. In the streets of Brooklyn, O'Malley was burned in effigy. Ebbets Field and the Dodgers' office at 215 Montague Street were picketed. Fans carried signs that said: 'O'Malley—Brooklyn's Hitler," "O—Biggest Bum of Them All."

On October 10, 1957, the Milwaukee Braves defeated the New York Yankees, 5–0 to win the World Series. New York City had lost two baseball teams and now for the first time since 1949 was without a world championship baseball team. On that day, the Fifth Avenue Association celebrated its fiftieth anniversary, and Mayor Wagner rode in the parade and served as Grand Marshal.

Arthur Daley wrote in the October 14 *New York Times*: "Other teams were forced to move by apathy or incompetence. . . . The only word that fits the Dodgers is 'greed.' New York balked at twelve acres. Los Angeles enthusiastically proffered three hundred acres. This is the biggest haul since the Brink's robbery—except that it's legal." On October 16, the Giants traded minor league franchises with the Red Sox. The Giants obtained the San Francisco Seals and their ball park in exchange for their holdings in Minneapolis.

Mayor Wagner announced that a committee of citizens headed by attorney William Shea would begin working immediately to secure a new National League team for New York City. The new team would be the New York Mets. The ball park would be named Shea Stadium in honor of the man that Wagner appointed to head the committee to bring National League baseball back to New York City.

But that was five years in the future. The fall of 1957, with the move of the Dodgers and Giants to California, found New York City without National League baseball for the first time since 1882. The move would have negative economic effects all over the city. In 1957, Dodger attendance was 1,026,158, including eight games at Jersey City. The Giants drew 653,903 at the Polo Grounds. Nearly half those who attended the games paid a thirty-cent subway or bus fare to travel to the ball parks. The New York City Transit Authority estimated that exclusive of bus fares to Ebbets Field "there would be an annual revenue loss of three hundred thousand dollars in passenger fares." Charles Patterson, chairman of the Transit Authority, said, "We are hopeful that increased attendance at Yankee games will offset the losses to a considerable degree."

Newspaper sales, restaurants, hotels, trains, planes—all were adversely affected by the move. Merchants in the vicinity of Ebbets Field and the Polo Grounds looked forward to the building of apartment houses to cushion the loss of Dodger and Giant fan revenues.

WOR-TV and WMGM radio, outlets for Brooklyn Dodger baseball, switched to alternate programming. WPIX-TV, which carried about one hundred forty Yankee and Giant games each year, increased Yankee coverage.

Some of the writers and photographers who covered the Dodgers and the Giants were left without work. Some switched to soccer or to bowling; newspapers had to fill space and give the writers and photographers something to do. There would be a two- to three-week lull whenever the Yankees were out of town. The time of a New York City baseball team at home every day of the season was over.

In that America of 1957, Elizabeth Taylor was twenty-four years old. *Life* magazine cost twenty-five cents. *Peyton Place* and *The Hidden Persuaders* were best-selling books. There were fifteen thousand parking meters in New York City and many drivers coveted the Buick B-58 that featured a dynastar grille, twin tower taillights, and a B-12000 engine. In Manhattan, a building boom had created 154 new dwellings since World War II. In the suburbs around the city a housing boom was underway. Major league baseball players earned a minimum salary of $6,000 while ground beef cost thirty-three cents a pound and one could purchase a pound of Eight O'Clock coffee at the A&P for seventy-three cents. The developing National Football League had sold more tickets before the 1957 season began than it had managed to sell for an entire season a dozen years before.

The time would be marked in the memory of millions, however, not by these things but because it was the final year of the Brooklyn Dodgers and the New York Giants. For millions, the move of the teams to California was a personal betrayal, an emotional relationship suddenly and cruelly severed. For many it was the end of their love affair with baseball. Never again would they attend a game. For some there was relief that they had kicked the habit, grown up, lost the need, the compulsion to study box scores, to stay up at night listening to games. No longer would there be protracted and passionate arguments about the relative merits of professional athletes who played a toy game.

Who was the better center fielder—Duke Snider, Mickey Mantle, or Willie Mays? The fights over Yogi versus Campy—who was the better handler of pitchers, the more accomplished clutch hitter—were over. Reese versus Rizzuto versus Dark—these arguments belonged to another time. Maglie, Newk, Reynolds? Who was best? Did Preacher throw a spitter? Who was faster, Mays or Mantle? Which outfield was the best—Pafko-Snider-Furillo or Woodling-Mantle-Bauer or Mueller-Mays-Irvin? Did Red Barber know as much about baseball as Mel Allen? Was Gil Hodges as strong as Hank Bauer? Such comparisons and fierce declarations of loyalty would be no more.

Some would grudgingly switch their allegiance to the New York Yankees. Still others would later become fans of the New York Mets. Some would become interested in other sports and become followers of the New York Knicks, the New York Rangers, the New York Giants, the Jets, the Islanders, the Cosmos. Some would tarry a while and become attached to the Giants of San Francisco and the Dodgers of Los Angeles. The move concluded an era. The coming of the jet, transcontinental sports, shifting franchises, changing demographics, transitory loyalties was upon us.

"The move was good for the National League," is the view of Peter O'Malley, son of Walter, now president of the Los Angeles Dodgers. "Visiting clubs immediately doubled the revenue they received when they came out to play the Los Angeles Dodgers. It was good for the American League, too. They immediately followed us out here," continued O'Malley, who remembers playing catch as a teenager at Ebbets Field with Roy Campanella and Gil Hodges. "It was good for everybody except those loyal Dodger fans we left behind in Brooklyn."

One of those loyal Dodger fans was often taken to Brooklyn's games by his mother. "I was educated by the Dodgers," says Elliot Goldstein, who is now Elliot Gould and who, like the Dodgers, changed his name and his address. "They were something you cared about, and you learned to figure batting averages and earned run averages. When they took them away, they took away Brooklyn's identity."

Buzzy Bavasi moved west with the Dodgers. "I'd never been to Brooklyn in my life 'til I got the job there in 1951 as executive vice president. Those years and moments are times . . . I would never trade. Walter O'Malley made a fortune in Los Angeles, but I don't think he would have given up one moment of Brooklyn for all the pennants he won. Someday the borough of Brooklyn will get all the credit it deserves from baseball people. Brooklyn was baseball."

Howard Golden, who today occupies the same position John Cashmore held, borough president of Brooklyn, still feels the repercussions of the move. "To this date," says Golden, "I get letters from people from all over the country asking me when is Brooklyn going to get a Dodger team again. The move took away a morale, they took away a pride, they took away a common topic of conversation. Whenever you walked into a taxicab, a luncheonette, a corner grocery store—the conversation was always around the Brooklyn Dodgers and the other teams . . . we lost something in New York City.

"If you go around the neighborhoods of Brooklyn, the people there still equate what O'Malley did with the knife that struck on Pearl Harbor. . . . I truly believe and I've spoken to old-timers about this, that there was no way that political pressures could've been brought to bear on him, including the age-old theory that had they built on the Atlantic Avenue terminal site, he would have stayed. O'Mally was a businessman, a banker. He was a person with great foresight and he sensed some of the problems that Brooklyn and the East Coast would be encountering, and he saw the potential and growth factor in the California market. He didn't go to San Francisco. And he didn't go to Oakland. He chose L.A. In retrospect, he chose the area which provided the greatest potential. . . . Politicians could only do so much. They could have given away a stadium. They could have said we'll build one for x million dollars and we'll give you a nominal rental deal. That would not have been practical or fair to the taxpayers. And I don't think it would have done any good. O'Malley did not want to be the tenant or the landlord. . . . It's like that song: they could've offered him Queens and Manhattan, and the

Bronx and Staten Island, too. Having done his demographic studies of L.A. and Brooklyn, he made his move. He chose L.A."

The last year of the Brooklyn Dodgers and the New York Giants was the first year of Tony Kubek as a New York Yankee. "Their move had no real impact on me. I just knew we had another game to play tomorrow and another pennant to win. . . . Maybe it was a cold thing but that was how people were brought up in the Yankee organization. I had no real concern for the Dodgers and the Giants. I was just trying to make the team and stay up. I had come through the Yankee farm system that was so rich in layers of talented players."

The reaction of Red Barber, who began broadcasting for the Dodgers in 1939, was a stark counterpoint to that of Tony Kubek. "I saw baseball in New York City," said Barber, "between the Dodgers and the Giants and from time to time the Yankees, when baseball was at its peak. It was sad to see it end. While there was every reason for Walter O'Malley to leave Brooklyn—he was hemmed in, he couldn't get any more real estate, the days of Ebbets Field were finished, the park was about to fall down . . . when those teams went to the Pacific Coast, there was a deep wound inflicted in baseball in Brooklyn especially that has not healed to this day. . . . Ebbets Field meant so much to me that I never went back to look at the place after it became a ghost. I never have gone back because I can still see Ebbets Field. As far as I'm concerned, it's still standing. . . . There are a lot of people who used to be fans who said to heck with the Giants and the Dodgers and with baseball and they meant it."

The man they called the "Dook of Flatbush," Edwin "Duke" Snider, said: "I hated to leave Brooklyn. I was born and raised in Los Angeles so at least I was glad the move was to my part of the country, but those years in New York City were something, something special. . . . Someone once asked me if I wanted to be twenty-five years old again. Sure I would, but not if it took away all those years in Brooklyn. I wouldn't trade those years for anything."

To this day, former Dodger star Carl Furillo maintains, "O'Malley put the buck in front of everything else. The players thought only of baseball. We thought we'd never move. It seemed the whole team belonged to Brooklyn."

WOR-TV brought the Dodgers to their adoring public from 1949 to the final game. Jack Carney was a witness and a worker through all those years as the Dodger dugout cameraman. "The move was like saying good-bye to your best friend who you were never going to see again," Carney said. "Get out of here and go to California and never come back. We don't want to see you. I don't think any of those true Dodger and Giant fans ever got over it. I know I never will because from that moment on I was firmly convinced that sports was big business and that baseball was not what I had thought it was when I was a kid. They did it for a buck and nothing will ever change it. They could play in California for hundreds of years and it'll never be the same."

The Times

The period of 1947 to 1957 will always be remembered in the phrase "after the war." Air conditioning and television were just catching on. It was the time after World War II and before the Age of Aquarius. It was an era of post-war, cold war, and Korean war. People talked about Joe McCarthy, Milton Berle, Marilyn Monroe, and Mamie Eisenhower.

On March 15, 1947, the "Betty Joe" completed the longest non-stop flight of an American fighter plane in history. The "Betty Joe" flew 4,978 miles from Hickham Field in Hawaii to LaGuardia Airport in Queens, New York. It was the same Hickham Field that had been bombed by the Japanese on December 7, 1941, triggering United States entry into World War II.

So on a clear August 2, 1947, New Yorkers were delighted to view the one hundred fifty aircraft that flew over the city. The planes were there to celebrate the fortieth anniversary of the United States Air Force and to underscore its strength. The USAF planes were complemented by "Dam Busters" from Great Britain's Royal Air Force. Pilots informed ground control that they could clearly see the *Queen Elizabeth* pulling out to sea, the Times Tower on Broadway, and the police information booth north of it.

New Yorkers felt safe and secure watching the planes form steel silhouettes in the pale blue sky over Times Square. Austerity was ending. It was a time of accessories for women—brass buttons, alligator bags. Crinolines returned. Nylon stockings became available in large quantities. Sales of lingerie items were at an all-time high. With the good times returning, dressing up was the vogue. Women wore fitted print bodices and sported full, long skirts. Bold black and white prints were very popular.

It was a time for hats. Some women wore Panama hats topped with veils. Those women who were less conservative engaged in flights of fancy. They wore hats shaped like bowls or pyramids or turbans and accented these with stuffed birds or wax fruits or barnyard fowl feathers.

Men, too, wore hats most of the time. Advertising intensified the reasons for wearing them. "You're way off base without a hat," said an ad trading off baseball lingo which appeared in the 1947 New York Yankee World Series program. "A survey of two hundred sixty-eight doctors shows medical authorities agree that head colds, skin disturbances, early baldness and other respiratory and skin diseases may come as a result of going without a hat in bad weather."

Teenagers bought bobby sox, a more fashionable form of sweat socks. Laced two-colored shoes called saddle shoes were in style. Males had their hair cut short in crew cuts or burr type, close-cropped hair styles reminiscent of the days of the war. Others wore their hair slicked back and greased with any one of a dozen best-selling hair tonics.

It was a time of eagerness and expectation, of the return of familiar things. "Near You" and "Peg 'O My Heart," a couple of nostalgic songs, were the best-selling records of 1947.

It was a time of fads, of Three-D Movies, Silly Putty, and chlorophyll. In 1952, eleven toothpastes and powders, thirty-one tablets and lozenges to sweeten breath, four mouthwashes, three deodorant sticks, eight dog foods, and one brand of cigarettes all contained chlorophyll, a green chemical substance that was billed as a miracle sweetener and freshener.

In New York City epidemic scares came and went in those years. In 1947, a massive drive was started to encourage citizens to undergo an examination for venereal disease. In the first six months of 1946, thirty thousand cases of VD were reported. In April of 1947, a second victim died of smallpox. Mayor O'Dwyer appealed to the public to obtain vaccination against the disease. Thousands rushed in, depleting the vaccine supplies in a couple of days. In 1955, it was estimated that there were ten thousand cases of tuberculosis in New York City.

Newspapers devoted much space to the symptoms and effects of the disease. Mayor Robert F. Wagner and Manhattan Borough President James Lyons were the first two persons to be X-rayed as part of the drive to contain the tuberculosis menace.

For students in the New York City schools, it was a time of pranks, of innocence, of culture of a sort. School officials inserted into the curriculum whole hours devoted to music appreciation. Students were taught to memorize tunes and composers by working the song titles into a spell/sound format: H-U-M-O-R-E-S-Q-U-E spells "Humoresque" . . . "Humoresque," was written by Dvorak. C-O-U-N-T-R-Y G-A-R-D-E-N-S, "Country Gardens . . ." There are many who still recall the bouncing ball repetition of the lyrics of that song.

Seeking surcease from the rote-learning atmosphere of the public schools, the kids of that time, who were disguised with such nicknames as "Itchy" or "Blueie" or "Heshie" or "Biggie," would enter the cool darkness of the movie theaters. Randolph Scott or John Wayne was always tall and manly and at war. For the kids, it was obligatory to avoid paying full price and to manage to gain admittance into the movie house for the under-twelve price. Once this was accomplished, the next step was to avoid the white-uniformed matron, who brandished a flashlight, so that they could sit in the adult section. "Ammunition" was also part of the ritual. The kids would load up with "Goobers" or "Sno-Caps" to throw at what they perceived as the "enemy"—the female types in the audience. Some Dodger and Yankee and Giant fans still recall going to the same movie day after day and sitting in the same seat, fearful of jinxing their favorite team out of a winning streak.

Change was also part of the times. A total of five hundred forty thousand veterans received loans and purchased homes in 1947. On a thousand acres of land near Hempstead, Long Island, a builder named William J. Levitt developed two-bedroom bungalow-type homes. They were 25 x 30 feet, had asphalt floors, and sold for $6,900—about what each New York Yankee received as the winner's share for the 1947 World Series. Thousands of veterans bought the Levitt homes.

In 1948, Columbia introduced the 33-1/3 long-playing record. In 1949, RCA pioneered the 45 RPM disc. What was called the "Battle of the Speeds" was underway. The casualty of the record war was the 78 RPM record. By 1955 it was no longer produced.

Demographic changes were at work in New York City. In 1947, it was estimated that two thousand Puerto Ricans were arriving monthly. There were no restrictions on their immigration. Most of them settled in a section of Harlem called "Little Spain." Gradually they moved to the Jackson Avenue area of the Bronx, to lower Manhattan, to Washington Heights, to the Atlantic Avenue area of Brooklyn close by the site Walter O'Malley would covet as a new playing field for the Dodgers.

Industry was converting to peacetime production—plastics, television sets, automobiles, frozen foods, home appliances. Take-home pay and minimum hourly wages were increasing. By 1949, the average family income after taxes had risen to $4,000; the minimum wage was 40 cents an hour.

New ways were advertised in the signs in the New York City ball parks: "No Foolin' Shave Electrically No Fuss," "Botany Ties—wrinkle proof," "Gas the Wonder Flame That Cools as Well as Heats." A full-page ad in the 1947 Brooklyn Dodger World Series program described the offerings of the Bedford Radio and Television Company, which was located one block north of Ebbets Field. The ad spoke about "thrilling entertainment from three television stations in New York every day." It spotlighted the Model 1000 Philco black and white television set, which could be purchased for $395.00. A Crosley set of the same size and characteristics cost a bit less. That 1947 World Series program depicted Joe DiMaggio and Pee Wee Reese with cigarettes self-consciously propped in their mouths. "ABC —ALWAYS BUY CHESTERFIELD," said the advertisement. A couple of pages away was an ad for another brand: "LS/MFT (Lucky Strike means fine tobacco). So round, so firm, so fully packed—so free and easy on the draw—Lucky Strike."

For millions of people that time was their "lucky strike." Prosperity made it the best years of their lives. And if they happened to live in New York City and root for the New York Yankees or the Brooklyn Dodgers or the New York Giants, it was a time of delight. Glittering stars, dynamic and intimate baseball, day after day, year after year, prevailed. Never before and never again would teams and the players on those teams dominate the sport, the psyche of fans, and the spirit of a city as did the New York City baseball teams of that era.

Except for 1948, each of those eleven years from 1947 to 1957 saw a New York City baseball team competing in the World Series. The New York Yankees won nine pennants and seven World Series —five of them in a row. The Dodgers won six pennants and one world championship. Three times they finished second. In 1950 and 1951, they were dramatically beaten by a home run in the last game they played, denying them pennants. The Giants won two National League championships and one World Series. Thirteen Most Valuable Player awards, ten earned run titles, eight Rookie of the Year honors, seven home run titles, five no-hitters, and four batting championships were collectively recorded by the players on those New York City teams.

Through the long and steamy summer nights and in the blaze of its days, from early spring to the winds of autumn, baseball dominated New York City. The deeds and the personalities of the Dodgers, the Giants, the Yankees transformed the huge metropolis into a small town of neighborhood rooting.

For a nation as well as a city at a crossroads after the death and disruption of a world at war, baseball brought reunion with normalcy, constancy, controlled and familiar excitement. Baseball was a sport played and viewed from childhood on. It was the fidgety anticipation during the playing of the national anthem, the camaraderie of the seventh-inning stretch, the familiar taste of hot dogs and mustard, the record of the program, the yearbook, the box score, the scorecard. It was the crack of wood against ball and the smack of ball against leather, the fraction of the plate shaved close, the fielder magically in position for the leap, the stab, the catch. Baseball was the ceremonious regularity of the set lineup and the fixed positions, four men in the infield, three outfielders, the pitcher throwing the ball on a white line from the mound to the plate to the catcher. It was the flawless geometry of the diamond and the green outfield pastureland, each team being allowed its three strikes, four balls, three outs.

Baseball was the comforting regularity of one dugout along the third base line and the other facing it along the first base line, alternately filling up and spilling out between innings as the sides changed from offense to defense to offense. And it was the individual battles of pitcher against batter and the varying degrees of intensity of time used up, shadings, nuances, tempo set by players and not the clock.

The season—April, May, June, July, August, September—gave plenty of time for personalities to emerge, for fans to learn the names and the styles and the strategies of the players and the teams. The major league tradition of eight teams in each league facing each other twenty-two times, half the time at home, half the time at the other club's park, was appealingly symmetric. The names of the teams in both leagues which most schoolboys could recite by heart, and the uniforms—white for the home team, dusty gray for the visitors—underscored the sport's familiarity.

Baseball dominated. Hockey was a foreign sport. The National Basketball Association, founded in 1946–47, was a metaphor for elongated men in sloppy shorts participating in an indoor sport, a college game. Some of its teams were located in minor league baseball cities: Rochester, Ft. Wayne, Syracuse, Minneapolis. The National Football League had a dozen teams struggling to make an impression. The season was short. The announcers pontificated. The rules were complicated. Tennis and golf were the preserves of the well-to-do. Soccer was an ethnic, immigrant game. Compared with baseball, the other sports came across in the newspapers, on the radio, and later on television as a hodgepodge of scrambling figures and shifting personalities and franchises.

Baseball was the national pastime. It was a game with easily identifiable heroes in tempo with the rhythm of the times. For a nation eager for heroes, baseball met the need. For a city eager for entertainment when the lights went on again after the darkness of World War II, the Dodgers, the Giants, the Yankees, their rivalry, their successes, their innovations, their stars, attracted the fanatical attention of millions.

During the war, many New York City players were in the armed forces. President Franklin Delano Roosevelt had written his "Green Letter" to baseball Commissioner Landis on January 15, 1942: "I honestly think it would be best for the country to keep baseball going." And despite the number of major leaguers in the service, the gas shortages that kept people at home, the reduced attendance, baseball kept going.

In 1945, the final year of World War II, the Brooklyn Dodgers took their spring training in Bear Mountain, New York, and their hitting practice at West Point. Lee Scott, the Dodger traveling secretary of that time, remembers a song:

> *Only 45 minutes from Broadway*
> *Bear Mountain's covered with snow*
> *Down at Asbury Park, it's dead after dark*
> *And the temperature's twenty below*
> *Oh we sure miss those Florida moon beams ...*

With the war's end, more than fifteen million men and women returned from the service. Some of them were ballplayers.

Prominent Dodgers who served in the Armed Forces included Rex Barney, Hugh Casey, Ed Head, Kirby Higbe, Cal McLish, Gil Hodges, Bobby Bragan, Dolf Camili, Billy Herman, Cookie Lavagetto, Gene Mauch, Eddie Miksis, Pee Wee Reese, Mickey Owen, Stan Rojek, Jackie Robinson, Pete Reiser, Joe Hatten, Gene Hermanski.

Giants in the Armed Forces included Dave Koslo, Sid Gordon, Johnny Mize, Willard Marshall, Walker Cooper, Clint Hartung.

Among the Yankees who served were Bill Dickey, Joe DiMaggio, Tommy Henrich, Phil Rizzuto, Tommy Byrne, Johnny Lindell, Ken Silvestri.

Some of these players went from farm teams right into the service. Others were traded or retired on their return from World War II. Seventy-one major leaguers missed the 1942 season; 219 were in the Armed Forces in 1943; the number increased to 242 by 1944, and in the final year of the war 385 major leaguers were in military uniforms. The GI Bill of Rights mandated that all clubs pay service returnees one year's salary at the same pay scale as when they went into the Armed Forces.

The Uniform Player's Contract, a single-spaced, four-page document, detailed the relationship of a player to a club. A reading of the contract provides many insights into those days. The third clause is entitled, "Loyalty ... the Player agrees to perform his services hereunder diligently and faithfully, to keep himself in first class physical condition and to obey the Club's training rules, and pledges himself to the American public and to the Club to conform to high standards of professional conduct, fair play and good sportsmanship." A clause for "Moving Expenses" stated, "In the event this contract is assigned by a major league club during the playing season, the assignor Club shall pay the player his reasonable and actual moving expenses resulting from such assignment up to the sum of $500."

A message to "Dodger rooters everywhere" from Branch Rickey carried with it the feeling of those post-war years. The Dodger president's message was addressed "to the most loyal and appreciative fans in baseball," and went on to express the hopes ". . . that the peace that has been wrung so hard from the wartime years will be permanently insured; that the coming season will bring triumphs early and many, for your Dodger heroes who made Brooklyn and the Dodgers known in every corner of the globe will be as intolerant of defeat in baseball as in else . . ."

"There was a great deal of excitement in the city," recalls Stan Lomax, who covered the Dodgers for a time as a sports writer for the *Journal-American.* "The war was over. The Dodgers got a hype with the new players and new ownership. They'd been saying they were going to be a winner for fifty years, but now they were going somewhere. The Giants were the old-liners. And they had their heroes. Mel Ott was the manager there and he was a god there and he should have been . . . there was never a lovelier man that ever lived. In a rough tough game, Mel was a gentleman. He never said or did anything nasty, and he played the game the way it said in the book. The Yankees and their fans were the carriage class. They expected a good team; they always had one. They went out to applaud their team rather than to root for them."

In those days many of the players lived fairly close to the parks in which they played. In many instances they rode public transportation to and from the ball park. Brooklyn Heights, close to the East River and the Brooklyn Bridge, was the location of the Hotel St. George, the Hotel Bossert, and the Towers Hotel. These residences were a short walk from the main office of the Dodgers at 215 Montague Street. Leo Durocher had a suite at the Bossert, as did Johnny Podres, Carl Furillo, and Gino Cimoli. Joe Black lived for a time at the Hotel

St. George. The hotels were convenient, just a twenty-minute subway ride to the Lincoln Road Station and a two-block walk to Ebbets Field.

The more zealous fans would arrange their schedules to be able to go to Eastern Parkway or Lincoln Road or Empire Boulevard and Ocean Avenue. There they would wait and tag along on the walk of their favorite players to the ball park.

Some of the Dodgers lived in the Bay Ridge section of Brooklyn. "The (Duke) Sniders, (Tommy) Holmes, (Rube) Walkers, (Carl) Erskines all lived there," recalls Reese. "I lived there happily with my family on 97th Street and Ft. Hamilton Parkway. It was a safe neighborhood. People didn't pester for autographs. It was a good place for my family to be protected while I was on the road."

Jackie Robinson and his family were the first blacks to live on Snyder Avenue in East Flatbush, a short walk from Samuel J. Tilden High School. And there were many who lingered on the sidewalk in front of his home yearning to see number forty-two, to talk to him, to manage to get an autograph.

Giant players lived at the Somerset Hotel on 72nd and Columbus, the Braddock at 126th and Eighth Avenue, and the Colonial at 124th and Eighth Avenue. As time passed, a changing neighborhood and bigger salaries and growing families encouraged most of the players to purchase homes in Westchester and New Jersey. The same pattern existed for Yankee athletes who lived at the Concourse Plaza on the wide, tree-lined Grand Concourse near 161st Street. Eddie Lopat and others moved into suburban homes in Bergen County.

In those days, New York City baseball was a ceremony of shared and familiar ritual. Those who rooted, those who wrote and spoke about the players, and the players themselves were bonded together through the long seasons. "Writers and players stayed with the same team for a decade or more," recalls Jack Lang. "They would be together each year from March to October. Our families grew up together. Those were the best days we ever had."

Spring training was ritual. The teams would go south with virtually every spot on the roster taken, especially on the Dodgers and the Yankees. There were never wholesale turnovers. "How was your winter?" was a phrase equivalent to today's workers inquiring of one another, "How was your weekend?"

A DiMaggio, a Furillo, a Rizzuto, a Robinson, a Westrum, Berra, Campanella would be a fixture. Their spots in the batting order, their positions on the field, the affection of the fans for them and the respect of the other players would be guaranteed.

Barnstorming north was also a ritual. "We would leave Vero Beach, Florida," said Lang, "and go to St. Petersburg, play two games and start north . . . Jacksonville, Mobile, Biloxi, New Orleans, up north through Alabama and Georgia and finally wind up in Washington. It would take ten, twelve days through ten or twelve cities." The writers and the players would be together in two or three private cars. "We would eat and drink," said Lang, "and play cards. It was before TV or movies on a train. You really got to know the ballplayers. We thought it was fast then. Nowadays you don't even see each other."

The road trips made for more closeness. "The farthest trip back then was to St. Louis or Chicago," said Monte Irvin. "It was seventeen, eighteen hours by train. You'd sit down with the writers, play cards with them, talk to them. You'd develop an intimacy with them, and they found out a lot of things about you and you found out a lot of things about them. That was a time for old stories. Some of the greatest anecdotes would come out then."

Lang recalls "Leaving New York City to go on a road trip we'd get on a train about 7:00 P.M. We were like members of the same family, the writers and the players. We'd have a couple of drinks, a bottle of beer was fifty cents. We thought it was an extravagant price in those days, but it was on a train so we paid it. The food in the dining cars was like eating in the best restaurant in the best hotels. There was elegant service. The Dodgers had the edge because they had the most black players. The porters treated us better than anyone else. When dinner was over, we had the rest of the night. We played cards in the club cars . . . nobody went to bed . . . we played cards and talked. . . ."

Arthur Richman worked for the *New York Mirror* for twenty-one years. He began as an office boy in 1942 and moved up to write a

column called the "Armchair Manager" that analyzed the results of
New York City baseball games. The time comes back to him in a
stream of consciousness—the train rides, the breakfasts, the lunches,
the dinners, the sitting around playing cards.

"Each club had two Pullman cars to itself. We had a private
dining car. Clubs would print up their own menus. 'The New York
Giant menu' . . . a good steak was three dollars. There would be bar-
bershop quartettes. Kenny Smith of the *Mirror* would bring along his
accordion. Sometimes the train would stop at some God-knows-where
waterhole and Eddie Brannick (the traveling secretary of the Giants)
and myself would run out in the middle of the night to get some sand-
wiches. The dining room was closed on the train . . . we'd all stay up
all night, throwing the bull."

"There were three cars on a train," Lomax remembrs. "X 1, X 2,
X 3. The regulars were in X 1; the scrubs were inX2, and the writers
were in X 3. If I wanted to interview a player, I would just walk into
the next car. I could interview him all night long."

New York City newspapers sold baseball and New York City
baseball sold newspapers. The teams competed for coverage; the
newspapers fought for scoops and readership. The *Daily News*
printed an oversize box score complete with the day's batting averages. In the metropolitan New York City area there were more than a
dozen newspapers, and baseball reporting was the premier assignment
for anybody covering sports. Even little Ebbets Field had a press box
that accommodated one hundred writers. "Back then," said Jack
Lang, "people lived to read about baseball in the newspapers."

It was a time without air conditioning in most of the neighborhoods, of cramped families in small apartments. After the summer's
sun had gone down, the streets were always crowded with the old-
timers straining for a breeze on the folding chairs in front of the
squalid tenement buildings. At about 8:30, many would make the walk
to the neighborhood candy store. A standard line of the time was "I'm
waitin' for the *News* 'n *Mirror*." Some who were not even baseball
fans, but were sent out by parents who were, waited. They were
given specific instructions on which edition of the newspapers to buy
—"the ones that have the complete box scores." At one point, with

respective circulations of two million and one million, those New York City tabloids ranked one-two in the United States in sales.

The radio in the candy store spilled out the sounds of Mario Lanza's "Because of You," or Frank Sinatra's "From This Moment On." Those who waited would muse about the day's baseball action, purchase a pack of Lucky Strike or Old Gold cigarettes, drink a lemon coke or an egg cream. There are still those who remember the taste of those chocolate egg creams, the feel of the cellophane cigarette package wrappings, the rough newsprint touch, the bold, black look of the headline on the back page: "DODGERS CRUSH CARDS, 14–3." Many still remember the walk past the Left Field Bar, past Ben and Sol's Delicatessen, to the large newsstand on Eastern Parkway in Brooklyn and the wait for the 9:00 P.M. newspaper drop.

"Those newspapers gave a real portrayal of what was going on," said Monte Irvin. "If a player didn't perform well, the writers traveling with the team, for example, did not try to smooth it over. They would write, 'He's a bum; he's got to go today.' They'd try to stir something up. It helped to build up the rivalry between the teams. The players all read the papers."

Dick Young of the *Daily News* was perhaps the most widely read baseball writer. Young fueled the fans' ferocious appetite. A highly skilled writer with a sense of humor and perspective—and also controversy—Young was a baseball writer's writer. "If Red Barber was the best radio announcer," said Lang, "then Dick Young was probably the best baseball writer that ever lived. Nobody ever wrote a game story as good as he did."

Young's fellow writers on the *News* included Joe Trimble, who covered the Yankees, and Jim McCulley, who was assigned to the Giants.

The other by-lines are still remembered by those who eagerly read every word of baseball news: Arch Murray, Milton Gross, Jimmy Cannon, Sid Friedlander, *New York Post*; Arthur Richman, Dan Parker, Ben Epstein, Gus Steiger, *New York Mirror*; Jack Lang, *Long Island Press*; Tommy Holmes and Harold Burr, *Brooklyn Eagle*; Joe Reichler, Arthur Daley, Roscoe McGowen, *New York Times*; Herb Goren, Bill Roeder, Joe Williams, Frank Graham,

Barney Kremenko, Red Smith, Tom Meany, Jimmy Powers, Mike Gaven, Kenny Smith.

Fans read these writers and argued about their skills, their styles. Writers personalized players, gave them nicknames that remain forever. Branch Rickey, aka "The Mahatma" was coined by Tom Meany; Dusty Rhodes, aka, "The Colossus of Rhodes," was a name invented by Arthur Daley; Ben Epstein of the *Mirror* gave Eddie Lopat the nickname "Junkman." Sal Maglie was dubbed "The Barber" by Jim McCulley of the *Daily News*.

"WAIT TILL NEXT YEAR"—that plaintive cry of Dodger fans—appeared annually in the *Brooklyn Eagle*, which was primarily a home-delivery, afternoon newspaper. "The *Eagle* headlines," notes former reporter Sid Frigand, "were looked upon as indicators of what had happened, what was going to happen to the Dodgers. For many in Brooklyn who had lived through a childhood and adolescence of miserable Dodger teams, the great teams of Robinson, Hodges, Reese, and Snider were viewed as Brooklyn's revenge on the world."

"THIS IS NEXT YEAR!" the front page of the *Daily News* screamed in bold black type the glorious morning after the Dodgers won Brooklyn's only world championship. The one-star edition of the *News*, which sold for four cents, devoted the rest of the front page to a photograph captioned: "Johnny is the Boy For Me"—a reference to winning pitcher Johnny Podres being engulfed in a bear hug by catcher Roy Campanella after the last out in the seventh game at the Stadium. Not to be outdone by its tabloid rival, the *Mirror* proclaimed in four different type faces across its front page: "WORLD CHAMPS! DODGERS DOOD IT. BUMS AIN'T BUMS—ANYMORE! BEDLAM IN B'KLYN ON 2–0 WIN."

Ironically, when "Next Year" arrived for the Dodgers, it was the last year for the *Brooklyn Eagle*. It went the way of the *Journal-American* and the *Sun*. "The newspaper folded in the black," says Frigand. "It was a fairly conservative newspaper. It just did not want to bother with unions anymore." Frigand remembers: "The *Brooklyn Eagle* knew the Dodgers were more than just a team for those who lived in Brooklyn." Its personalized grabber headlines praised and panned the "Bums." Such headlines as "EGAD MEN, WAKE UP" (after a painful Dodger loss), or "WE'RE COOKIN' TODAY" (commenting on Cookie Lavagetto's 1947 World Series pinch-hit double that ruined a no-hit bid by Bill Bevens) were featured in newspapers all over the country.

In 1947, there were 38.5 million households in the United States, and radio linked them in a global village. There were 9 million radios in autos, 21.6 million in stores, factories, offices. All but four million of the American households had at least one radio.

Radio back then was the sound of "Captain Midnight . . . brought to you by Ovaltine . . . Jack Armstrong, the All-American boy . . . have you tried Wheaties? . . . the Children's Hour and its sponsor Horn and Hardart . . . Grand Central Station." Lunchtime when the kids came home from school was a time for Lorenzo Jones and his wife Belle. There was also "Our Gal Sunday" who lived in Black Swan Hall, located in Cripple Creek, Colorado. And "Who knows what evil lurrrrrrks in the hearts of men? The *Shadow* knows! Hmmmmmmmm —hmmmmm—hmmmmmmmmmm." Radio was always on, always ritual. And in New York City, baseball on the radio was a dominating sound.

Followers of the New York City teams could go to a butcher shop, a candy store, a laundromat, moving from one to another virtually without missing a pitch. What the Yankees, the Giants, the Dodgers were doing, had done, would do was broadcast into bars and beauty parlors. On the job and in school rooms, there was always the sound of baseball.

The era when games were mostly at night was in the future—the most western baseball franchise was in St. Louis. Baseball was easy to keep up with even at night. In doorways, on stoops, on fire escapes, or lying in bed in their own apartments, on the steamy summer nights, fans would listen to the play-by-play. Some kept score. Others just visualized the action. They knew what the outcome of a game was before they went to sleep. It was immediate—the results, the standings, the statistics, the next day's probable pitchers.

"It was a golden era of broadcasters," Monte Irvin said. "Red Barber and Mel Allen . . . it was impossible to choose between them as to who was number one. Russ Hodges did a fine job with the Giants, but he didn't have quite the style or the publicity. Mel Allen had that golden voice. We thought he used to root more than anybody. Red did less rooting. Mel was strictly a homer, but he was a truly fine announcer. Red and Mel are in the Hall of Fame already. Russ will make it in time."

"The "Voice of the Yankees," Mel Allen personified Yankee baseball. Haughty, explosive, with a total command of every aspect of language and baseball, his mellow Alabama accents still ring in the ears. Allen began his broadcasting career in 1939. At his peak he received one thousand letters a week.

"The fans accused him of being prejudiced for the Yankees," said former Yankee star pitcher Ed Lopat. "How could he be otherwise! One year we won thirty-nine games in the seventh, eighth, and ninth innings. He had to get riled up."

Allen marveled at the accomplishments of the talented Yankees. He labeled home runs in deference to sponsors: "Ballantine Blasts" and "White Owl Wallops." He captured the excitement of a ball streaking toward home run territory in the phrase: "Going, Going Gone!"

"He changed the whole style of broadcasting," said Don Carney, WPIX vice president of sports. "Announcers before Mel were pretty much straight reporting. He dramatized events. He lived and breathed baseball and he made the fans feel what he felt."

Walter Lanier "Red" Barber was born on February 17, 1908, in Columbus, Mississippi. He began his broadcasting career for station WRUF in Gainesville, Florida, in 1930. He worked for Larry Mac-Phail in Cincinnati in 1934 and was brought to Brooklyn to become New York City's first sustained radio baseball announcer in 1939.

"There had been a gentlemen's agreement among the three New York City baseball teams," noted Stan Lomax, "that they would not have day-by-day radio broadcasts . . . only features. Larry MacPhail broke the agreement with Red Barber. The Giants and the Yankees hollered, but MacPhail didn't care."

The Brooklyn ear had some difficulty getting attuned to Barber's southern vernacular. "He speaks some foreign langwidge," one fan observed, "and I don't get the pernt."

Ultimately that fan along with millions of others got the point that Barber was one of the most talented and knowledgeable of sports announcers. The "Old Redhead" spoke of black-eyed peas and the "rhubarb patch" (a condition of controversy). He described "Bedford Avenue Blasts" (home runs into Bedford Avenue), and "F.O.B." (bliss for Dodger fans—the bases full of Brooklyns). He used such phrases as "Oh, Doctor" and "tearing up the pea patch," a more genteel way of characterizing the commotions that continually cropped up at Ebbets Field. Barber was always in "the catbird seat," always in control. He had the uncanny ability to retain a sense of humor and his composure amid the most uproarious conditions. His narrative skills and down home manner made him the "Voice of Brooklyn." And there are many who still remember him selling the Old Gold cigarettes, giving us "a treat instead of a treatment."

"Red did an especially wonderful job with women," says Stan Lomax. "Proctor & Gamble was one of his first sponsors, and I saw the bags of mail that he got, I mean, great big bags of mail. He came up with the idea for Ladies Day in New York City. He brought the ladies into the ballpark. 'C'mon in,' he'd say, 'and we'll all have a very nice time. Pee Wee Reese is a very handsome guy.' Red was a great salesman for the Dodgers and he didn't slug you with it. He was really the first continuous play-by-play baseball announcer in New York City."

Just how many he converted into lifelong lovers of baseball can never be precisely calculated, but the figure must reach into the hundreds of thousands. Just as Barber's southern-accented broadcasts brought a feeling for baseball into so many homes, the Dodgers' extensive southeastern radio network created vast numbers of Brooklyn fans with southern accents. Nat Albright handled the play-by-play for fans throughout North Carolina, Florida, and Virginia, creating perhaps more southern Brooklyn Dodger fans in those days than there were fans of any other major league team.

In 1954, Barber left the Dodgers and joined the Yankee broadcasting team. It was as if he had been traded. Some loyal Dodger fans could not accept the old 'redhead' describing Yankee baseball. "Red was exceptional," recalls Don Carney, who worked with Barber as a Yankee broadcast director. "He was the greatest on radio. He loved it, for he had no limitations. He could describe a game any way he wanted to at any pace. He was a master of the language; he told me he preferred radio. When he was on TV he was always partnered with another broadcaster and it intruded on his way of thinking. He really didn't like to share a mike with another broadcaster because it hampered him."

Barber was the ultimate professional, the perfectionist. "I worked day and night to learn my business," he says, "and I respected it to the end. When I left, it was almost the end of professional broadcasting, then the jocks took over. I thank the almighty for the timing of my years. If I started out today, I couldn't even get a job. I didn't win twenty games or hit .350, but I worked harder at my trade than any announcer I know about.

"I have been grateful to God that the timing of my life and my professional work was when it was, when things were very simple. The depression was on . . . the owners then only got the money from the spectators who paid their way to get in. They got something from the concessionaires. They got something from an occasional ad on a fence . . . radio rights were nothing . . . television wasn't even dreamed about and the other means of getting money was to sell a ballplayer or trade a ballplayer and get some money thrown in. It was very much a game—not what it is today, a cold capital gains business."

NBC initiated TV sports coverage with primitive transmission in 1939. In Manhattan, in 1947, there were twelve thousand television sets. Robert S. Stanton was the announcer as NBC covered every home game of the Giants. With only two cameras in operation, Stanton described the events on the field in a slow, studied voice, lest the picture lag too far behind his narration.

By mid-1948, there were 325,000 TV sets in the United States. Half of them were located in the metropolitan New York City area. The Roosevelt Hotel in Manhattan installed television sets in forty of their rooms and raised room rates three dollars. The average price of those primitive sets was $400.

"In those days," Sid Frigand recalls, "it was really prestigious if somebody built the set for you. That made you different from everybody else who had a manufacturer's set. So many of those sets were so bad that the pictures were so wavy that you couldn't see a damn thing. It was better to listen to the game on the radio."

When WOR-TV pioneered local TV baseball coverage in 1949, only one out of ten persons in the country had viewed the new medium. Coverage was basic. One man sat behind the chicken wire behind home plate with a single camera. "Then they added a camera in each dugout," said Jack Carney. "We used the old RCA cameras with a turret that you had to flip back to get a wide shot. There was no zoom lens at the start. The lens had to be flipped when you were not on the air—otherwise the audience would see the flip which was actually the changing of the turrets on the camera. And how they complained when they saw that flip!"

Comedian Fred Allen cracked, "There are millions of people in New York City who don't even know what TV is. They aren't old enough to go into saloons yet." Allen's comment poked fun at the superabundance of TV viewing, especially baseball viewing, that took place in local bars. Seats close to the sets were reserved by bartenders for their regular patrons. Newcomers were carefully positioned in less choice locations in the back of the bar, away from the TV.

The sounds of beer and baseball were part of the times: Ballantine Blasts and Schaefer Slams. The commercials were live. "Schaefer beer was a big sponsor of the Dodgers," recalls Jack Carney. "I can still taste the beer that was left over from the shows that I drank with guys like George Shuba and Wayne Belardi."

The practice of superimposing the names of batters on the TV screen was instigated by fans in bars. "Some guy at the end of the bar," recalls Don Carney, "would complain that he could not hear the sound on the screen and wanted to know who was at bat. We used a black piece of cardboard with white printing on it. If we didn't get the names spelled right or if we didn't have the right size, we'd get calls. They were always complaining—'I can't read the name—do something about it.'"

By April of 1953, the number of homes with TV had climbed 40 percent from January of the year before. Almost 20 million TV families existed; 44 percent of the homes in the United States had a set. In New York City, engineers muffled the sound and threw "snow" on the screen to reduce the freneticism and to censor the language and gestures of such figures as Charlie Dressen, Leo Durocher, Carl Furillo. The first color TV sets were produced in 1954 and sold for about a thousand dollars each. The season of 1954–55 was the first color season. NBC programmed about twelve to fifteen hours a week.

"I think the Dodgers more than any other team made women regular baseball fans," said Sid Frigand. "Housewives, who for years heard the droning on the radio but had never been to a game, were finally able to see what they had heard. They were glued to the sets . . . and then they started coming to the park in big numbers."

In addition to Mel Allen and Red Barber and Russ Hodges, who used phrases such as "Bye, bye birdie" to characterize a home run and "five thousand Chesterfields," a reward to a player who had hammered a home run, all types of personalities and programs entertained the baseball listening and viewing audiences.

There was Al Helfer, Ernie Harwell, a young Vin Scully—he arrived on the scene as a protégé of Red Barber in 1950—a heavy Connie Desmond—the freckled announcer who began his baseball descriptions in 1943. Perhaps the only authentic New York City accent belonged to Frankie Frisch. One of the first of the ex-ballplayers to go into sportscasting, he is remembered describing Giant baseball in a stretched-out speech pattern and for the phrase, "Oh, those bases on balls!" Others included Jim Woods, Joe Garagiola, Curt Gowdy, Andy Baruch of Lucky Strike Hit Parade fame, and Joe E. Brown, who did a pre- and postgame show for the Yankees and some play-by-play. Laraine Day, Mrs. Leo Durocher, prettified the home screen doing a pregame show, "A Day in the Life of the Giants." Even the taciturn (in those days) Yankee Clipper, Joe DiMaggio, got into the act. He had a brief stint as a television commentator on Yankee games.

Whole programs were devoted to baseball. One of the most popular was "Today's Baseball." It came on the air on radio station WMGM at 7:00 P.M. and was a re-creation of the day's Dodger game. Marty Glickman, Burt Lee, Jr., and Ward Wilson were among those who handled the play-by-play. "Gorgeous Gussie" Moran, a former tennis star whose lace panties had created a stir, provided the color commentary. The "instant replay" of its time, "Today's Baseball" was total simulation. A crack of a wooden block beneath the microphone re-created the sound of a home run; crowd noise tapes of varying intensity provided atmosphere.

During the early '50s, many fans were intrigued by the "Mystery Dodger," a sort of baseball quiz show. The *Brooklyn Eagle* published a photograph of an old Dodger and each day a piece of the photograph would be peeled away revealing more of the player. Tied in with this was a program on WOR-TV which gave fans the opportunity to guess the identity of the obscure Brooklyn player that the photograph showcased. The whole package was essentially a promotional venture for the newspaper and the television station and one that attracted a great deal of fan interest.

One of the most popular baseball television personalities of the time was Happy Felton, a bespectacled fat man in a Brooklyn Dodger uniform. His broadcasting roots were in children's programs, and he went on to become the genial host of pre- and postgame shows at Ebbets Field, performing as if he still had an audience of children. The "Knot-Hole Gang" was broadcast thirty minutes before the game began. Felton would have a Dodger star work out with and tutor aspiring major leaguers who came from the hundreds of youth leagues in New York City. When the Dodger games were concluded, Felton came back on the air with a program entitled "Talk To The Stars." In-depth and sometimes humorous interviews with players were the basis of the show. "Happy did not know that much about baseball," recalls Jack Carney, "but he had the ability to put it over and to entertain."

Scoreboard watching, subway riding, following the accomplishments of the Montreal Royals, the Newark Bears, and the Jersey City Giants—the top farm teams of the Dodgers, Yankees and Giants—were other rituals of those days.

Ball park scoreboards were operated manually. Fans at a game watched the scores of other games develop inning by inning as operators working behind the scoreboard dropped the numbers into the slots. A "2" in the first inning for the Cardinals might be followed by a "1" for the Cubs. This contemporaneous baseball—the contest being played at Ebbets Field, the Polo Grounds, Yankee Stadium—and the ebb and flow of the games on the scoreboard fascinated fans. The numbers would stay up, strung out, three innings, five, six . . . and if an inordinate amount of time elapsed between the dropping of numbers into the slots, fans would notice. They would speculate and argue with each other as to how many runs had been scored, what was happening in St. Louis, or Boston, or Cincinnati.

"The manual operators at Ebbets Field were real teasers," said Jack Lang. "If the Dodgers were playing a contender, the operators would hold the number, tease the fans and the players. There was a lot more romance back then and a lot more excitement. Today electronic scoreboards have mostly replaced the manual operation. Games don't unfold. You just get the inning and the score and not the whole picture."

Trains transported hundreds of thousands to the New York City ball parks. There are still those who remember riding the Brighton Beach Express into the dazzling daylight as the train powered out of the dark underground tunnel into the Prospect Park Station near Ebbets Field. There are still those who recall how they purposely sat on the left side of the train as it came from the underground to the 161st Street elevated line station to be able to catch a glimpse through the opening of the grandstand and bleachers of the players in Yankee Stadium taking batting and fielding practice.

"How many people had cars in those days?" said Arthur Richman. "Everybody seemed to ride the subways. There were kids with Giant caps, with Dodger caps, with Yankee caps, people with brown bags with their lunch going to games." Subways were for arguing about the New York City baseball teams, for anticipating what would happen at a game, for reviewing what had happened.

"I remember going home at four in the morning after the final edition of the *Mirror* had been put to bed," said Richman. "The subways were crowded. Sometimes you couldn't even get a seat, people worked nights. People would be reading the papers finding out what happened in the night games."

Some diehard Giant fans traveled to Jersey City and a good many Yankee rooters made the trip to Newark when the 'big' clubs were on the road. The fans went to preview the up-and-coming players on the powerful farm teams. Box scores and stories about the doings of the

Bears, the Royals and the 'little' Giants were eagerly read by fans in the New York City newspapers.

It was also a time of parades and decorations. Baseball seemed always to be dressing up New York City, making it festive and alive. On April 17, 1956, Johnny Podres, the hero of the 1955 World Series, the man who had won the final game to give the Dodgers their first and only world championship, rode in an open convertible heading a parade down Flatbush Avenue to Ebbets Field. Podres had been drafted and was wearing his Navy uniform. He helped hoist the Dodger championship banner. In the autumn of 1956, presidential candidates Dwight D. Eisenhower and Adlai E. Stevenson toured Flatbush Avenue in open cars just before the World Series. It was a few weeks before the election and the exposure and identification with baseball was a predictable campaign technique. The two candidates argued about who would attend the first game. Eisenhower did, and Stevenson was able to get his exposure at the second game.

There were parades for clinching pennants, for winning World Series, for no-hitters. During those autumns New York City was lit up in red, white, and blue buntings at the ball parks and in the neighborhoods along main streets. Store windows, especially along the Flatbush Avenue and Fulton Street parade routes, featured banners, pictures of Dodgers, an autographed ball, a bat—the symbols of baseball. Signs like: "Congratulations National League Champs"; "Yankees Did It Again—Best Wishes to the Bronx Bombers"; and "Manhattan Salutes the Miracle Giants" were hung in bars all over the boroughs.

In those eleven years from 1947 to 1957, Edmund Hilary climbed Mt. Everest and Roger Bannister ran a four-minute mile. Clothes were mass-produced for the first time in junior sizes. Citation won racing's Triple Crown. Albert Einstein and George Bernard Shaw died. The mambo gave way to the creep; hot jazz replaced cool jazz, and rock 'n roll drowned out virtually all other music. The "New Look" came and went; 33⅓ and 45 RPM records were introduced. Television antennas were installed on millions of rooftops. There were fifteen million homes with TV in 1952; twenty-six million in 1954; forty-one million in 1957. The first successful kidney transplant was made. A baby boom began. Suburban housing developments flourished. And the Yankees were left at the end of the era as New York City's only baseball team.

For many who lived through that time, the images still tarry in the memory. It was a time when World Series tickets were always being printed each season for one, two, or all three New York City teams. It was a time when the major "league leaders" listed in the newspapers were always dominated by the players on the New York City teams. Monday, September 13, 1954, for example, listed Snider, .342; Mays, .340; Mueller, .331; Robinson, .315 in the National League and Noren, .325; Berra, .310; Bauer, .304 in the American League. Under the column for RBIs, Snider, 123; Hodges, 119; Berra, 112; Mantle, 105 were listed. Three of the top four home-run hitters for the date were New York City players: Hodges, Mays, Snider.

The look and style of the players, the number on their uniforms, their nicknames were as familiar to fans as their own telephone number or address.

Eddie Lopat, spinning the slow curves off the corner of the plate with workmanlike precision; Jackie Robinson, the scowl, the swing, the slide, the stolen base; Joe DiMaggio, boldly noble, gliding after the white sphere in the green pastureland of the outfield; Roy Campanella, brawny and beaming, swinging the heavy bats coming up to the plate; Leo Durocher, foulmouthed and frenzied, jutted jaw, scheming to win; Carl Furillo, taking charge in right field, sturdily proficient, daring runners to take chances with his arm; Preacher Roe, a cowboy in a Dodger uniform, wiping the perspiration into the spitball; Casey Stengel, juggling, jawing, having fun and winning; Monte Irvin, solidly professional, whacking the ball and driving in the big runs; Allie Reynolds, flaming the ball in, starting, relieving, winning, winning; Pee Wee Reese, a gentleman shortstop with more than just a touch of class; Willie Mays, losing his cap and basket catching the ball; Johnny Mize, digging in and pounding the ball; Billy Cox, sad and skinny, with the magic glove; Gil Hodges, heroically strong, playing it straight, busting open games with his bat. . . .

Pee Wee Reese number 1, Carl Furillo number 6, Vic Raschi number 17, Allie Reynolds number 22, Whitey Ford number 16, Joe DiMaggio number 5, Jackie Robinson number 42, Duke Snider number 4, Carl Erskine number 17, Yogi Berra number 8, Gil Hodges number 14, Mickey Mantle number 7, Don Newcombe number 36, Tommy Henrich number 15, Phil Rizzuto number 10, Billy Cox number 3, Joe Black number 49, Willie Mays number 24, Ralph Branca number 13, Elston Howard number 32, Jim Hearn number 7, Roy Campanella number 39, Jim Gilliam number 19, Sandy Koufax number 32, Bobby Thomson number 23, Don Mueller number 44, Sal Maglie number 39, Monte Irvin number 20, Sandy Amoros number 15, Hank Bauer number 9, Joe Collins number 15, Gil McDougald number 12 . . .

Oisk and Newk, Pee Wee and Skoonj, Ski, Campy, and Preacher, Casey (Stengel) and ("You") Casey, the Commerce Comet and King Kong and Joe Di, the Springfield Rifle and the Reading Rifle, Shotgun, Jumbo Jim, Bullet Bob, the Super Chief, Spec, the Yankee Clipper and Joltin' Joe, "Barney" Shotton and "Rex" Barney, Westy, Blacky, Whitey, Dixie, Pistol Pete and Handy Andy and Abie and Buddy, the Peepul's Cherce, Cookie, Sandy, Smokey, the Old Reliable and the Old Perfesser, Scooter, the Junkman and Steady Eddie, and more. Yogi, Jolly Cholly, Bobo, the Lip, the Brat, the Hondo Hurricane, Mandrake the Magician, the Barber, Moose, Hot Rod and Lucky Lohrke and the Big Cat and the Bull, Junior, Bucky, the Flying Scot . . . and another Duke, another Whitey, another Sandy . . . nicknames, standards, personalities, identities.

For many, that time of their life had the best day, the best year, the best month, the best hitter, the best pitcher, the best moment, the best catch, the best announcer, the best base stealer, the best manager . . . the best of everything.

It was a sensitive, even delicate situation. It had to be handled inning by inning, game by game, month by month. It was there all the time because when Robinson came, he came to stay.

— RED BARBER

The Pioneers

In April of 1947 there were sixteen blacks in organized baseball. Half of them were in the Dodger organization. Branch Rickey had signed Dan Bankhead, who would pitch ten innings late in the season. John Wright, Roy Parlow, Don Newcombe, and Roy Campanella were also a part of the Brooklyn organization. Hank Thompson and Willard J. Brown would join the St. Louis Browns in July. "Brown said he was thirty-eight at the time," recalls Arthur Richman. "He may have been older. He was powerful when he hit, but he did not hit often enough." The Cleveland Indians had signed Larry Doby, and he would play in twenty-nine games for them in 1947.

But Jackie Robinson was the main man, the first of the black stars who would change forever the way things were in major league baseball. He came to his role as history's messenger after having been a star athlete at UCLA, an officer in the United States Army, a premier shortstop with the Kansas City Monarchs in the Negro Leagues. Before he was cast in the role of black pioneer, before he broke baseball's color line, there were bittersweet foreshadowings.

On July 27, 1943, with the United States locked in a life-and-death struggle with the Axis powers in World War II, a wire service dispatch announced that three Negro National League players would be given tryouts with the Pittsburgh Pirates. The three players—Roy Campanella and Sam Hughes of the Baltimore Elite Giants and Dave Barnhill of the New York Cubans—never received their tryouts.

Three black players were given tryouts by the Boston Red Sox at Fenway Park in 1945. They were told that they would be contacted if a decision were made to sign them. They were never contacted. The three players were Marvin Williams, Sam Jethroe, and Jackie Robinson.

On August 28, 1945, at the main office of the Brooklyn Dodgers at 215 Montague Street in Brooklyn Heights, an historic meeting took place. Branch Rickey met with Jackie Robinson. Both men were fiercely competitive. Both were highly sensitized to baseball's color line.

Rickey came to the meeting after engaging in months of discussion on the problem of the black in baseball. He had served on a Committee for Unity formed when the New York State Antidiscrimination Law was passed. The other members of the committee included Bill Robinson, the black tap dancer, New York Yankee owner Larry MacPhail, Judge Jeremiah Maloney, and *New York Times* sports columnist Arthur Daley. The meetings, the studies, the statistical analyses frustrated Rickey. He was a man who prided himself on doing, not dwelling. He realized the potential source of major league baseball talent which the black player represented. He also was motivated by a principled desire to do what he thought was long overdue.

"One day at 215 Montague Street," Stan Lomax recalls, "Rickey brought out a bunch of receipts for railroad fares, hotel bills. He had scouts watching Cuba and the Negro Leagues." Ricky had triggered the Dodger organization into a search for the most talented, the most exciting, the most intelligent, the best black ballplayer available. The search brought Jackie Robinson to the August 28 meeting.

Robinson entered the meeting with the knowledge that more than 60 percent of the players in the major leagues were southern born, that there had been other meetings, other discussions with blacks that had led nowhere. He remembered his "tryout" at Boston's Fenway Park.

The world later learned the details of the Rickey-Robinson meeting and the role-playing the two men assumed in the trial run aimed at breaking new ground in race relations and baseball. Rickey snarled and shouted. He cursed. He questioned and taunted Robinson. Rickey was the snarling waitress, the bigoted sportswriter, the prejudiced hotel clerk, the profane and biased ballplayer. "Not only will you be on trial," he told Robinson, "but all of black society. You must be a man big enough to bear the cross of martyrdom. You must not fight back. You must turn the other cheek."

Robinson, who grew up in the slums of Pasadena, California, grudgingly agreed. "I'll turn the other cheek," he said, "for as long as it is necessary, but when it's no longer necessary, I'll be my own man."

Contract terms were agreed upon. Jackie Robinson would receive a $3,500 bonus and $600 a month and would play in 1946 for the Montreal Royals, the top farm team of the Dodgers. If all went well, he would be the first of his race to play major league baseball in 1947. The official announcement that Robinson had been signed was postponed until October 23, 1945.

The news of Robinson's signing became the most talked about and debated sports topic in years. Rickey was labeled "The Great White Father" by some newspapers. Robinson was called "The Black Meteor." Minor League baseball commissioner William Bramham issued a statement from Durham, North Carolina: "Father Devine will have to look to his laurels, for we can expect a Rickey Temple to be in the course of construction in Harlem soon. Whenever I hear a white man, whether he be from the north, south, east or west, protesting what a friend he is to the Negro race, right then I know the Negro needs a bodyguard. It is those of the carpetbagger stripe of the white race, under the guise of helping but in truth using the Negro for their own selfish interests, who retard the race."

The press reacted coolly, at best, to the news of Robinson's impending debut. *The Sporting News* claimed that "Robinson's abilities would make him eligible for a trial with a Class B farm club if he were six years younger." *New York Daily News* sports editor Jimmy Powers wrote ". . . we would like to see him make good, but it is unfair to build high hopes and then dash them down . . . he is a thousand to one shot to make the grade." Joe Williams, a New York City sportswriter, wrote, "Blacks have been kept out of big league ball because they are as a race very poor ballplayers."

A couple of storied stars expressed misgivings. Cleveland Indian pitcher Bob Feller claimed that Robinson had "football shoulders." "He's tied up in the shoulders and can't hit an inside pitch to save his neck. If he were a white man, I doubt if they would even consider him big league material." Feller had pitched against Robinson twice in off-season exhibitions. Hall of Famer Rogers Hornsby observed, "Ballplayers on the road live close together . . . It won't work." The darling of Dodger fans, Dixie Walker, said, "As long as he's not with the Dodgers, I'm not worried."

Rickey was called an opportunist. Some said he was an ultra-liberal. But there were those who praised him for his courage and for his sincere desire to solve a sociological problem. Georgia-born Rudy York, stalwart first baseman of the Detroit Tigers, said, "I wish Rickey all the luck in the world, and I hope Robinson makes good." Rickey insisted, "I signed Jackie Robinson for just one reason . . . to win the pennant. I'd play an elephant with pink horns if he could win the pennant."

The first pennant Jackie Robinson helped win was the one recorded by the Montreal Royals in 1946.

Opening day of the 1946 International League baseball season was the first opening day in four years that the United States was at peace. Thousands of black and white New Yorkers took the day off and traveled through the Hudson Tubes to witness the debut of Jackie Robinson at second base for Montreal. Mayor Frank Hague of Jersey City declared a holiday. Schoolchildren were given the day off. Many of them were in the ball park. With the war over, with all the lessons of democracy seemingly having been taught, a new world quality attached itself to that early spring day in the stadium named for the president who led us through the war and died before the peace. Jackie Robinson's middle name was Roosevelt, like the late president and the stadium he was to make history in.

Rickey had told Robinson "Run those bases like lightning. I want you to worry the daylights out of those pitchers. Don't be afraid to try to steal that extra base . . . just go out there and run like the devil."

Montreal blitzed Jersey City, 14–1. Robinson ran like the devil and hit like a siege gun. His walking, daring, taunting leads flustered Jersey City pitchers into committing two balks. He stole two bases. He notched three singles. He smashed a three-run home run. He was a presence and a force. He completely dominated the game. He began the season that way and never let up.

"The most significant sports story of the century was written into the record books," Joe Bostic commented the next day in the *Amsterdam News*. "Baseball took up the cudgel for democracy and an unassuming Negro boy ascended the heights of excellence to prove the righteousness of the experiment. And prove it in the only correct crucible for such an experiment—the crucible of white-hot competition."

On July 8, 1946, with Robinson stealing bases, slashing hits, scoring runs, stoking Montreal's pennant romp, a special steering committee season of major league baseball was held in Chicago.

The committee agreed that "one or two Negroes ought to be allowed into the major leagues," but it had no specific recommendations for the moment. It reasoned that there were not enough Negro ballplayers of major league caliber. It stated that the Negro Leagues were already very profitable and that there would be a lessening of profits if the major leagues were opened up to blacks. The committee also claimed that "outside agitators were trying to break down the segregation barriers and these people were not necessarily interested in baseball but in other things."

Robinson ignored the rhetoric, and the dugouts that displayed watermelons and shoe shine kits. He played baseball. Gambling, battling, triggering the Montreal offense, he pushed the Royals to a fifteen-game lead by August 1 and to a runaway International League pennant victory. He led the league in batting with a .349 average, paced the league in fielding with a .985 percentage, and stole forty bases. The Robinson effect paced Montreal's Little World Series triumph over Louisville. A quota on blacks allowed to attend the games in Louisville was just another example of the cruel reality Rickey had warned Robinson about.

"Mr. Rickey was very paternal without being paternalistic," said Rachel Robinson. "He felt he was not only the initiator of the idea but he felt responsible for seeing that it worked not just for the team and for himself, but for Jack. It wasn't as if he had set Jack up and then said, 'Okay, if you do it, fine—if you don't do it, it's not my fault. I gave you the opportunity.' Mr. Rickey allied himself with Jack. He operated in such a way that he tried to anticipate the problems."

Sportswriter Tom Meany gave Rickey the nickname, "The Mahatma." Meany got the idea from John Gunther's phrase describing the Indian leader Mohandas K. Gandhi as a "combination of God, your own father, and Tammany Hall." Rickey needed his total combination of traits to help smooth the path for Robinson. He was aware of the problems of white prejudice, yet he did not overlook the potential problems of excessive black passion for Robinson.

On February 5, 1947, Rickey met with a group of prominent Brooklyn black leaders. He spoke to them about "the weight of responsibility that rests upon the shoulders of leading Negro citizens of this community. . . . We don't want any Negro to add to the burdens of Jackie Robinson. We don't want Negroes to form gala welcoming committees, to form parades to the ball park every night. We don't want Negroes to strut, to wear badges . . ."

Rickey warned the black leaders about jealousy and sensitivity. "We don't want premature Jackie Robinson Days or Nights. We don't want Negroes in the stands gambling, drunk, fighting, being arrested. We don't want Jackie wined and dined until he is fat and futile . . . We don't want what can be another great milestone in the progress of American race relations turned into a national comedy and an ugly tragedy."

The black community agreed with Rickey. Its leadership coined the slogan: "Don't Spoil Jackie's Chances."

A few of the players on the Dodgers balked at the idea of Robinson joining the team. "Bobby Bragan went to Branch Rickey," Monte Irvin notes, "and said he could not play baseball on the same team with a black man. Rickey told Bragan, 'I've got Bruce Edwards, I've got Gil Hodges. You're the third string catcher and you're expendable.' The Alabama-born Bragan's response was 'I live down in Ft. Worth, Texas. My friends there would never forgive me.' Bragan was that blinded," said Irvin.

Rickey sent Bragan down. "After a year or two," Irvin notes, "Bragan realized what his attitude was. Later he became a Pacific Coast League manager and went out of his way to help black players coming up." Bragan eventually remarked, "Not only was Robinson a hell of a ballplayer, he was a hell of a man."

On April 9 and 10, 1947, the Dodgers and the Montreal Royals featuring Jackie Robinson played two exhibition games at Ebbets

Field. Thousands wore "I'm for Jackie" buttons. Petitions were circulated urging the Dodgers to purchase the contract of Robinson from Montreal and make him a member of the Brooklyn team. On April 9, Commissioner "Happy" Chandler suspended Dodger manager Leo Durocher for the entire 1947 season for "conduct unbecoming to baseball." On April 10, the reporters in the Ebbets Field Press box were still gossiping about "The Lip's" departure when a Rickey assistant in the sixth inning passed out a release dwarfing the Durocher story: "Brooklyn announces the purchase of the contract of Jack Roosevelt Robinson from Montreal. . . . He will report immediately. Signed, Branch Rickey."

The *Amsterdam News* of April 11 reported that Branch Rickey had met secretly with his coaches in his Forest Hills home and that all of them were in favor of making Robinson a member of the Dodgers. "Now I can relax," Robinson was quoted in the article. "I have a few days before the season opens and I'll be ready then. The time element in making good won't be a factor anymore."

The legal tool that broke baseball's color line was the Uniform Player's Contract of the National League of Professional Ball Clubs. Dated April 11, 1947, the "parties" were the Brooklyn National League Baseball Club, Inc. and Jack Roosevelt Robinson of 1588 W. 36th Pl., Los Angeles, California. Robinson's social security number, 551-14-1990, his clear and strong signature, Rickey's scrawled name, and the tall signature of National League President Ford Frick were all on the contract.

In that April of 1947, black Americans all over the country mused about what might have been and what would be. Amidst all the news about rookie prospects, managerial shifts, the excitement of a new baseball season, the Branch Rickey announcement that Jackie Roosevelt Robinson, grandson of slaves, would open the season at first base for the Brooklyn Dodgers eclipsed all else. "I'm thrilled," Robinson said. "It's what I've been waiting for. I'm just going to take a cut at the ball every time a good one comes over the plate, try to connect, run as fast as I can and play the game hard and clean."

April 15, 1947, was Opening Day of the baseball season. In New York City the day began with brilliant sunshine and then turned raw. Workers building the Brooklyn Battery Tunnel were on strike. At the United Nations a lengthy meeting focused on the establishment of an organization to control atomic energy. Former President Herbert Hoover and a delegation from the United Nations led by Russia's Andrei Gromyko were among the 39,444 fans at the Yankee Stadium opener. The Philadelphia Athletics behind Canadian war hero Phil Marchildon topped Spud Chandler and the Yankees 6–1. The Giants played in Philadelphia and lost 4–3 as Schoolboy Rowe outpitched Bill Voiselle.

The only New York City baseball team Opening Day victory belonged to the Dodgers. Joe Hatten beat Boston's Johnny Sain 5–3 before 26,623. Many of the fans showed up in their most fashionable spring clothes. Many of the fans sat in the outfield box seats that had been constructed by advancing the left-field and center-field stands fourteen feet. Some of those who attended the game were not even baseball fans but had come wearing "I'm for Jackie" buttons, to witness the debut of twenty-eight-year-old Jackie Robinson.

"I was scared and I was there," recalls Stan Lomax. "The general feeling was that we've got a keg of dynamite here—is anybody going to touch off the fuse?"

In his first at-bat Robinson hit the ball sharply to shortstop. He sped down the line. Unable to brake himself, he touched first base and continued running for a few more steps. The throw and Robinson arrived at first base at about the same time, but umpire Al Barlick called him out. Robinson scowled, took a step toward Barlick, and then remembered. Rickey had taught him well. He trotted back to the Dodger dugout, unhappy but restrained. In his second appearance at the plate, he flied out to left field. His final time up he hit into a double play. Robinson had not gotten a hit, but he had smashed the color line in baseball once and for all.

The next morning Arthur Daley wrote in the *New York Times*: "The debut of Jackie Robinson was quite uneventful even though he had the unenviable distinction of snuffing out a rally by hitting into a double play. . . The muscular Negro minds his own business and shrewdly makes no effort to push himself. He speaks quietly and intelligently when spoken to. . . . 'I was nervous in my first play in my first game at Ebbets Field,' he said with his ready grin, 'but nothing has bothered me since.'"

Sid Frigand, the former *Brooklyn Eagle* writer, looks back at Robinson's historic debut: "There was a great feeling of pride that it happened in Brooklyn. Its traditions were not that liberal but the borough rooted for an underdog. Jackie Robinson was an underdog."

Stan Lomax believes that not only Brooklyn but the entire city of New York provided a receptive climate. "Color doesn't matter with a New Yorker—if he's good they'll applaud. If he's bad, they'll boo, but New Yorkers give a guy a chance to prove himself."

In the seventh inning of the second game he played, Robinson recorded the first of his 1,518 major league hits. He bunted the ball down the third base line. Bob Elliot flubbed a barehanded attempt to come up with the ball and Robinson had a bunt single. "The Negro isn't exactly wearing out the ball," the *Brooklyn Eagle* commented the next day, "but he's still under heavy pressure."

Rachel Robinson remembers the pressure: "It was post war, and we could not get any housing. We did not have much money. We could only afford one room in the Hotel McAlpin in Manhattan. It was tough living in that one room, contending with reporters, making formula for three-month Jackie, Jr., hanging diapers in the bathroom.

"Both of us were strangers to the city. We didn't have friends. We had no relatives in New York City. Jackie, Jr., caught a cold on opening day when I took him to the ball park. I was worried about the child. I was worried about the experiment of Jack. He still had to win a spot on the team.

"Jack and I could not even go out and eat together. In the back of the McAlpin, there was a cafeteria on a side street. One of us would mind the baby. The other would go out and eat and then we'd switch off. I didn't get sitters. I did not want to leave my baby with anyone. I would not miss a game. It was like going to work with your husband. I held on to Jack. He held on to me. The baby was part of the whole unit. In those first couple of years, my world, my whole context was the family and the ball park. We couldn't take advantage of the city. We didn't even have a car. We'd take bus rides just to get some recreation. The black newspaper reporters were closest to us of anyone. They followed us, and they helped us."

On April 18, Robinson blasted the first of his 137 career home runs as the Dodgers defeated the Giants, 10–4, before 37,546 at the Polo

Grounds. The new Dodger manager, Burt Shotton, and the huge Harlem contingent at the ball park were delighted.

"Robinson was an all-around person whom everybody could be proud of whether he or she was black or white, yellow or red," observed former Mayor Wagner. "I can never remember anybody in New York making any trouble—in other cities, yes, but not in New York City."

In games against Philadelphia, there the invective of the prejudiced major league manager that Rickey had warned about came out full force. "Hey, nigger, why don't you go back to the cotton field where you belong? Hey, snowflake, which one of those white boys' wives are you shacking up with tonight?" Alabama-born Philly manager Ben Chapman orchestrated the hate language as the Dodgers tried to concentrate on baseball and beating Philadelphia. The abuse of Robinson went on for two days. His bathing habits, his sexual preferences, his ancestry, his physiological makeup—all were characterized in the most unseemly language.

When Robinson had first reported to the Dodgers, second baseman Eddie Stanky had told him, "I don't like you but we'll play together and get along because you're my teammate." In the third game of the series with Philadelphia, Stanky could remain silent no more. "Listen, you yellow-bellied cowards," the Alabama-born ballplayer shouted, "Why don't you pick on someone who can fight back? You know Robinson can't. What kind of men are you, anyway?"

Branch Rickey had remarked about Robinson: "Here is a man whose wounds you could not feel or share." The Chapman incident altered Rickey's view. "Chapman did more than anybody," said Rickey, "to make Dixie Walker, Eddie Stanky and other Dodgers speak up in Robinson's behalf. When Chapman poured out that string of unconscionable abuse, he solidified and unified thirty men, not one of whom was willing to sit by and see someone kick around a man who had his hands tied behind his back."

On May 9, 1947, Stanley Woodward revealed in a *Herald Tribune* article how a strike against Jackie Robinson by the St. Louis Cardinals had been aborted. The strike had been planned as a protest against Robinson being in the Brooklyn Dodger lineup. The strike had been planned for May 6—the first 1947 meeting between the

Dodgers and Cardinals. The Woodward story reported that National League president Ford Frick sent the following message to the Cardinals:

"If you do this, you will be suspended from the League. You will find that the friends that you think you have in the press box will not support you, that you will be outcasts. I do not care if half the League strikes. Those who do it will encounter quick retribution. They will be suspended, and I do not care if it wrecks the National League for five years. This is the United States of America, and one citizen has as much right to play as another. The National League will go down the line with Robinson, whatever the consequence. You will find that if you go through with your intention that you have been guilty of complete madness."

Red Barber recalls the 1947 baseball season. "It was a sensitive, even delicate situation. After all, I had the mike, and I had the southern accent, and I had millions of people listening to every word I said. And this thing was not something you were suddenly confronted with one day and then didn't have to worry about anymore. It had to be handled inning by inning, game by game, month by month. It was there all the time because when Robinson came, he came to stay."

"The more they rode Jackie Robinson," said Roy Campanella, "the better he played." He played like a man possessed. He fought back against the black cats that magically appeared in opposition dugouts, the elevators in hotels that suddenly malfunctioned, the restaurants that ran out of food, the tags of opposing fielders that were more like gloved punches, the racial taunts, the long, cool stares, the silences. All the speed and skill that had enabled him to star in football, basketball, tennis, broad-jumping, and baseball at UCLA were let out full throttle.

"He did things that if you read about them," recalls Ron Gabriel, who spent so much time at Ebbets Field as a teenage Dodger zealot, "you wouldn't believe them. If you saw it on TV, you'd think it was trick photography . . . you had to see him at the ball park to appreciate it."

Dancer Bill "Bojangles" Robinson called him "Ty Cobb in technicolor." Jackie Robinson played in one hundred fifty games in 1947—more than any other Dodger. He batted .297. He led the league in stolen bases and won the Rookie of the Year award. He pushed Brooklyn's attendance to 1,807,526—the first of ten straight million-plus years for the Jackie Robinson Dodgers. On the road, the Dodgers drew nearly two million more. Robinson's presence helped account for the National League ten-million-plus attendance figure, its highest to that point in history.

In June of that first momentous year, he startled everyone by scoring all the way from first base on a sacrifice by Gene Hermanski in a game in Chicago. Another time he dashed to second base on a walk. He stole home and for a brief instant the loyalty of the hometown fans in a game in Pittsburgh. Walking leads that terrorized opposing pitchers, football-like slides that intimidated infielders, clutch hit after clutch hit, evasive tactics on run down plays—these became part of the Robinson mystique and style.

"He created tension in pitcher, in fans," said Mrs. Robinson. "He hoped to get pitchers so rattled that he'd upset them into mistakes. That hatred of him in that context was also complimentary. He was a danger and a threat in a work sense. That style fit with his personality . . . the ball park was an outlet for his daring. Mr. Rickey and the coaches encouraged the explicit development of the style."

A powerfully built, ebony-skinned man with the number forty-two on his back, Jackie Robinson was paradoxically a man apart and a pied piper. Wherever he went, he attracted a crowd. When he moved with Rachel and Jackie, Jr., in the middle of the 1947 season to a Brooklyn tenement apartment, the street on which he lived was often a congregating place for the curious. His five-block walk from the subway to Ebbets Field was always jammed with autograph seekers. Whenever he played, thousands of non-baseball fans would come out to get a glimpse of the black pioneer.

Gradually, with each hit, with each stolen base, with each run batted in, with each smart fielding play, Robinson became accepted. "As he saw he was succeeding," recalls Rachel Robinson, "he began to feel more comfortable." On the streets of Brooklyn, Manhattan, the Bronx, kids who had modeled their stances after Stan Musial or Johnny Mize or Joe DiMaggio began to raise the bat high over their right shoulder and play Jackie Robinson.

The Brooklyn Dodger office at 215 Montague Street received

more than five thousand requests for all types of social and commercial appearances for Robinson. Gangs of autograph seekers and mobs of celebrity followers pursued him wherever he went. "The way things are now," Rickey said, "he's a sideshow. Give him a sporting chance." Rickey told reporters, "If I had my way about it, I would place a cordon of police protection around him so that he might be a ballplayer."

Sid Frigand feels that "the credit has to go to Rickey not only for just bringing Robinson to the majors . . . but also for doing the right things when he spoke to reporters. Rickey never put it into a moral frame, a righteous sense," said Frigand. "He always stressed that Robinson was a fine ballplayer, that it was good for baseball. Had he turned what was happening into a racial crusade, the results might have been different."

There were still those who could not accept the fact that Jackie Robinson, a black man, was succeeding in what had always been a white man's game.

Two years to the day that Robinson had appeared in a Montreal uniform in exhibition games against the Dodgers at Ebbets Field, Brooklyn was scheduled for a three-game exhibition series against the Atlanta Crackers. The grand dragon of the Ku Klux Klan, Dr. Samuel Green, declared that it was illegal for interracial teams to play in Georgia. He threatened to take steps to block the Dodgers from playing. He warned that there would be violence. About fifty thousand spectators appeared for the three-game series. For the Sunday game about fourteen thousand blacks showed up. They spilled out of the section reserved for them and watched the baseball action a dozen deep in the outfield. The threatened violence never took place.

The crowd reaction to the black players was in itself a sociological statement. Lang remembers the Dodgers of Brooklyn barnstorming into Birmingham, Alabama, on a Wednesday afternoon in the spring. "The outfield stands, the cheaper seats were all crowded with blacks who had come out to see Robinson. The grandstand seats had perhaps a dozen people. It was the whites back then who were showing their feelings by boycotting the game."

Lang, today a *New York Daily News* sportswriter, remembers the games in Cincinnati: "Charter buses in those early days of Robinson and Irvin and Campanella and Newcombe used to arrive from all over the south to see a Sunday doubleheader. There was always a jammed ball park. The people made it into a festival, a coming together.

"Generally, there would be an announcement in the seventh or eighth inning of the second game—'Bus leaving for Memphis in fifteen minutes, train leaving for Mobile in ten minutes.'

"The park would grudgingly start to empty out. Some stayed and missed their train or bus. They stayed to see Robinson hit one more time or Newcombe pitch one more inning.

"You were sitting in on history being made. And you had to be sympathetic if you were fair-minded. The blacks had been mistreated and all they wanted was a chance to play ball."

In 1950, a letter signed by the "Three Travelers" was sent to the Dodgers, the Cincinnati baseball team, the Cincinnati Police Department, and a Cincinnati newspaper. The letter threatened the life of Jackie Robinson and claimed that if he played at Crosley Field against the Reds, he would be shot by a marksman positioned in one of the buildings that crowded close to and overlooked the little ball park.

Before the game, FBI agents patrolled the buildings and the ball park. They interviewed Robinson, trying to reassure him.

In the clubhouse, after the agents had left, outfielder Gene Hermanski suggested that all the Dodgers wear number forty-two. "We'll be able to protect Robby that way." Robinson grinned. "Now if you'd brought along a little soot to paint your face black and practiced walking pigeon-toed, you could wear number forty-two and be of some help."

There were thousands of blacks in the ball park. Many of them had traveled long distances from the south to watch Robinson, Campanella (who joined the Dodgers in 1948), and Newcombe (who joined the Dodgers in 1949). The FBI was concerned about the threat to Robinson's life and the possible violent aftermath if there was an attempted assassination.

Robinson won the first game of the scheduled doubleheader with a home run. The ball landed not far from the vicinity where a gunman might have been lurking. Robinson crossed home plate and shook hands with Cal Abrams, who had been on base when Robinson hit the home run. "My God, Jack," said Abrams, who was Jewish, "Let's get into the dugout quick. If they are ever gonna shoot the two of us, now's the time!"

The hits, runs, stolen bases were measurable. In 1949, he batted .342 to lead the National League. It was the first of six consecutive .300 seasons. From 1947 to 1953, he averaged better than one hundred runs scored per season, and close to seventy bases on balls. Twenty times in his career he stole home. What Jackie Robinson could do on a ball field was a matter of record. What he was as a person still arouses controversy.

"He was aloof to most of us," said sportswriter Jack Lang, "except for those he thought were for civil rights before it became popular in politics. He was close to certain writers, none of whom traveled regularly with the Dodgers, except for Roger Kahn who traveled with us for one and a half years of active coverage. Where Robinson would have CBS broadcaster Edward R. Murrow as his guest in the Dodger clubhouse, Carl Furillo would have some guy named Tex who owned a pizza place just off Eastern Parkway. Jackie was far above the other players educationally."

Irving Rudd said, "There was a lot of respect, but also a lot of ambivalence in his relationship with the other blacks on the Dodgers. They were not home and home visitors."

A part of it all and yet a man apart, Jackie Robinson is recalled by his wife Rachel as a person whose behavior was often misunderstood. "Jack was not a socializer," she said. "He was not one to hang out with the boys, or have a beer on the corner. That behavior was often misunderstood as snobbishness, aloofness. He'd make a beeline for home after a game or a golf driving range where he'd go hit his golf balls before dark. That was his way.

"He never expected a fair share from some writers. He'd ridicule them and write them off. Dick Young was one. Jimmy Powers changed over the years and became very much a supporter. Jack was trying to do something very important. . . . If you're suspicious of some . . . you don't let yourself get in a position where they can do you in. . . . Some of the tension between him and the press was that they wanted to talk about the score; he wanted to talk about social issues."

The walk, the look, the voice of Jackie Robinson became as familiar to New Yorkers as number forty-two's exceptional playing skills. In 1948 he became a WMCA radio sports commentator. By 1950, although there were still traces of prejudice against him, he began to receive the financial rewards that he had so convincingly earned on the ball field.

His 1950 salary was $35,000—tops to that point in Dodger history. On March 10, New Yorkers could purchase a Jackie Robinson jacket at Macy's for $6.95 or a cap for 98 cents. In April, three years after he had broken baseball's color line, he signed to do the film version of his life story for $50,000 and a share of the film's profits. The *Life* magazine cover of May 8 had a picture of Jackie Robinson and the headline "Star Ballplayer Stars in a Movie." *The Jackie Robinson Story* premiered at the Astor Theater in New York City on May 17, 1950. Newspaper ads for the film said:

"They'll shout insults at you . . . they'll come in at you spikes first . . . they'll throw at your head . . . but no matter what happens, you can't fight back.

"Yes only in America could a man have the courage, the will and the greatness to face such overwhelming odds with only a ball . . . a bat . . . and a glove . . . and win.

Jackie Robinson—

The Pride of Brooklyn—

as himself."

By 1953, with seven teams playing black players—a total of twenty-three in the major leagues—Robinson was able to become his own man. "As he fitted in, some of that deep-down resentment started to surface," notes Stan Lomax. "He remembered all of those who had treated him nasty. He had a sullen feeling against them. He started to become testy and outspoken, and who could blame him?"

Rachel Robinson said, "A mythology exists that there was a conversation between Branch Rickey and Jack in which Rickey said, 'take the gloves off now.' That never happened.

"It was always understood between the two of them that Jack would go along with the program for a limited time. As he began to feel more and more in control of the situation, as he proved himself as a ballplayer, he knew that it was time to be himself. Mr. Rickey did not give the signal. It was Jack's own timing. He determined it. It was very hard for a man as assertive as Jack to contain his own rage—yet he felt the end goal was so critical that there was no question that he would do it. And he knew he could do even better if he could ventilate, express himself, use his own style."

An incident at the Chase Hotel in St. Louis revealed Robinson's new assertiveness. "Our colored players stayed at separate hotels when we were in St. Louis," recalls Lee Scott, former Brooklyn Dodger traveling secretary. "That was the way it was. Dorothy Dandridge was performing at the Chase Hotel where the bulk of the team stayed. I asked the manager, 'How about our getting our colored players into the hotel?'

" 'They're colored,' he said. 'I can't do it.'

" 'How about Dorothy Dandridge? She's colored.'

" 'But she's an entertainer,' the manager said.

"I said, 'What do you think ballplayers are?'

"That kind of floored him. He said, 'Okay, Lee, on the next trip, bring them in. But tell them to have room service.'

"On the next trip, Jackie Robinson, being the stubborn guy that he was, had me sit at a table in the dining room with him and Campy. The waitress didn't know what the hell to do. 'It's all right, honey,' I said, 'Mr. Robinson (that was also the name of the hotel manager) said it's all right.' We never had any trouble after that."

The black ballplayers that followed Jackie Robinson into baseball are mixed in their feelings toward him. "The most vocal, the most articulate of them," says Rachel Robinson, "is Joe Black. He has said time after time that without Jackie the others would not have had the opportunity. Some of the others claim that they will not attribute their success, even their opportunity, to him. 'I made my own way,' they say. . . . Some of the early conflict and tension with Roy Campanella dealt with who got selected first to break the color line. Campy grew up with baseball and was a great player by the time he was nine years old. That was his life. Jack came in much later. Baseball was not one of his primary interests. He got the pioneering role. That created envy and a lot of ambivalence."

National League Most Valuable Player in 1951, 1953, and 1955, Campanella lived by the creed "To play this game good, a lot of you has got to be a little boy." At five feet nine inches and close to two hundred pounds, Campy supplied a great deal of the power of the Dodgers. Stan Lomax remembers Campanella. "On Tuesday nights, in Dexter Park, on the Brooklyn–Queens border, the Philly Stars used to come over and play. Campy was the catcher and he was the star of the Stars. You knew once the color line was broken, somebody would grab him."

Rickey signed Campanella a short while after he signed Robinson. Campanella spent 1946 with the Dodger farm team at Nashua, New Hampshire—the lone black on the nineteen-man roster. Walt Alston was his manager. In 1947 he was with the Montreal Royals. In 1948 Rickey assigned the "man from Nicetown" (Campy was raised in Nicetown, Pa.) to the St. Paul team in the American Association. The Mahatma wanted Campanella to break the color barrier there. After thirty-five games, Campanella had slammed thirteen home runs and was called up to the Dodgers where he was to star for the next decade.

Four times he hit more than thirty homers a season and led the league in fielding. Three times he drove in more than a hundred runs and batted over .300. He hit more home runs than any other catcher in Dodger history. The beaming, broad man with the number thirty-nine on his back added another dimension to the Dodger team. A kind and compassionate handler of pitchers, a man for the young players to come to talk to, his spirited optimism would always buoy the team in times of slump or crises. Campy had spent so many years in the Negro and minor leagues that he deemed it a privilege to be in the majors. He would tell the old stories of catching both ends of a doubleheader in the Negro leagues, running for a bus, sleeping sitting up in the bus and then catching another doubleheader the next day in another city a few hundred miles away. "Being up in the big leagues is heaven," he would say. "I can't complain."

On January 28, 1958, Roy Campanella was severely injured in an automobile accident. He was all set to move with the Dodgers to Los Angeles. "I'll never quit," he had joked. "They'll have to cut the uniform off my back." The accident left the once powerful slugger paralyzed from the waist down. "He's been in that chair, twenty,

twenty-one years," notes Stan Lomax, "and he still smiles, he never complains."

The only mild grousing that Campanella, who was admitted to baseball's Hall of Fame in 1969, engaged in during his career was over the roles that black ballplayers should take. Unlike Robinson, Campy was willing to wait. "I'm not a man for controversies," Campanella said. "I shy away from them like the plague." Robinson acknowledged "everyone wants to conform," but his whole being marched to an inner drum of conscience that made him speak up, refuse to 'Wait 'Til Next Year' when it came to social issues.

"There was always a coolness between Robinson and Campanella," said Stan Lomax. "One was fiery and the other was calm."

Campanella acknowledged the differences. "Jackie was a politician, wanted to be a politician. I didn't. I would exercise my vote and urge all blacks to exercise their vote but I'd be darned if I'd get on a soapbox and preach for one party or another."

"There was a real clash with Jack and some of the other black players," says Rachel Robinson, "[between] his political involvement and their lack of involvement, his political identification with social issues and their not understanding why he cared . . . his efforts to draw them in . . . and their saying, 'Why are you doing this?' . . . Willie Mays has said, 'I look at my house. I look at Jackie Robinson. I look at the dollars in my pocket. I look at Jackie Robinson.' Yet Willie has never contributed to the Jackie Robinson Foundation."

Those who saw Jackie Roosevelt Robinson play will never forget the pigeon-toed walk, the shuffled feet, the bluff, the dash, the stolen base, the crowd's roar. "The worst time with the Dodgers," recalls former Polo Grounds ticket taker and watcher Joe Flynn, "was when Robinson came in and all the blacks would come to the Polo Grounds. All of a sudden, he'd get a hit or steal a base and they'd belt you on the back of the neck. They'd knock you over. They were great, great fans. They sure loved him!"

Near the end of his career his reflexes had slowed and he played most of the time at third base because of reduced mobility. His hair turned white and his weight was well over two hundred pounds. The newspapers called him the "old, fat, gray man." He was only thirty-seven. The last game he ever played was on October 10, 1956. It was the last World Series game the Brooklyn Dodgers ever played. Robinson was the last Dodger to bat. He struck out.

The girl he met when she was a freshman and he was a senior and star athlete at UCLA remembers Jackie Robinson: "He was so concerned with other people, and I remember him for his bigness," says Rachel Robinson. "I remember him for being deeply religious. He would never articulate or conceptualize his great belief in religion, God, destiny, that he was on a mission doing God's work, but he felt it.

"He would say in times of trouble: 'God's testing me,' but he never took the passive attitude of 'it's God's will.' He was a warm, affectionate, demonstrative person. . . . If you are going to carry out a mission, your children do not have as much of you as if you were someone else . . . yet our children had a great deal of him in concentrated doses.

"In remembering him, I tend to de-emphasize him as a ballplayer and emphasize him as an informal civil rights leader—that's the part that drops out, that people forget, and we're trying to keep that part alive. My memories of him are very good, very satisfying to me.

"Jack was persistence in the face of enormous obstacles," Rachel Robinson continues. "He pursued excellence. Jack presented a model for persistence, for survival, a model for being able to sustain yourself without too much outside support. He contributed to black participation in baseball in many ways that never happened before. There are many spin-offs that we cannot trace . . . blacks as spectators, as participants. It may be even showing up in the arts and in so many places, the thread that goes back to Jack. . . . When I travel, people will stop me and say, 'I feel so much better about myself because Jack lived.' "

On July 8, 1949, a black pitcher faced a black batter for the first time in the history of major league baseball. The pitcher was Don Newcombe of the Dodgers. The batter was Hank Thompson of the Giants. A failure with the St. Louis Browns in a brief trial in 1947, Thompson had been signed along with Monte Irvin in 1948. Each player was given $5,000. "We lost money," says Irvin, "but we knew we'd gain money in the long run if we made the Giants."

Irvin was a thirty-one-year-old rookie. "I'm just a little bitter about it," he says. "If I'd have had the chance I could have come right out of high school and played major league ball."

When Irvin and Thompson reported from Jersey City to the Giants in 1949 there were sixteen major league teams with a total of four hundred players. Three teams had a grand total of seven black players. "Durocher did not make Rickey's kind of speech to us," recalls Irvin, now an assistant to the Commissioner of Baseball and a member of the Hall of Fame. "He said, 'Conduct yourself like gentlemen. If somebody does something, don't go out of the way to turn the other cheek. Give it back to them one for one!'"

Durocher told Irvin and Thompson not to complain too much, and he gave the Giant pitchers orders to protect them. Irvin recalls: "The opposition used to get delight in throwing at us and knocking us down. Durocher said, 'We're either a team or we're not a team. You wear "Giants" across your chest and you're part of the team . . . we'll take care of you.'

"Leo took us around and introduced us to everyone. I got close to Lockman, Lohrke, Hartung, Rigney. They were kind and helpful. The fact that they were as friendly as they were made it easier, made it much easier. Thompson and I did not have the difficult time that Jackie Robinson had had a couple of years earlier. In fact, whenever we came in contact with Robinson, we would talk and he would always have stories to tell. We were always sympathetic to the fact that he had such a difficult time.

"Stoneham was a big factor, too," observes Irvin, who played in thirty-nine games in 1949. "When the Dodgers signed Robinson, you just knew Horace Stoneham, being the benevolent man that he was, would be the second to sign black players . . . plus at that time the Giants needed players. They weren't doing well, and they needed a shot in the arm, and he saw the potential. He also would not stand for any hostility toward us from the players and he made that clear."

Irvin remembers that there was not overt hostility in 1949, but there was a disturbing atmosphere:

"You'd walk into a room and they'd walk out. You'd sit down on a train and one person, maybe two, would get up and walk away. This was 1949 in the United States of America. It was just the thing to do for some. It's always been this way. Let it be this way forever. There was no sense of fair play. That was the role these fellows were supposed to have, beneath you. I do believe, however, that some of the mean and underhanded and nasty things they did they had to have second thoughts about afterward. I do believe that many of them who were prejudiced were sorry afterward they behaved that way."

A late start and injuries truncated Irvin's major league career. From 1950 to 1953, he batted .299, .312, .310, .329. In 1951, he led the league in runs batted in and stolen bases. His last year as a New York Giant was 1955. He put in one more year with the White Sox and then was finished as a major leaguer. "My career was condensed," said Irvin. "I started late and finished early." He still wonders what he would have accomplished had he had a full shot as a major league ball-player. In 1973, Monford Merrill Irvin, born February 25, 1919—one month after Jackie Robinson—was admitted to baseball's Hall of Fame.

On May 14, 1935, Jack Schwarz joined the New York Giants as manager Bill Terry's secretary. In 1936, the farm system of the Giants had originated with one team—Greenwood, Mississippi. The following year the Greenwood franchise was moved to Ft. Smith, Arkansas. The Giants began another minor league club in Blightville, Arkansas, and they purchased the Albany, New York, baseball team and moved it to Jersey City, creating their first Triple A franchise.

During the years of World War II, the Giants curtailed their minor league operations. After the war they, along with other major league teams, expanded their minor league operations. One of the first players to come out of the Giants' farm system to star in the majors was Bobby Thomson.

By 1950 there were sixty minor leagues. The Giants had twenty-four farm teams and were always grappling with the problem of staffing them completely. "In the early months of 1950," recalls Schwarz, "there was a vacancy at Sioux City, a Giant farm team. They needed a first baseman. At that stage of the season it was difficult to get one. Horace Stoneham said to me, 'Your only shot is the Negro leagues. Why don't you try Alex Pompez?'"

Schwarz contacted Pompez, a leading figure in black baseball circles. Pompez recommended a veteran first baseman on the New York Cubans. That team was scheduled for a series against the Birmingham Black Barons. Schwarz sent two scouts to evaluate the first baseman on the New York Cubans.

"I didn't hear anything for about ten days," said Schwarz, "and then I got a call from one of the scouts, Bill Harris. 'That first baseman can't help Sioux City,' he said, 'but they've got a little black outfielder on Birmingham that's better than Bobby Hazle.' Cincinnati had signed Hazle that summer and given him a $35,000 bonus," noted Schwarz.

"Then I got a call from the other scout, Eddie Montague. 'You must get this outfielder on the Birmingham Black Barons. You must buy him—he can't miss.' "

What followed were many long distance telephone calls to ascertain if the Birmingham owner was willing to part with the outfielder. It was determined that the Boston Braves were also interested in obtaining him. Their offer, according to Schwarz, was $7,500 cash and another $7,500 if they kept the player for thirty days. Mr. Hayes, the Birmingham team owner, did not like the offer. He had sold players before to white clubs, and when they didn't keep the players they came back to him after being paid a salary so high that he couldn't match it, and the players became dissatisfied.

"The Giants offered Hayes $10,000 cash," Schwarz continued. "Montague had said that the player would be in the Polo Grounds in two years, and that was good enough for me. I got a hold of Chub Feeney, who was then vice president of the Giants, and we made the deal and then we went in to get Mr. Stoneham's approval, but we had already made the deal."

Nevertheless, the black outfielder never played for Sioux City. "I always suspected," says Schwarz, "it was because they didn't want a Negro. There had never been one in their league." Instead he was sent to Trenton in the Interstate League.

"It was something like Jackie Robinson breaking into the major leagues. I was there by myself. I stayed at segregated hotels and was picked up and dropped off before and after games. But I wanted to play so bad that those kinds of things didn't worry me," recalls the outfielder from Alabama, Willie Mays.

When Mays reported to Trenton, the team was in third place. At season's end, they finished first. "He moved them up three notches by his play," Schwarz said.

"The next spring Mays was moved to Minneapolis. An exhibition game was scheduled between Minneapolis and Sioux City as it had been every year," Schwarz continued. "On every lightpost, there was publicity about the game that would feature Willie Mays. He was hitting well over .400 at the time. Sioux City was selling the game on the basis of a player they wouldn't give a chance the year before. They never got a chance to see him play in Sioux City. Durocher called up in the afternoon before this night game was scheduled. He wanted Mays for the New York Giants. They found him in a movie theater and told him to get on a plane and come to New York City."

Garry Schumacher, publicist for the Giants at the time, recalled the arrival of Mays: "The Giants were on their way from Chicago to Philadelphia to finish the last three games of a road trip. I was by the front door of the Giants office on Times Square. Suddenly this Negro kid comes in. There were always a lot of kids coming around, some of them wanted tickets, some of them wanted tryouts. He was carrying a few bats in one hand and a bag in the other which contained his glove and spikes. He was wearing the most unusual cap I ever saw. It had a bow in the front and a little belt in the back, and it was plaid colored. When I found out who he was, I took him to meet Mr. Stoneham. We bought him some clothes and then sent him to Philadelphia to join the club. He was wearing the new clothes when he left, but funny thing—he refused to take off that funny cap."

Willie Mays became a New York Giant after appearing in only 116 minor league games. He had batted .353 at Trenton and came up from Minneapolis with a .477 batting average—a drop from his peak of .500. He went hitless in his first twelve major league at-bats, cried in the dugout, and told Durocher to send him back to Minneapolis. "You're my center fielder," Durocher said, "and that's all there is to it."

Mays stayed for twenty-two seasons, a fixture among the superstars of major league baseball, one of the most cherished of all those who played for a New York City baseball team. Images of his playing stickball in the streets of Harlem, running out from under his cap pursuing a fly ball, swinging the bat with natural force and gusto, pounding one of his 660 career home runs still linger in the memory. "Willie could do everything from the day he joined the Giants," Durocher said. "He never had to be taught a thing. The only other player who could do it all was Joe DiMaggio."

Monte Irvin remembers Mays from the moment he first came up to the Giants. "When you saw Willie, you knew that he was going to be a real star. He could run, hit, field, throw, but you did not know he would be the home run hitter he became. What surprised all of us was that he developed all that power. He was not that big, but he was tremendously strong and coordinated. As a person, he was just a kid, happy-go-lucky, all the time. . . . Everybody loved him because he was a rare talent. He made it easier for other blacks coming up later on. Having him on your team playing center field gave us confidence . . . We figured that if a ball stayed in the ball park, he would catch it."

Mays arrived in the major leagues four years after Jackie Robinson. "You could never get away from the fact," observes Stan Lomax, "that Robinson was the pioneer. When Mays came up, a lot of the animosity towards blacks had been toned down. But I don't think Willie ever realized that he was a colored man. I don't think Willie ever thought of or feared the fact that he was black in a white league. He wasn't grown up when he first came to the Giants. I don't even think he'd seen an inside house toilet. He played the way he did for the fun of it. He was a guy who played ball as if he were still on the sandlots. He was never an 'I' guy. He was great for the morale of the club, trying to win for his team. He was accepted immediately."

Born Willie Howard Mays, May 6, 1931, in Westfield, Alabama, Mays was a natural. Five times he led the league in slugging percentage; four times he won the home run title; twice he was voted the Most Valuable Player. Winner of the Rookie of the Year award in 1951 and the batting title in 1954, the Hall of Famer was the most beloved player of his time. "Jackie Robinson rubbed it in," a player from that era said. "Mays smoothed it out."

In 1953, there were seven clubs with a total of twenty-three black players. None of them was on the New York Yankees. Jackie Robinson appeared on the television program "Youth Wants to Know."

"I have felt deep in my heart," he told moderator Faye Emerson, "that the Yankees for years had been giving Negroes the runaround." Controversy constantly clung to Robinson. His comments became grist for newspaper columns and the subject of protracted and passionate arguments among New York City baseball fans. "As Robinson got older," recalls Stan Lomax, "he got testy. He didn't like the Yankees anyway." The television station and the Dodger office received many phone calls and letters reacting to the Robinson comment. He did not back down. He issued a statement declaring that he felt the Yankee management was prejudiced against black ballplayers.

The executive chiefly responsible for the absence of blacks in the Yankee lineup was George Weiss. "Boxholders from Westchester don't want them," the taciturn Yankee general manager said. "They would be offended to sit with niggers. I will never allow a black man to wear a Yankee uniform." Southpaw Eddie Lopat won sixteen of twenty decisions in 1953 and topped the American League in earned run average and winning percentage. He pitched for the all-white New York Yankees against the Jack Robinson Dodgers in the 1953 World Series. "You had nothing to say if you were a player and you wanted a black player on your team or not," notes Lopat. "It was the front office. A player was just a player—a cog in a wheel. It was not like it is today where they can say anything they want and get away with it."

Eight years after Jackie Robinson had broken the color line, Elston Howard, a black man, joined the Yankees in spring training in 1954. "The next thing we knew," said Lopat, "he was leaving. Some of us talked up to Case [Stengel] and said, 'Hey, Case, we can use this man. He can help us.'

"Case said, 'I have nothin' to do with this. They want to switch him to a catcher.'

"Well, Elston was a guy who showed you a good bat, could play the outfield and first base," Lopat continued. "They sent him to Toronto and it was out of the organization. He came back the MVP. He was a swell guy. He joined us the following spring. The players said, 'No matter what kind of spring he has, he's staying. He can help us.' "

Born February 23, 1929, Elston Howard was the antithesis of

Jackie Robinson. Robinson was a liberal; Howard was a conservative man. Robinson was flash and fire; Howard was steady and stoical. Dodger manager Charlie Dressen had remarked of Robinson: "He reminds me of a sign I once saw in a locker room. 'We supply the equipment. You supply the guts.' Robinson does not need a sign like that. He's got the equipment and the guts." Casey Stengel's early characterization of Howard was: "When I finally get a nigger, I get the only one who can't run." Howard let the remark pass. Robinson always mentioned it when talking about Stengel.

Howard was a slow runner, but that was his only drawback. He could hit. He could throw. He could handle pitchers. He could lead. He became one of Stengel's favorites. "You can substitute," the old perfessor said, "but it's tough to replace. With Howard, I have a replacement not a substitute." 'Ellie' Howard played the outfield, first base and catcher. It took him seven years to become the regular Yankee catcher. Yogi Berra—not the color of Howard's skin—proved to be the roadblock.

"Club owners who went after black players at the start had a pipeline into a bunch of number-one draft choices in a couple of years," said Jack Lang. "They were a goldmine of talent." Six Most Valuable Player awards were achieved by the black New York City ballplayers: Robinson (1949), Campanella (1951, 1953, 1955), Newcombe (1956). Later Howard would become the first black MVP in the American League. In 1947, Jackie Robinson won the Rookie of the Year award, then Newcombe in 1949, Mays in 1951, Joe Black in 1952, and Jim Gilliam in 1953.

Gilliam was the bat boy for the Baltimore Elite Giants in the old Negro leagues. When he was seventeen years old, he was promoted to the regular second base position and dubbed "Junior." The name stayed with him.

A warm, gentlemanly man, Gilliam never played less than 144 games a season during his first 11 years as a Dodger. "He was probably the closest thing to the perfect ballplayer I ever saw," said his former manager, Walt Alston. "In all the years, he never missed a sign. He played anywhere I wanted him to. He was a manager's delight."

Gilliam always maintained that "one of the greatest things in my life was coming to the Brooklyn Dodgers and rooming with Jackie Robinson. I learned a lot about life on and off the field from him."

In 1975, Gilliam signed his autograph "Jim." When asked if the "Junior" had changed to "Jim," he responded "I sign Jim because it's three letters and Junior is six. The Junior will never change to Jim, but I don't care what you call me as long as you keep on calling me for a few more years."

He had only a few more years to be called. In 1978, he died. "I don't know what Gilliam's career average was or how many hits or home runs or RBIs he had," said his former teammate, Pee Wee Reese. "I don't know anything about his 'statics' as Dizzy Dean used to say, but I do know he was a great man to have on the ball field. He never complained. He had the greatest attitude I ever saw. He did so many things for you to win a game that you'll never be able to find in the 'statics.' " A third baseman, a second baseman, a left fielder, a right fielder, a center fielder—Gilliam was never out of position.

By 1959, the Boston Red Sox had signed Pumpsie Green and every major league team had at least one black player. By 1960, the Negro American League had ceased operation. And Opening Day, April 15, 1947; and Ben Chapman and the aborted strike of the St. Louis Cardinals; and black cats mysteriously appearing on baseball fields were no more. The Aarons, the Banks, the Brocks, the Gibsons, the Jacksons, the Parkers who followed in Robinson's historic path changed baseball forever. They brought with them a verve, a talent, a style that enriched the game.

On October 24, 1972, Jackie Robinson died. He was fifty-three years old and had lost the sight in one eye. "He was discovered to be a diabetic the year after he finished playing baseball," said Rachel Robinson. "The question is—was he a diabetic before then and burning up all the sugar? He didn't have the symptoms of diabetes. He didn't have hypertension. It's possible that he was an incipient diabetic all along and that the symptoms came out when he was exercising less. What the stress contributed to the hypertension had to be a factor. He didn't die of heartbreak or pressure. He died of a very virulent disease that may have been advanced by the stress. He was struggling, fighting all the time. He would just not give up."

The Giants

For most of the 1880s, the New York National League baseball team played its games on a field at 110th Street and Fifth Avenue. The location was across from Central Park's northeastern corner. The land on which they played was owned by James Gordon Bennett, publisher of the *New York Herald Tribune*. Bennett had played polo on that field with his society friends, and that's how the ball field came to be called the "Polo Grounds."

The team received its nickname in the 1880s when manager Jim Mutrie, commenting on the size of his players and urging them to victory during a close game, shouted, "My big fellows! My Giants! We are the people!"

In 1889, the Giants moved to New York City plot 2106, lot 100, located between 155th and 157th streets at Eighth Avenue in upper Manhattan. The location was called the "new Polo Grounds." The baseball diamond was nestled in what was known in the 1880s as Coogan's Hollow, an area under Coogan's Bluff, a craggy rock cliff. The hollow and the bluff derived their names from James T. Coogan, Manhattan's first borough president.

A horseshoe-shaped stadium with Coogan's Bluff on one side and the Harlem River on the other, the Polo Grounds seated 55,987, the most in the National League. It was a four-story, misshapen structure with seats close to the playing field and overhanging stands that gave spectators a feeling of being close to the action.

There were 4,600 bleacher seats, 2,730 field boxes, 1,084 upper boxes, 5,138 upper reserved boxes, and 2,318 upper general admission ham's office was equipped with a well-stocked bar, and he would be joined by cronies for a drink or two, or sometimes a meal.

The first floor of the clubhouse contained the executive offices. On the ground floor were the dressing rooms of the Giants and the visiting team. The Giants were located on the first base side; the visitors dressed on the third base side.

"I remember getting to the Polo Grounds at ten in the morning," said Marvin Doblin, now an attorney, back then a kid from Queens who loved the Giants. "The players would pass through the gate near the right field Giant bull pen . . . they would walk across the field in their civilian clothes to the center field clubhouse. There were cheers for the Giants and boos for the other teams, especially the players on the Dodgers. Most of the players wore sports jackets and shirts without ties."

Magically the players would reappear fully uniformed and take batting, hitting, and fielding practice. "It was something," Doblin continued. "We saw them first as human beings in street clothes and then they were like gods in their uniforms."

Long steps ran up the stands from the field to the doors of the clubhouse. "The Dodger fans sat on the third base side of the steps," recalls former Flatbush favorite, Cal Abrams, "and the Giant fans sat on the first base side. They screamed their support or cursed players as they came out of the clubhouse doors. They screamed at each other throughout a game."

Big-time bookmakers worked their trade on either side of the clubhouse steps, taking advantage of the loyalties of the fans. Wagers were taken on the outcome of a game, the number of runs for an inning, whether a pitch would be a strike or a ball, anything the bettor desired.

The best seats in the house for Giant fans were behind the Giant dugout to the right of the screen. "It was a dollar and ten cents for general admission for those seats, but you had to come real early," recalls Doblin. "Reserved seats at the start were only for games with the Dodgers or for big games or for holiday times."

Polo Grounds signs included one in deep center field: "Put A Smile On Your Smoking, Buy Chesterfield." Another sign pro-

seats. The bulk of those who came to the Polo Grounds wer
in the remaining lower general admission section. The Harlen
way ran behind home plate, and Eighth Avenue was out
center field. East 155th Street and East 157th Street were loca
side first base and third base.

The visitor's bull pen was looked upon as a torture char
those mandated by their managers to sit there. Literally just
positioned in the boondocks of left center field with no shad
the sun, the bull pen presented an especially appealing targe
Giant fans who sat in the reserved seats in the left field corner
players with assorted projectiles was a favorite pastime.

Playing field dimensions were asymmetrical. A ball smack
or right center field would generally be caught, but the same
another park could go in for a home run. The center field
were 450 feet away from home plate. "I didn't like it too mu
Polo Grounds," said Dick Sisler, former National Leagu
could hit the heck out of a ball for four hundred feet or m
would be caught." It was 257 feet from home plate to the r
wall, which was 10 feet 7 ⅝ inches high. The left field wall
9 ¾ inches high) was 279 feet from home plate. The short
right field dimensions at the Polo Grounds facilitated w
known as "Chinese home runs."

The upper left field deck hung over the lower deck. It
tually impossible for a fly ball to get into the lower deck b
the projection of the upper deck. There were many argun
resulted because of the overhang, for if a ball grazed the fr
overhang, it was a home run. The double decks in right f
even. The short distances and the asymmetrical shape of the
resulted in drives rebounding off the left and right field wal
liard shots. Outfielders had to play the carom. Over the ye
hitters and fielders familiar with the pool table walls of the p
big advantage over opposing teams.

Positioned in a recessed area in back of center field b
monuments and plaques was the clubhouse building. There
conditioning, only fans. Horace Stoneham's office was on t
floor. He would watch the game through a pair of binocul

claimed: "Lanolize Your Shoes With Esquire Boot Polish." Back then there were no surgeon-general warnings and no one questioned what the word 'lanolize' meant. Other signs were painted on the concrete of the left and right field walls.

The ball park had been a summering place for many Broadway stars during the 1930s. Games began at 3:15 P.M., enabling celebrities and Wall Streeters to get to the park before the first pitch. The team had last won a pennant in 1937, but many of the fans had seen or heard of Giant legends—John J. McGraw, Carl Hubbell, Bill Terry, and Mel Ott.

"It's a different game today," said Joe Flynn, who worked as a ticket taker and watcher of ticket takers at the Polo Grounds until the day the Giants left New York. "In the old days, those fellows would get to the park at ten A.M. . . . they'd practice and then they weren't due back until one P.M. In the meantime, they used to go down to the saloon, and they'd be in there drinking. McGraw would be in uniform and would go down there and have maybe three or four whiskies and walk back into the Polo Grounds through the Eighth Avenue entrance. He didn't give a shit who saw him. He'd fight you in a second. He was a tough little bastard."

During World War II, the Giants were inept. They managed their best finish in 1942—third place. The area around the ball park changed in the years between the start of the war and its end. Once a melting pot of working class Jews, Italians, Irish, Germans, Greeks—by the mid 1950s these white ethnics formed a minority of the population. Southern blacks and Hispanics took their place.

In 1946, the Giants finished in last place. In 1947, they climbed to fourth place, recorded their all-time attendance high—1,599,784, and pounded a then major league club record of 221 home runs.

"The Giants had bought out the Minneapolis Millers in 1946," former "Jint" catcher Wes Westrum notes. "I automatically became their property since I was a member of the Millers. As a boy growing up in Minneapolis, the Giants were my personal favorites. On September 17, 1947, I was brought up to the big club. I joined them in Chicago. Mel Ott was the manager. He said, 'Don't be nervous. They use the same ball, the same bat, the same bases up here.' I caught Dave

Koslo in the second game of a doubleheader. I got a hit the first time up—to the opposite field. That was a game where Ernie Lombardi got his last hit—a double."

In July of 1948, the style and look of the Giants of New York changed. Leo Durocher left the Dodgers and crossed over to take charge at the Polo Grounds. He replaced Mel Ott, a Giant since 1925 when he arrived as a sixteen-year-old rookie carrying a straw suitcase. Ott was given a job in the Giant front office.

Former Giant equipment manager Eddie Logan was sixteen years old in 1925 when he was sent by John J. McGraw to meet Ott on the old Ninth Avenue El. "Who would have believed it," said Logan, "Durocher replacing Mel. On the day that it happened, Mel and I sat in the clubhouse for about seven or eight hours and we told each other the old stories."

Durocher was not concerned with the old stories or the old ways for the Giants. He immediately announced: "This is not my kind of team." He started to create the Giants in his image.

"Ott had been a gentle and nice man," said Westrum. "Durocher was the opposite. He was all out to win. I don't care if it was tiddly-winks. He wanted to win. It rubbed off on our ball club. He'd get under your skin."

The Giants finished in fifth place in 1948. Under Ott, they won 27 and lost 38. Durocher's Giants won 51 and lost 38.

The 1947 Giants were a collection of lumbering home run hitters. They could whack the ball but were limited in all-around baseball ability. The outfield of Bobby Thomson, Willard Marshall, and Sid Gordon recorded seventy-eight home runs. First baseman Johnny Mize clubbed fifty-one homers and led the league with one hundred thirty-eight RBIs. Catcher Walker Cooper had thirty-five home runs. Buddy Kerr played a steady but unimaginative shortstop. Bill Rigney played alongside Kerr. "Rig" was an unsteady and brittle second baseman. He hit seventeen home runs in 1947. Jack "Lucky" Lohrke was the third baseman. A rookie pitcher from Oregon named Larry Jansen won twenty-one of twenty-six decisions.

The franchise was one of tradition and continuity. The fans were loyal but traditional. "It never seemed to me," said Richie Ashburn, who came into the Polo Grounds many times in the uniform of the

Philadelphia Phillies and today is a broadcaster for the team, "that Giant fans were as involved emotionally or physically as some other fans. They never really affected a game, for example, at the Polo Grounds the way those fans at Ebbets Field could."

Giant fans were the businessmen. They were there at the Polo Grounds with their shirts and ties in the same box seats game after game. Tickets were passed down generation after generation, just like the team.

One family had owned the Giants since 1919—the Stonehams. In forty-five years, the team had employed just three managers: John J. McGraw, Bill Terry, Mel Ott. It was a clannish, Irish-dominated organization of Sheehans, Schumachers, Feeneys, Brannicks. Owner Horace Stoneham functioned as his own general manager.

Durocher retooled the Giants. Big Johnny Mize pounded ninety-one home runs in two seasons, but he was a defensive liability and could not run. Durocher paved the way for the "Big Cat" to move across the Harlem River to play for the New York Yankees. He peddled Walker Cooper, another whacker, to Cincinnati. He convinced Stoneham to purchase Hank Thompson and Monte Irvin, the first black players the Giants ever had. A member of the St. Louis Browns in 1947, Thompson's drinking habits and pugnacious attitude had marred his playing effectiveness. The Browns released him. Durocher thought Thompson was worth a second chance. "The Lip" was proven correct. Thompson added power and versatility to the "Jint" lineup.

In the winter of 1949, the look and the style of the team were completely revamped. A blockbuster trade sent Willard Marshall, Buddy Kerr, Sam Webb, and Sid Gordon to the Boston Braves.

A 1936 graduate of Samuel J. Tilden High School in East Flatbush, Gordon was Jewish and a favorite of New York City baseball fans, in the tradition of Andy Cohen and Harry Danning. In the 1920s, Cohen, a Jew, had played second base for the Giants; another Jewish player was catcher Harry Danning, who played for the team during the 1930s. A powerfully built, affable man, Gordon hit thirteen home runs in 1947 and then jumped to thirty-one in 1948. He was just rounding into slugging form when the Giants traded him.

"Before 1948 I could hit a fairly long ball but it always went to right or right-center," said Gordon. "At the Polo Grounds, right-center is just a big out. Coach Red Kress used to pitch batting practice and tried to get me to pull the ball to left. He started out by moving my right-hand grip on the bat around a little and then he opened up my stance—I now put my left foot toward third when I hit. I learned to roll my wrists more and step into the ball . . . and I got much better results."

Durocher called Gordon into his office that winter the trade was made with Boston. "I hated to let you go in the deal," he said, "but there would have been no deal if you were not included."

The deal gave the Giants a slick and professional double play combination—shortstop Alvin Dark and second baseman Eddie Stanky. Durocher's old 'brat' from the Brooklyn days batted in the lead-off position most of the time and teamed effectively with Dark, a skillful hit and run exponent, who batted second in the order. Dodger fans called Stanky, "Stinky." Durocher had better words for him. "Stanky couldn't hit or run or throw or field. All he could do was beat you." In the spring of 1950, another player with the will and the uncanny ability to beat the opposition joined the Giants.

Sal Maglie, banned for five years for jumping to the Mexican League in 1945, returned. He brought back with him a popping curve ball that would tease, tantalize, and torture National League batters. Oddly enough, Maglie was not impressive in spring training in 1950 and Durocher wanted to trade him. Instead he put "The Barber" in the bullpen for almost half the 1950 season. An eleven-inning win against the Cards in July was the first step in an eleven-game winning streak and the rebirth of Salvatore Anthony Maglie, born April 26, 1917, in Niagara Falls, New York.

"In his prime, he was sallow with sunken cheeks, black hair, black eyebrows," recalls Stan Lomax. "He looked like an undertaker coming in to pitch. He threw right under a batter's chin. He had a guy managing him who wanted him to be mean and worked on him to do it. Maglie was real intimidating. He took the fire right out of a hitter."

Durocher boasted, "If it's under 'W' for win, nobody cares how you did it." Tirades and tinkering characterized the Durocher way.

He moved players with his mouth and on the field. Hank Thompson, a .280-hitting second baseman in 1949 became a .289, twenty–home-run third baseman in 1950. Outfielder Whitey Lockman was converted into a first baseman; center fielder Bobby Thomson was turned into a third baseman.

"We realized that the Dodgers had a better organization," observes Monte Irvin, "and more talent. We realized we were the underdogs, but we were not underdogs as far as our fans were concerned. We had good fans and the fans the Dodgers had we didn't want anyway. They might have been loyal, but they were not that classy. Around the league, the borough of Brooklyn and its fans were looked down upon—they were considered second-class fans.

"The whole Giant team worked real hard," continued the soft-spoken Irvin. "Part of the effort was for our fans, part of the effort was the Horace Stoneham influence. He was a fair-minded owner. If you played real hard for him, he'd give you as much money as he thought you deserved. There was never any money problems with him. And there was Leo.

"Durocher developed a style of his own that rubbed off on the Giant teams. He used to draw fans to the ball park. They loved to see him go toe to toe with the teams we played against."

There was a hidden agenda to Durocher's toe-to-toe arguments with the umpires. "Whenever I argued with them," he said recently, "I'd try to get them near the line. Then I'd kick the lime off the line onto their pants. If they didn't get the lime off pretty quick, it'd burn a hole in their pants. They always tried to get out on the grass."

In 1950 Durocher celebrated his forty-fifth birthday by managing the Giants to a third place finish—their best since 1942. The "Jints" won eighty-six games, thirty-four of them from July 20 to Labor Day. "This proves," said Durocher, "that I can win anywhere if I have my kind of team." Westrum became the regular catcher and pounded twenty-three home runs. Lockman and Irvin batted close to .300. Thomson whacked twenty-five homers and drove in eighty-five runs. Stanky batted .300, led the league in bases on balls, assists, and put-outs. Jim Hearn, acquired during the season on waivers from the Cardinals, posted an 11–3 record. Maglie was 18–4, the top winning percentage in the league. Jansen won nineteen games. Hearn led the league in earned run average. Maglie was second and Jansen was fourth. They each pitched five shutouts.

By 1951, the personnel, the attitude, and the foundation were there. The Giants were primed for what would be known as the "Miracle Run." The team did not possess the talented set lineup of the Dodgers or the layer upon layer of skilled players on the Yankees. They had tradition, style, combativeness—and in 1951 they would also have Willie Mays.

The arrival of Mays on the fifteenth of May, 1951, solidified the Giants. He got off to a shaky start—0–12—and begged Durocher to send him down. Just as another Giant manager, John McGraw, refused to send a youthful Mel Ott to the minors, Durocher refused to listen to the pleas of his rookie center fielder.

Willie Mays' first hit was a home run off Warren Spahn at the Polo Grounds. He hit it over the roof.

"We had a meeting of the pitchers," Spahn recalls. "We knew Mays was having trouble, but we also knew the kid was a good hitter. Our pitchers decided that the best way to pitch to him was with curve balls, away. That's fine for them, they were right-handed. I tried to catch the outside corner of the plate with a curve. He went out after it and knocked a few seats out of the sundeck."

All around the league they marveled at his attitude, ability, and potential. In Pittsburgh's old Forbes Field, Rocky Nelson blasted a drive 457 feet to dead center field. Galloping back, Mays realized as his feet hit the warning track that the ball was hooking to his right side. The ball was sinking and Mays could not reach across his body and glove the drive. Just as the ball got to his knee level, Willy stuck out his bare hand and caught it. Durocher told all the Giants to give Mays the silent treatment when he returned to the dugout, but Pittsburgh general manager Branch Rickey sent Mays a note: "That was the finest catch I have ever seen . . . and the finest catch I ever hope to see."

He was only a rookie, but he stabilized and inspired the 1951 Giants. His arm, his bat, his glove, even his bare hand added a new dimension to the team. Mays was the extra ingredient that enabled the scrappy, efficient lineup to come together. Stanky batted in the lead-

off position and played second base. Alvin Dark, a great bat manipu-
lator, hit in the second spot and turned over the double plays at shortstop. Don Mueller, another skillful bat handler, was positioned in right
field and often hit third. The clean-up spot was reserved most times
for Monte Irvin, the left fielder, solid and skillful. Whitey Lockman,
a left-handed batter, played first base, and Bobby Thomson, a right-
handed hitter, handled third base. Westrum batted in the eighth position and intelligently handled the pitching staff. Mays roamed center
field, sometimes batting third, fourth, sometimes batting, fifth, sixth.
There was variation but there was constancy.

The storybook finish of the Giants—chasing, catching, and finally
crushing the Dodgers in the play-off with Bobby Thomson's "Shot
Heard 'Round The World" was called the "Miracle at Coogan's
Bluff." It was an astonishing feat, but it took a solid team to do it. The
Giants were solid. Second in home runs as a team to the Dodgers,
their pitching staff topped the league in earned run average.

Thomson hit thirty-two home runs. Dark had more doubles than
any other player in the league. Irvin was the National League RBI
leader, second in triples, batting .312. Stanky and Westrum finished in
second and third position in walks. Westrum also led National League
catchers in fielding and hit twenty home runs. Maglie was the money
pitcher. "The Barber" allowed the fewest hits of any pitcher per nine
innings, was second in ERA and complete games, third in strikeouts.
Jansen won twenty-three games. Hearn won seventeen. The "Big
Three" of the Giants pitching staff combined for almost 70 percent of
the team's ninety-eight victories. How many games Durocher shoved
into the "Win" column is a matter of conjecture, but his gambling,
driving, scheming attitude did not hurt.

In 1952, the Giants missed three key members of the 1951 pennant-winning team. Stanky was traded to St. Louis. Monte Irvin
broke his ankle in a spring training accident and only appeared in forty-two games. Willie Mays was around for just thirty-four games and
one hundred twenty-seven at-bats, then he was drafted into the Army.
Jansen had pitched himself out in 1951 and finished 1952 with a dis-
appointing 11-11 record and a 4.09 earned run average. A twenty-
eight-year-old rookie from North Carolina named Hoyt Wilhelm
with his knuckleball that darted, dodged, and defeated the opposition

was a major reason for the Giants finishing second. Wilhelm won fifteen games and saved eleven more, topping all pitchers in earned run average and appearances. Polo Grounds attendance dropped under the one-million mark.

The 1953 Giants finished in fifth place, thirty-five games in back of the pennant-winning Dodgers. Maglie and Jansen, nagged by injuries, were ineffective. Only two members of the pitching staff won more games than they lost. Ruben Gomez was 13–11; Al Corwin was 6-10. Attendance dropped below a million again. It was a season of disappointment for Giant fans. Durocher stormed about, fighting even more with umpires, arguing with players.

"If you have a winning team," Jackie Robinson observed, "nobody is better than Durocher. He had the knack of stimulating winning ballplayers, pushing them to heights that were sometimes beyond their ability. But with a losing team, Durocher would lose his composure. He got upset, he made players angry, causing some to play below their ability."

One Giant hero was gone and another one returned as the season of 1954 got underway. Bobby Thomson, who fired the "Shot Heard 'Round the World" in 1951 was traded to the Braves for southpaw Johnny Antonelli. And Willie Mays returned from the Army, bigger, stronger, more mature. The addition of Mays and Antonelli powered the Giants to the 1954 pennant.

Antonelli had signed with the Braves in 1948 for $65,000 and was one of the original "bonus babies." In 1954 he came of age. The stylish left-hander topped all National League pitchers in winning percentage, strikeouts, and earned run average as he won twenty-one of twenty-eight decisions. Gomez won seventeen games, and Maglie, coming back from his injuries, had fourteen victories. The Giants got a lot of help from their potent bull pen. Wilhelm won twelve games against just four losses, and right-hander Marv Grissom picked up nineteen saves. Hank Thompson and Alvin Dark combined for forty-six home runs. The man with the "seeing eye bat," Don Mueller, batted .342.

All of these performances were able to more than compensate for the retirement of Larry Jansen midway through the season. After his twenty-three-victory year in 1951, the stylish right-hander had slipped dramatically. A .500 pitcher in 1952, 11–16 in 1953, he quit after thirteen games in 1954. His earned run average for that last sad year as a New York Giant was 5.98.

The force of the '54 Giants was Willie Howard Mays. By the All-Star break, he had slugged thirty-one home runs—a pace that put him ahead of Babe Ruth's sixty-home-run year. Willie wound up the year with forty-one homers and led the league in batting with a .345 average—three points ahead of his teammate Don Mueller. Mays was first in doubles and in slugging percentage, scored 119 runs and drove in 110 more. He struck out just 57 times in 565 at-bats. He had the numbers—the power, the clutch hitting, the average, the versatility. Half the 1954 season he clubbed the ball so hard and so far and so often that he threatened Babe Ruth's home run record. Then Durocher told him to switch his style, to become the catalyst not the cannon. Racking up singles, doubles, triples, Mays powered the Giants to ninety-seven wins and a five-game winning margin over the Dodgers.

He was listed in the lineup as the center fielder, but anything hit near him was fair game. It seemed to the opposition that there was glue in his glove, lightning in his arm, mercury in his legs, and radar in his head as he ranged the vast Polo Grounds' center field and raced back like a hawk for fly balls, charging in after line drives like an infielder. Exuberance and pride in his craft characterized Mays. Years later he would say "I was the best player I ever saw." There were very few who would argue the point—especially if they were members of the Cleveland Indians of 1954.

The 1954 World Series was the biggest financial windfall for the players competing in it up to that point in history. The winner's share was $11,500 a player—for some, more money then they had earned for the entire season. The losers received $6,700 each. Dramatically staging what would be called the "Little Miracle of Coogan's Bluff," the Giants copped the winner's share. Winning the first four games from the Cleveland Indians, the Giants became the first National League team since 1914 to accomplish a sweep.

The Indians had been picked as odds-on favorites to win the series. Paced by one of the great pitching staffs in history, they had during the regular season been victorious in more than seven of each ten games they played. The Yankees won 103 games. Cleveland won 111. Early Wynn and Bob Lemon each recorded twenty-three victories. Mike Garcia was a nineteen-game winner and had the American League's top earned run average. Bob Feller won thirteen of sixteen; Art Houtteman notched fifteen wins. A combined 16-6 record was posted by Indian relievers Don Mossi, Ray Narleski, and Hal Newhouser. Cleveland had pitching; it also had power. The Indians slugged more home runs than any other American League team; they had the batting champ, Bobby Avila, the home run and RBI leader, Larry Doby, and a couple of other sluggers named Al Rosen and Vic Wertz. The Giants had Willie Mays and Dusty Rhodes.

A Giant since 1952, James Lamar Rhodes batted .345 in 1954, slugged 15 homers and drove in 50 runs in just 164 at-bats. As things turned out, the regular season was just a warm-up for the good-natured native of Mathews, Alabama.

"Dusty was a nature boy," says Lomax. "We used to get a lot of guys like him from up the hill, behind the railroad tracks. Leo stood for his idiosyncracies because Dusty produced for him. Today as a designated hitter, he'd bat .600."

"Leo kept me around," Rhodes reminisced, "because he said he liked the way I looked. I dressed up the hotel lobbies."

Joel Amalfatano was a teammate of Rhodes. "Dusty was a free-spirited individual," said Amalfatano. "He was ahead of his time. He loved to hit. He didn't care too much about the other parts of the game."

The first game of the World Series was played on September 29 at the Polo Grounds. A triple by Vic Wertz with two out in the first inning put Sal Maglie and the Giants behind, 2–0. The score was tied as the Giants tallied twice in the third inning off Bob Lemon. The power-pitcher Lemon and the curve-balling Maglie matched pitch for pitch as the innings moved along and the shadows of autumn began to gray in the Polo Grounds.

In the top of the eighth inning, Doby walked. He moved to second on an infield hit by Rosen. Bald Vic Wertz came to the plate. The powerful Pennsylvanian had driven in the only Cleveland runs and had singled in the fourth and singled in the sixth. Playing percentages,

Durocher removed Maglie and brought in southpaw Don Liddle to pitch to the left-handed-hitting Wertz.

Liddle's first pitch was tagged. The ball leaped off Wertz's bat and like a cannon shot headed for the distant reaches of center field. Mays took off the instant his instincts told him where the ball was headed. Back, back, back, he raced toward the bleacher wall. The ball was dropping and Mays was still running. Approaching the warning track —his number twenty-four lined up almost with home plate—Mays stretched out his arms as the ball went over his shoulder. On the warning track, he whirled, twisted toward the plate, and fired the ball back to the infield. His cap fell off. He fell to his knees. The throw came in to Davey Williams in back of second base. The Indians did not score that inning.

The catch and the throw would go down in World Series history as one of the great moments. As things turned out, what Mays did changed the momentum of the two teams and gave the psychological advantage to the Giants.

In the bottom of the tenth inning, Mays walked and stole second. Hank Thompson was intentionally passed. Durocher removed Irvin, who hadn't gotten a hit all day, and replaced him with Dusty Rhodes. The free-swinging Alabaman popped Lemon's second pitch down the right field line. Dave Pope, the Cleveland right fielder, propped himself against the wall, just 260 feet from home plate. Pope waited against the wall, bracing himself to catch the ball. He didn't catch it and neither did the fans in the first row of seats where the ball landed. The ball rebounded out onto the field and landed near Pope's feet. Giant fans rejoiced. Their special weapons—Mays and Rhodes —had produced, and their not so secret weapon—the Chinese home run—had claimed yet another victim. As Rhodes crossed the plate, Lemon threw his glove into the air and mumbled to himself as he hurried to the center field clubhouse. It took the Giants three hours and eleven minutes to record their 5–2 victory. Rhodes was just beginning, but for Cleveland, it was all over.

Johnny Antonelli was matched up against Cleveland's Early Wynn in the second game. Indian lead-off batter, Al Smith, smacked Antonelli's first pitch for a home run, but that was the only scoring

Cleveland did. Rhodes took over again. In the fifth inning Mays walked. Thompson singled. Durocher called on Dusty again to replace Irvin. Wynn remembered what had happened to Lemon. He buzzed a fast ball high and tight that sent Rhodes tumbling out of the batter's box onto the ground. Rhodes slapped Wynn's next pitch into center field for a single. Mays scored and the game was tied. Antonelli's ground out scored Thompson with the second Giant run. Rhodes clinched the Giant victory with a seventh-inning clout that landed on the right field roof. Antonelli went the distance in the 3–1 Giant victory, walking six, yielding eight hits, but striking out nine.

The series moved to Cleveland for the next two games. Even playing in their own ball park was not an edge for the Indians. If Rhodes had stayed in New York City they might have had a chance.

In offices and bars in Manhattan, much of the baseball talk focused on Dusty and Willie. After the third game, Hoyt would be a new topic of conversation. Cleveland fans groaned as the Giants scored six times in game three before the Indians even got on the board. The "Jints" notched a run in the first on two singles and an error. Mays, with the first of his three hits in the contest, drove in Lockman for the score. With the bases loaded in the third inning, Durocher once again called on Dusty to replace Irvin. The twenty-seven-year-old Southerner delivered again, slashing a single to right to score two runs. His third pinch hit of the series tied the record set by Bobby Brown of the Yankees. In the eighth inning, Ruben Gomez was tiring. The Indians had seen Rhodes; they had seen Mays; now they would see butterflies. Knuckleballer Hoyt Wilhelm had the Cleveland batters chasing the air as he retired the last five hitters to nail down the 6–2 New York victory. Garcia, Narleski, Houtteman, and Mossi were all used by Indian manager Al Lopez in the losing cause.

Both managers gambled in the fourth game. Durocher could afford it. The Giants were hot and with a three-game lead, he had little to lose. "The Lip" pitched "Little" Don Liddle, yielder of the tremendous first-game shot to Wertz. Lopez, backed against the wall, went with his best. Bob Lemon started with only two days' rest.

Giant bats staked the 5 foot 10-inch, 165-pound Liddle to a seven-run lead after five innings. The Giants scored twice in the second inning and once in the third on a Willie Mays double. Hal

Newhouser, a major league pitcher since 1939, replaced Lemon with the bases loaded in the fifth. "Prince Hal" walked in the fourth Giant run. Irvin was the next scheduled batter. Most of the 78,000 in attendance expected James Lamar Rhodes. Rusty sat. Irvin came up to hit. He slapped a single to score two more runs, and the Giants scored another to cap their seven-run cushion. Wilhelm and Antonelli, who was credited with a save, protected the lead as the Polo Grounders won, 7–4. Cleveland fans went home wondering how the Indian pitching staff which allowed just 2.78 runs per game during the regular season could have been racked by the Giants for twenty-one runs in four World Series games.

In 1954, the Giants had the spotlight of the baseball world on them. In 1955, the Yankees and Dodgers took it away, transforming the "Jints" into the stepchild of New York City baseball. It was a year of utter bliss in Brooklyn, climaxed by the Brooks' first and only World Series victory over the hated "enemy" Bronx Bombers. For the fans of the Giants, there was a sense that the team was coming apart. They finished in third place and drew just 824,112 to the Polo Grounds. Many came just to see Mays, who had another banner year—fifty-one home runs, a .312 batting average, and inspired play in the field that gave him a league-leading twenty-three assists. But Maglie, who won nine of fourteen decisions, argued with Durocher and was sent to Cleveland late in the season. An ailing Irvin was farmed out to Minneapolis. Antonelli, Hearn, and Ruben Gomez were subpar, losing more games than they won. Sid Gordon came back for the last sixty-six games of his career and batted .243.

At season's end, the Giants were eighteen and a half games out of first, in third place with slim prospects for the future. Durocher quit. Bill Rigney replaced him. "The Cricket" succeeded "The Lip." "When Leo went away," recalled Garry Schumacher, "it was the end of the carefree youth of Willie Mays. He became more serious and playing ball was not as much fun for him as it had been."

In 1956 and 1957, the Giants finished in sixth place. Both years they were twenty-six games out of first place. Their home attendance sagged to just above six hundred thousand each of those last two years.

Babe Ruth used to refer to people with the greeting, "Hiya, Kid" because he could not remember names. Mays, who at the start of his career employed the appellation, "Say Hey" because he did not know the names of all he met, was now the leader of the Giants. He recorded seventy-eight homers in those last two years and still made those incredible plays in the field. The Giants of New York had Mays but not much else.

Westrum appeared in only sixty-eight games in 1956 and sixty-three in 1957. Players named Bill Sarni and Valmy Thomas did most of the catching. Dusty Rhodes lost the magic in his bat. He hit .217 in 1956 and .207 the following year. Whitey Lockman was relegated to a utility role. Wilhelm, 4–9 with a 3.83 earned run average in 1956, was traded. Alvin Dark and Don Liddle were traded. The team came apart at the seams. Name veterans like Red Schoendienst, Ray Jablonski, and Hank Sauer were acquired, patches for the fraying fabric. Bobby Thomson came back and played eighty-one games in 1957 and batted .242. The Daryl Spencers, Foster Castlemans, Danny O'Connels were stopgapped into the positions that Alvin Dark and Eddie Stanky once played with such skill and verve.

When the team moved to San Francisco, the players still wore "Giants" across their uniform chest, but the franchise was struggling for an identity. It was a maudlin finale for the sports organization that once had been the apogee of New York City baseball.

The Dodgers

On a cold and windy April 9, 1913, almost twelve thousand paying customers entered the grand and ornate rotunda to get through the turnstiles to watch the first regular season game ever played at Ebbets Field. The park was built on four and a half acres of the lowest slope of Crown Heights on filled-in marshy swampland called "Pigtown" by neighborhood people. Built at a cost of $750,000, the park derived its name from Charles H. Ebbets, who rose from his job selling peanuts and scorecards to become president and principal owner of the team. The Dodgers lost 1–0 to the Phillies; the most spectacular fielding play was made by a Dodger outfielder. His name was Casey Stengel.

Over the years, the little park fused Flatbush with Gowanus, Red Hook, Greenpoint, and Brownsville. It hosted Italians, Jews, Poles, Irish, blacks, the hoity-toity, clerks, bankers, kings—all of whom had as much fun being there with each other as they did viewing the baseball action.

It was an antique of a ball park that in its prime seated 32,000—the least in the National League. A large sign placed there by the New York City Fire Department said that attendance of more than 33,000 was not permitted, but there were many times the sign was ignored, especially when the Giants came to play. On August 30, 1947, for example, an Ebbets Field single-game attendance record was set when 37,512 jammed into the park to watch the Dodgers battle the Giants. On September 24, 1940, a night-game attendance record was set— 35,583. Some days hundreds stood in the aisles and on the rooftops of nearby apartment houses to see Brooklyn baseball. A closed-in place, a sandlot stadium located at the intersections of Bedford Avenue (beyond right field), Montgomery Street (in back of left field), Sullivan Place (behind first base), and McKeever Place (in back of third base and the left field stands), Ebbets Field was a people's park.

It was called the home of "Dem Bums," a nickname the Dodgers had picked up or earned, depending on one's perspective, when an excitable fan during the depression years used to scream out his anger at the inadequacies of the team. He would squeeze the chicken wire screening in back of home plate and bellow, "Ya bum, ya. Yez bums, yez!" Bums meant Brooklyn. Bums meant Dodgers. And Bums they were called in newspaper headlines and stories; cartoonists vied with each other to create the most appropriate caricature. Cartoonist Willard Mullin developed a national reputation for his interpretation of the Brooklyn Bum.

Ebbets Field was a park of intimate dimensions so that "when you had a box seat," according to Red Barber, "you were practically playing the infield." Former Dodger publicist Irving Rudd recalls, "You could see the tan in a player's face from a good seat, the cords in his neck." Sal Maglie, who pitched there both as a Giant and a Dodger, remembers Ebbets Field "as a place where you were never secure. A game was never settled until the final out because the place was so small."

Brooklyn Borough President Howard Golden muses: "Whether you sat in the box or reserved section, or you sat in the bleachers, you were part of the action. I remember sitting in the top row of the bleachers as a kid, happy to sit there with my lunch and to spend my dime for a soda. You'd go out and spend a weekend there. Part of our upbringing and education for a whole generation took place at Ebbets Field."

The 40-foot-high screen in right field was just 297 feet from home plate, a favorite target for left-handed pull hitters. The distance from the plate to left field was 343 feet to the wall (9 feet 10½ inches) that had to be cleared for a home run. Dead center field was 405 feet from home plate.

It was claimed that half the fans on any given day walked in off the street from their homes located in the residential neighborhoods that ringed the ball park, and that after a game they could all be home within twenty minutes.

For those who came by car, there was limited parking, just one small lot on Montgomery Street. However, the area around the park was the hub of much public transportation. The IRT subway stop was two and a half blocks away. The Prospect Park BMT subway station was a walk of a block and a half. Fans came to Ebbets Field on the Flatbush Avenue bus, the Reid Avenue bus, the Empire Boulevard bus, the Franklin Avenue trolley.

The arguments, odd happenings, and odder characters that congregated at Ebbets Field prompted Red Barber to refer to the ball park as "the rhubarb patch." Opposing players employed earthier expressions. It was a place of curiosities and a home for the curious.

"Whether we won or lost," recalls Wilhemena Brandt, who worked the Dodger switchboard from 1941 until the day they left Brooklyn, "every day was a busy, big day on the switchboard that was located right next to the visiting clubhouse at the corner of Bedford Avenue and Sullivan Place. Fans called up with every kind of question you could imagine, like the wives who wanted their husbands paged to make sure they were at the ball game like they said, or the lady who wanted to know when to put the pot roast on."

The circular entrance rotunda was a grand and aesthetic touch when the park first opened in 1913. In the '40s and '50s it proved to be an obstacle course. Fans went around in circles attempting to determine which entrance to use to enter the actual ball park. Pushing, shoving, name-calling, and fist fights were logical outgrowths of the frustration.

Some fans enjoyed picking on those athletes who could not fight back. The visitors' bull pen was a bench close by the reserved seats in the left field corner. A daily assortment of tomatoes, raw eggs, half-filled paper cups, hot dog buns, and other items were gleefully tossed at the visiting athletes by the "Flatbush faithful." The biggest barrage was usually fired at Giant players.

The noise level at the park produced earaches. It spilled out onto Bedford Avenue and into the surrounding neighborhood. It was possible five blocks away to tell if the Dodgers were doing well or not in a particular game by the rise and fall of the sounds.

Former Dodger general manager Buzzy Bavasi recalls, "You'd call the fans at the park by their first name. You'd turn the lights on for a night game and fifteen thousand would come out just to see why the lights were on."

Jim Thomson was in charge of stadium supervision and management. "You either got along with the fellow sitting next to you," he said, "or you fought him. There was no in-between. There was always a brawl of some kind at Ebbets Field."

Ebbets Field was part of the life of Dodger fans, a second home. Jackie Robinson and pitcher Russ Meyer "got into a brawl in Philadelphia," recalls Thomson. "The Phillies and Dodgers then came back to play at Ebbets Field. We had only sold about two thousand seats for the game. The next morning there were lines halfway around the block. The fans all wanted to see the continuation of the fight between Meyer and Robinson. That's what made Ebbets Field. The fan became part of the player's life."

The press box at Ebbets Field was located just about ten feet above the left field stands. And in this area resided journalism critics. "There was a guy," Jack Lang recalls, "who day after day used to holler insults up to us. He especially had it in for Herb Goren of the *New York Sun*. 'Hoibie, you were wrong again yesterday, you idiot,' he would yell."

Tex Rickards was the public address announcer in that Coney Island of ball parks. "He had worked at Ebbets Field for fifteen dollars a day," said Lang, "for as long as anyone could remember." Rickards had a wonderful sense of perspective that perfectly fitted the context of Ebbets Field. His convoluted malapropisms made him another one of the prized characters of Dodger fans. "A little boy has been found lost," and "Will the fans along the railing in left field please remove their clothes," were just two of his more famous lines.

One day during a frenetic pennant race, some of the Dodgers, according to Jack Lang, noticed that the number of the Cub pitcher performing in a crucial game in Chicago had not been posted on the scoreboard. They asked Rickards, who sat on a little chair next to the Brooklyn bench, to find out the name of the Chicago pitcher. Rickards used the dugout phone to call Dodger publicist Frank Graham, Jr., in the press box. Graham informed Rickards that he did not know who was pitching but would call back with the information. A few minutes later, Lang said, Graham called back.

"Bob Rush," announced the voice of Graham.

"Hi, Bob Rush," responded Tex Rickards, "How you doin'?"

Disorientation was just one of the traits that enabled Rickards to lay claim to his reputation as one of Ebbets Field's outlandish characters. He also had a faulty memory. One day a new catcher came in for the Dodgers. His last name was Livingston.

"What's this guy's first name?" Rickards shouted at the Dodger bench.

"Stanley," answered one of the Dodgers.

With all the assurance in the world, in a deep and resonant voice, Tex Rickards announced to the Ebbets Field crowd: "Now catching for the Dodgers—Stanley Livingston."

Others who changed from mild-mannered civilians to eccentrics in the telephone booth that was Ebbets Field included the successful businessman who blew a whistle until he ran out of breath. Then as his second act he would switch to releasing previously inflated multi-colored balloons. The most famous whistler was Eddie Batan. His "peep-peep, peep-peep" pleaded for the Dodgers to launch a rally. Another character was a primitive precursor of the "Cookie Monster." He was passionately involved with Dodger outfielder Harry "Cookie" Lavagetto. The fan would run up and down the aisles bellowing, "Cookie! Cookie! Cookie!" And there was Abe, the gambler. A large, serious man, he stationed himself in the stands behind third base, collecting and dispensing money for the bets he had made.

One of the prime tourist attractions at Ebbets Field was Hilda Chester. A rather large woman with a leaning toward flowered print dresses, she was a Brooklyn favorite and anathema to the opposition. Equipped with a large sign proclaiming "Hilda is here," and armed with a large cowbell in each hand, she would ring her bells, creating earaches and producing support for the Dodger cause. "She would shake that bell," recalls Horace Stoneham's wife, Valeda, "until you were just ready to jump. She was the Dodgers' biggest rooter."

Hilda was a sensitive, caring lady," said Irving Rudd. "Once in a while some people didn't understand her and would talk to her as if she were some demented asylum inmate. She would tell them to talk nicely. She was a dame who just wanted to ring a cowbell. Once TV came in she became self-conscious."

The Dodger batboy of that time was another character. Nicknamed "The Brow" because of his furrowed forehead and the tricks he could perform with a pen, he personally autographed baseballs for fifty cents each. His customers would then sell the autographed base-base with the "authentic Dodger signatures" to eager collectors. At World Series time tourists would cheerfully pay as much as fifteen dollars per ball. "The Brow" at work was an artist in his deft and swift imitations of the signatures of Dodger favorites. A "Duke Snider" leaned to the left, southpaw style. "Gil Hodges" was signed with a flourish. The autograph of "Roy Campanella" was written in a cramped catcher's style, leaning to the right. "Pee Wee Reese" displayed excellent penmanship and the "P" and the "R" were created out of sweeping loops.

Former Dodger outfielder Cal Abrams remembers an autograph seeker who probably never heard of "The Brow." "For twenty straight games," Abrams said, "one kid got my autograph on a penny postcard. Finally I had to satisfy my curiosity. I asked him why he was doing it. 'I need thirty Cal Abrams so I can get one Carl Furillo,' the kid said."

Another group of characters were the members of a little musical band that Red Barber dubbed the "Dodger Sym-phoney," in his phrase, "a little rag-tag group that just made a lot of noise." They were all Italians, and they came from the same neighborhood in the northern section of Williamsburg, Brooklyn. The five original members included Brother Lou Soriano, Jerry Martin, who played the snare drum, Jo Jo Delio, a clanger of cymbals, Paddy Palma, whose specialty was the bass drum, and Phil Cacavalle, trumpet man.

"It was a real cockamamie band," says Jerry Martin. "None of us read music, but we made a lot of noise and all the Dodger fans used to fight to come sit near us. After a while, everybody wanted to get in the act and a lot of them did." Martin maintains that Shorty Laurice, a diminutive figure who wore a stovepipe hat, was added to the Symphoney by Walter O'Malley. "That Laurice," Martin still gripes, "wasn't even from our neighborhood. He just sucked his way in." Laurice became the leader.

Chased all over the park by security personnel in the early years, eventually the little band, through the intervention of Jack Collins, Dodger business manager, was given seats 1–8 row 1, section 8, behind the Dodger dugout. "We had a lot of fights with people who came and tried to take our seats over the years," said Martin.

The efforts of the Sym-phoney were part-time; they played at night games and on weekends. "We all held down full-time jobs so we played when we could," said Jerry Martin. "Sometimes we'd travel with the team to Boston or Philadelphia. They paid us nothing. We paid our own way. They didn't even give us pretzels."

The brassy sounds and oddball routines of the Sym-phoney carried through the summer afternoons and evenings through the park into the bleachers and out into Bedford Avenue. "They could hear us good—Ebbets Field was closed in, it was a bandbox," said Soriano. When they weren't in their seats behind the dugout, they wandered through the stands, pied pipers in street clothes. "We never needed police protection at Ebbets Field," Martin said. "Everybody loved us."

Only umpires and opposing players were irritated. When the little band disagreed with an umpire's call against one of the Dodgers, it musically protested to the tune of "Three Blind Mice." The big number of the Sym-phoney, however, was a song called "The Worm Crawls In." (Its real name was "The Army Duff.") The number earned the affectionate devotion of Brooklyn Dodger fans and the irritated antagonism of opposition ballplayers. Numerous choruses were played as an accompaniment to the self-conscious strides of an opposing ballplayer who was headed back to the bench after an unsuccessful turn at bat.

The climax to the tune and the cat-and-mouse game between band and player was the "bang" timed on the bass drum at the very instant the derrière of an opponent touched down to the dugout bench. "They'd go to the pump [water cooler] or walk around," Soriano said. "We wouldn't hit it. They'd think we forgot about them. We never forgot. We had patience. Big Johnny Mize gave us the most trouble. But he like the rest of them used to finally sit down and we'd go BANG!"

Once things went "bang" around the Dodger Sym-phoney. "I had brought my brother to a game," the excitable Soriano recalls. "He was a little odd. He was a Giant fan. Whitey Lockman hit a home run to put the Giants in the lead. My brother grabbed the cymbals and started jumping up and down and banging them together. He was dancing all around, he was so happy. The fans behind us got pissed off. 'What the hell you bringin' Giant fans wid' ya?' one of them yelled. I said, 'Don't mind him—he's my brother and he's crazy!' "

The biggest controversy the Sym-phoney was ever involved in took place when the musicians' union insisted that the Dodgers pay union scale for a standby band. "They thought the Sym-phoney was employed by us," Walter O'Malley recalled, "and they insisted they would strike Ebbets Field unless we agreed. We decided on a Music Appreciation Day. Anyone with a musical instrument was admitted free. They came with cornets, drums, calliopes, old wash boards. There was some racket and a lot of fun. The *Daily News* the next day said that was the best way they ever saw to break a strike threat— treat it with a sense of humor."

Poignant, slapstick, satirical, dumb, good-natured, unintentional . . . humor pervaded Ebbets Field. An advertisement on the thirty- foot-high right field wall said: "THE DODGERS USE LIFE- BUOY." One morning early arrivals saw the work of what they assumed had to be a Giant fan who sneaked in while Brooklyn slept. Under the sign, the anonymous artist had scrawled in red letters: ". . . AND THEY STILL STINK!" In 1947, with Durocher suspended for the entire season by Commissioner Chandler, the "faithful" brought homemade signs to Ebbets Field: "OPEN THE DOOR CHANDLER," "WE MOURN OUR LOSS," "LET LEO OUT!" "CHANDLER FOR DOG CATCHER."

"HIT SIGN, WIN SUIT," was the most famous sign at Ebbets Field. Located at the base of the scoreboard, approximately four feet high and forty feet wide, the space was rented by Brooklyn clothier Abe Stark of 1514 Pitkin Avenue. With Furillo positioned at least half the time in front of the sign, which was situated almost four hundred feet from home plate, there were very few who were ever entitled to the free suit. The sign and the name on it became so popular that many claim Abe Stark's climb through Brooklyn politics to the borough presidency was helped by it.

Signs dominated Ebbets Field, Atop the scoreboard was the Schaefer Beer sign. The "h" lit up to indicate a hit and the "e" lit up to denote an error. Other commercial writing included: "Bulova—Official Timepiece—Brooklyn Dodgers"; "Once again you're clean—Gem Blades"; "Stadler's Winthrop Shoes"; and "Van Heusen Shirts."

It was claimed that Ebbets Field was a place where anything could happen and where everyone wanted to be. This was more fact than claim. In 1951, for example, the tiny ball park drew almost two million paying customers. Five times in the 1947–1957 era, the Dodgers led the league in home attendance. Ebbets Field was an attraction for visitors from all walks of life, from all over the world.

When Douglas MacArthur was relieved of his command in Korea by President Harry S Truman, one of the first places the controversial general visited was Ebbets Field. He delivered a speech that began, "I've been told that one has not lived unless one has been to Ebbets Field and has watched the Dodgers play baseball." Publicist Irving Rudd claims, "I slipped him the line."

Rudd arranged for famed commentator Ed Morrow to visit the ball park and mingle with the players in the clubhouse. Rudd remembers Dodger utility infielder Rocky Bridges shouting at Murrow as he left, "And good night and good luck," the broadcaster's famous closing line. Other celebrity visitors to Ebbets Field included former Governor of New York State Averell Harriman and columnist Walter Winchell.

Governor Harriman, a shy and dignified man, "asked a lot of intellectual questions and hardly spoke above a whisper," recalls Rudd.

Winchell visited Ebbets Field sporting a gray fedora and an expensive silk suit. In the '40s and '50s, Winchell was known and feared for his ability to create or destroy celebrities and for his Sunday radio show that began at 10:00 P.M. with these lines: "Good evening Mr. and Mrs. North and South America and all the ships at sea . . . Let's go to press." In 1948, Winchell was the highest-paid newscaster in America. ABC paid him five hundred twenty thousand dollars. His sponsor, Jergens Lotion, provided a sum almost as huge to the quick-talking gossip journalist. "Winchell mesmerized and boggled the Dodger players in the clubhouse," according to Rudd. "He had such power and fame that the players did not know how to act.

He wound up devoting a whole column to his visit to Ebbets Field."

One August morning in 1952, Rudd was awakened by Dodger president Walter O'Malley and told to rush down to Ebbets Field. "The King of Iraq," (Faisal II) O'Malley said, "has come to the United States and has indicated he wants to visit our ball park." The seventeen-year-old king had been invited to the United States by President Truman. Rudd said, "Here was a king who knew nothing about baseball, but he had heard about the Dodgers and Ebbets Field. I got to the press gate about eleven and suddenly a whole bunch of cars pulled up. These big guys, State Department security men, got out and there's this nice-looking guy with a big hat. He was about five foot five, five foot six, and the same size as me. And here I am, a nice Jewish kid from Brooklyn saying 'How do you do, Your Majesty'—it was like you read in the books in school. There I was with a real live king!"

It was a weekday afternoon. Rudd was the only official member of the Dodgers present. "So I had no choice but to walk him on the playing field. Suddenly I'm pointing out the bases. I'm telling him about the outfield. Then a whole bunch of photographers and a news-reel crew starts shooting. They shout, 'Irv, point again. Take his arm. Do this. Do that.' I'm dying. I told a couple of the Ebbets Field employees, 'get Buzzy [Bavasi], get Fresco [Thompson], [Dodger vice-presidents], get somebody!' and the cameras are poppin', and this 'n that."

Rudd peered over to the Dodger dugout thinking he could at least introduce the king to one of the Dodger coaches. "It's a little after noon," Rudd recalls, "usually the first guy up the steps with a bag of balls was coach Jake Pitler. On this day, up the steps comes Jackie Roosevelt Robinson—in the flesh. I said to myself, glory be, I'm saved.

"Your Majesty, I want you to meet a real fine gentleman. 'Hey, Jackie, Jackie, I'd like you to say hello to the King of Iraq.' Jackie and I used to kind of kid each other a lot and that must be why at that moment he gave me a withering look as if to say what the hell is he up to now. But I did convince Jackie I was on the level. Later the king was on Jackie's radio show."

Another special part of the Ebbets Field atmosphere was the nicknames. Part of the reason for the nicknames was the intimacy of the ball park. Part of it derived from the passionate emotional attachment of the fans to the players. And part of it was the inability and/or unwillingness of Brooklynites to bother with the finer points of articulation and diction.

Fred "Dixie" Walker came to the Dodgers in 1939 from Detroit and played at Ebbets Field until 1947 when he was traded to the Pittsburgh Pirates for Billy Cox. ("Name eight Dodgers without Cox" was a popular joke of the time.) Of "Dixie" Walker, Frank Graham observed, "Dodger fans yelled to him when he was in the lineup and yelled for him when he wasn't." A big, smiling blond, he was dubbed "The People's Cherce."

Cal Abrams was "Abie." Abrams played for the Dodgers from 1949 to 1952. "I got cheated three times of a World Series share. In 1950, Sisler hit the home run to give the Phillies the pennant. In 1951, Thomson hit the home run to give the Giants the pennant. In 1952, the Dodgers won the pennant but they traded me early in the season to Cincinnati." Abrams came back to Ebbets Field with the Dodgers in 1951 after hitting .477 on a western trip and inspired the *Daily News* headline: "MANTLE, SMANTLE, WE'VE GOT ABIE." Abie lost his batting eye shortly afterward by hiring himself out as a Coney Island batting range instructor. Batting against a machine, he fouled up his fluid swing and eye-hand coordination.

Kirby Higbe, a portly pitcher, became Kirby "Higelbee." Carl Erskine was "Oisk." Roy Campanella was "Campy." Don Newcombe was "Newk" and Carl Furillo was "Skoonj" in tribute to his Italian love of scungili. Gene Hermanski was "Ski" and there was The Preacher and Robby and Shotgun and Sandy and Pistol Pete. . . .

One of the true favorites of Dodger fans was Harold Henry Reese, born July 23 in Ekron, Kentucky. Boyhood skill with marbles and his 5-foot 10-inch, 160-pound frame earned him the nickname "Pee Wee."

"I always felt that he held the Dodgers together," said Sid Frigand. "He was somewhat less than bigger than life among all those stars and he had that nice quality of steadiness."

A lifetime .269 hitter, the man they also called "The Little Colonel" averaged almost a walk a game during his sixteen years as a

Dodger. Others on the team hit peaks and valleys—Reese was the solid man, just getting the job done day after day, season after season.

He had very few enemies and his gentlemanly manner earned him a lot of friends. Once Dodger manager Charlie Dressen brought in Clyde King to relieve. When King finished his warm-up tosses, he explained to Pee Wee that he was not quite ready. "Go back to your shortstop position and stall around a bit, Pee Wee, I'll try to sneak in a few extra practice pitches."

Reese sauntered back to his position and called "time," complaining that he had gotten something in his eye. He went over to Billy Cox for aid. Reese's protestations were so convincing that King, instead of taking the extra warm-up pitches, headed over to third base to see if he could be of any assistance.

On July 22, 1955, one day after he had collected his two thousandth hit, the handsome Kentuckian was given a birthday party at Ebbets Field. "It was the first and only night up to that time where fans were asked not to kick in," notes Irving Rudd. "All they were asked to bring was a cigar, a cigarette, a lighter, candles—anything they could light up for Pee Wee."

Rudd remembers Dodger executive Buzzy Bavasi asking him how much he thought the Dodgers would draw that night. "I said, 'Maybe twenty thousand or so.' He said, 'Anything over eighteen thousand, I'll give you a buck a head.' I wished I had gotten it in writing. We pulled thirty-three thousand. We sold out at seven P.M.! We closed the gates that night. At the Prospect Avenue station of the BMT and the Franklin Avenue exit of the IRT you had to show your ticket as you left the subway or you were not allowed to get on the street. There were cops lined all the way down Franklin Avenue turning people away from the park."

Bloomingdale's and Wallach's donated clothing. Grossinger's gave Reese a lifetime pass to its hotel and a set of golf clubs. "Chock Full O' Nuts contributed two two-hundred-fifty-pound cakes, each with thirty-six candles on them," said Rudd, "plus tons of coffee. Nathan's gave pounds and pounds of hot dogs. All the old timers returned—even Larry MacPhail was there." A congratulatory telegram from Vice President Nixon and a cablegram from President Eisenhower were read to the festive crowd.

The poignancy of the passage of years was evident that night. In 1940, Dodger fans bragged about the "Gold Dust Twins"—Pee Wee Reese and Pistol Pete Reiser. A switch-hitting outfielder, Reiser led the National League in batting average and slugging percentage in 1941. He was an impassioned defensive player and crashed against the concrete walls of Ebbets Field going after fly balls. At the age of twenty-two, he was all through as a superstar. "Reiser could run, field, and throw," said Leo Durocher. "But that brick wall would never stop him. He thought he could go right through it. If he didn't run into the walls, there's no telling what he could have been."

Fifteen years after Reese and Reiser broke in as Dodger rookies, Reese was being feted at Ebbets Field and Reiser was managing at Thomasville, Georgia, in the lowest minor league.

Joint Masters of Ceremonies, Happy Felton and Dodger announcer Vince Scully, introduced Reese. "When I came to Brooklyn in 1940," he said, "I was a scared kid . . . to tell you the truth, I'm twice as scared right now." The lights were dimmed and with varying levels of competency but with the same high ardor, the fans of the Dodger captain sang "Happy Birthday Pee Wee, Happy Birthday to you. . . ."

Reese recalls the time. "With something that big going on, there was the thought you'd fall flat on your ass. There were so many people there. I remember Gene Conley was the pitcher for the Braves. He was a six-foot, six-inch right-hander. I didn't hit him too well. The first time up I got a two base hit, and I knew I would be okay." Reese collected two doubles and a single, and the Dodgers won the game, 8–4.

The zaniness that permeated Ebbets Field was there that night. "My daughter," Reese remembers, "was taken out to a large fishbowl on the field. The fishbowl had a lot of keys in it. She would pick a key and then a car would be driven out to her. If the key fit I was to get the car . . . but the key didn't fit. She went and picked another key and another car was brought out. I don't know how many times this was done. Looking back it was funny.

"She kept picking keys and they kept driving out another car. Finally someone decided to bring out one car and have her pick keys until the one key that fit the car was found."

It was not only the Reeses, Walkers, Higbes, Robinsons, and

Sniders that Brooklyn fans related to. Ebbets Field was a place where some players from the opposing teams were respected and responded to almost as well as those on the Dodgers. Brooklyn-born players who had defected to the "enemy" side fell into this category. Tommy Holmes says, "Brooklyn was my home and my second favorite team." A star for the Boston Braves, he was a special favorite of the crowd at Ebbets Field. "They always treated me very well," he recalls, "except one day I did especially well against the Dodgers and four fans followed me home to Bay Ridge, shouting 'traitor, traitor, traitor.'" Sid Gordon, a New York Giant, then a member of the Braves, was another home-grown favorite.

Bill Nicholson, a free-swinging outfielder for the Chicago Cubs and then the Philadelphia Phillies, had excellent rapport with the fans at Ebbets Field. They used to love to see him swing, especially when his bat failed to make contact with the ball—ten thousand, twenty thousand voices would shout, "swish, swish!" Bill Nicholson became "Swish" Nicholson all over the league.

St. Louis Cardinal star Stan Musial was first referred to at Ebbets Field as "Musical," for his name posed pronunciation problems. Though he racked up the Dodgers with his frozen rope hits, the Ebbets Field fans respected his ability. "The Man," a name connoting admiration, became Musial's nickname not only at Ebbets Field where it originated but throughout baseball.

Ebbets Field was Brooklyn's pride—a loud, lively, human symbol of the Dodgers. Hall-of-Famer Monte Irvin remembers the noise: "You could hear those Dodger fans, almost every word. They'd yell at us [the Giants], 'You're gonna get buried today. You'll never get back to New York alive. If you try and win today, we'll be waiting for you outside the ball park.' They tried to intimidate us. They hated the opposition but they sure loved Brooklyn."

Jack Carney remembers the atmosphere: "I was in a little alcove and worked off a wooden platform and a metal chair with the WOR-TV dugout camera. It was a front-row seat to history. The Dodgers weren't gettin' paid too much, but they knew they were accomplishing somethin' in baseball. The fans knew what they had. There was true spirit at Ebbets Field, not phoney adulation. And everybody there had a lot of fun."

Jim Gilliam remembered the fans: "They were the best. They knew the game for they had it for so long. They knew when a guy was in a slump. They knew when a guy was trying. You could come to Ebbets Field and watch a game but you couldn't say anything you wanted to about the Bums because their fans loved that team. I will always have a soft spot in my heart for Ebbets Field."

And Irving Rudd, the kind of man Damon Runyan would have liked, remembers the players: "Great guys, all of them. As Swift would say, 'There wasn't a rotter in the bunch.' "

On April 24, 1940, Pee Wee Reese replaced Leo Durocher as the shortstop of the Dodgers. "I really did not want to be a member of that team," he says. "I didn't know too much about them, but what I did know was that it had not been too successful an organization. I had the image of two or three guys winding up on the same base."

The assessment Reese had was based on fact. In 1890, 1899, 1900, 1916, and 1920, the Brooklyn National League entry had won pennants, but it had not done very much since. During much of the 1930s, the team, under control of a bank that went under the name of the Brooklyn Trust Company, was entrusted to the skills of cast-off and over-the-hill players. "Daffiness Boys" was their nickname. Reese's image of two or three players winding up on the same base actually did take place. In the days of Manager Wilbert Robinson ("Uncle Robby"), three players wound up on third base. "Leave them alone," Robinson bellowed. "That's the first time they've been together all year." The rotund Dodger manager helped contribute to the "loser" image of the team. He did not play personnel whose names he was unable to spell out on the lineup slip and there were those who said he left players out of the lineup for months because he just did not remember they were on the team.

Reese, judged too slight to play for the Boston Red Sox, was picked up by Larry MacPhail, who created a new image and new power for the Dodgers of Brooklyn.

MacPhail had left the Cincinnati Reds in 1936. Numerous verbal altercations with owner Powell Crosley and one well-publicized punch made his exit imperative. A large, red-haired man, MacPhail was recommended to Dodger owners George V. McLaughlin and Jim Mulvey by then Cardinal general manager Branch Rickey and

National League Commissioner Ford Frick. Signed as Dodger general manager on January 19, 1938, MacPhail received an unlimited expense account, raises in salary based on home attendance, and full authority on all matters dealing with the team.

MacPhail brought in Red Barber from Cincinnati to broadcast Dodger games and give New York City its first continuous baseball radio coverage. He staged a footrace between the slim Barber and his three-hundred-pound broadcasting colleague, Al Helfer. MacPhail paid Olympic track star Jesse Owens, $4,000 for a pregame sprinting demonstration. He gave Babe Ruth a job as a first base coach.

His flair for the unexpected and the unusual led him to spend $35,000 on paint and decorations for the old ball park. MacPhail brought in Gladys Gooding to play on the pipe organ he had installed at Ebbets Field. A standard joke of the time was: "Who played at first base for the Dodgers longer than anybody?" The answer was Gladys Gooding. Her box that housed the organ was located right at first base.

The master promoter literally lit up Ebbets Field. He installed the lights for night baseball. What happened at the first night game ever played in New York City underscored the cliché that "everything happens at Ebbets Field." On June 15, 1938, 38,748 sat through the tension of every pitch and contributed $100,000 in gate revenue as Johnny Vandermeer of Cincinnati pitched his second successive no-hitter.

The MacPhail Dodgers finished seventh in his first season, but MacPhail jacked up attendance from four hundred fifty thousand to seven hundred fifty thousand. He obtained Leo Durocher from St. Louis and made him player-manager in 1939. "MacPhail was half-madman, half-genius," Durocher was to observe later. MacPhail spent $50,000 for Dolph Camili of the Phillies, $90,000 for Billy Herman of the Cubs. Another $100,000 went to Philadelphia for Kirby Higbe, a portly pitcher. He made a trio of Brooklyn portly pitchers with the acquisition of Freddy Fitzsimmons from the Giants and minor-leaguer Hugh Casey for relief work.

The Brooklyn Trust Company, which had placed the Dodgers in care of MacPhail, groaned. More money was spent—some of it went to Detroit for Dixie Walker, some of it went to St. Louis for catcher Mickey Owen.

In 1941, the MacPhail Dodgers won their first National League pennant in two decades. They lost to the Yankees in the World Series, but Brooklyn fans were exultant. The Brooklyn Trust Company and executives George V. McLaughlin and Jim Mulvey were enraged. MacPhail's spending had exceeded the profits the pennant-winning team had earned.

World War II intervened and Larry MacPhail went where there was action. He left the Dodgers, enlisted in the United States Army even though he was over fifty years old, assumed the rank of major, and plotted his next move with another New York City baseball team.

Branch Rickey took MacPhail's place. When the man they called "The Brain" and "The Mahatma" became general manager of the Dodgers on October 29, 1942, he brought with him one of the most brilliant of baseball records. Rickey had invented the farm system in 1919 and in twenty-seven years of guiding the St. Louis Cardinals, had recorded six National League pennants and four world championships.

Both Rickey and MacPhail were shrewd and highly organized baseball men. Rickey's reputation as being a tough man with a dollar was a particularly appealing feature for the Brooklyn Trust Company, especially after MacPhail's lavish spending.

Preacher Roe was fond of telling a story about Rickey's frugality. A member of the Pirates in 1947, the skinny Arkansas southpaw won just four games and lost fifteen. Rickey "who could look inside a guy's muscles and see what was going on," according to Stan Lomax, "who could spot things in a man's play, a man's run, a man's throw that nobody else could spot," saw something in Elwin Charles Roe. The Dodger general manager engineered a trade with Pittsburgh. Roe became a Dodger. "Dixie" Walker was one of the players sent to the Pirates. Over the next half dozen years, the Preacher won ninety games against just thirty-three losses, but he always seemed to have trouble at contract time.

One winter Roe and Rickey had a few fruitless salary sessions. Rickey suggested that Roe go home and ponder what they had discussed. "I think I've made you a fair offer," said the man New York City newspapers called "El Cheapo." "By the way, I know how much you like hunting, Preacher. I've got two wonderful hunting dogs that I'd like you to have."

Roe went home and went hunting and thought about Rickey's salary offer. The hunting dogs turned out to be the best he ever had. "One day I got to thinkin' that Mr. Rickey couldn't be too bad a fella if he'd give me such good dogs. So I signed the contract and put it in the mail. A few hours later, those two dogs took off across the field and I haven't seen 'em since."

Rickey had learned quite a few things in his twenty-seven years with the St. Louis Cardinals. One of them was that hungry (and underpaid) ballplayers generally performed best. His dealing with Roe and other Dodgers was an application of one of his theories.

The highly motivated executive also drove himself and his staff at a dizzying pace. Those who worked with him at the Dodger offices at 215 Montague Street considered themselves lucky if they were able to get home for dinner even once a week. Rickey, who had a fondness for lighting and chewing Anthony and Cleopatra cigars, labored long hours building teams to last. He had learned that the best way to build a team for the future was to assemble a group of players of approximately the same age and plan for a decade or more of service from them. Campanella and Erskine joined the Dodgers in 1948. Robinson and Snider and Hodges had arrived the year before. Newcombe came in 1949 and Clem Labine and Billy Loes made the roster in 1950. Except for Robinson, who retired in 1956, all of these players—the virtual heart of the team—lasted up to and in some cases past 1957, the final year of the Dodgers of Brooklyn.

During the war years, nearly every major league organization retrenched its scouting and expenditures for the future. Rickey did the opposite. Thousands of letters went out to high school coaches asking for their recommendations for the best players available. Rickey also dispatched scouts to look at new sources of talent— blacks, Hispanics, college athletes. By 1946, the twenty-five minor league farm teams of the Dodgers were stocked with talent. From Montreal to Ponca City, from Abilene to Zanesville, talent was developing.

At Newport News in the Piedmont League, Jake Pitler managed a team that had fifteen players who were seventeen years old or younger. One of the players was Edwin "Duke" Snider.

They called him the "Dook of Flatbush" and the Brooklyn fans made him one of their favorites when he arrived as a twenty-year-old in 1947. A handsome, tempestuous left-handed power hitter, he would star in center field for each of the remaining eleven years of the Brooklyn Dodgers, Mantle and DiMaggio were reserved; Mays was a natural. Snider was like the people, the Dodger fans said. He had his highs and lows, he showed emotion, and he could slug the hell out of the ball. No Dodger ever hit more career home runs than Snider (389), recorded more extra base hits (814), more runs batted in (1,271). No Dodger aside from Zack Wheat ripped more doubles (343), recorded more total bases (3,669). The California-born "Dook" is also third on the all-time Dodger list of runs scored, fourth in hits, sixth in games played.

Players like Snider and an older, more polished performer at Montreal named Jackie Robinson prodded Rickey into declaring, "Two years after the war, we'll be fully developed. After that I envision pennants, pennants, pennants."

In 1946, one year after the war, the two teams of Rickey—the one he had built into the National League's most exciting and powerful team, the Cardinals, winners of pennants in 1942, 1943, 1944, and the team he was building, the Dodgers—met in the first National League play-off. "I owe it all to Rickey," was Cardinal manager Eddie Dyer's comment as the St. Louis team won the play-off.

"I was in charge of a banquet at the Hotel St. George for a World Series party after the play-off," recalls Lee Scott. "There were hundreds of writers invited. After we got beat, instead of them going to the St. George, they all took off for St. Louis for the World Series."

Rickey told Scott, "They won this time, but we'll be the power in the National League for years to come." Three quarters of the Dodger farm teams finished in the first division in 1947. The future was on the field.

Rickey was following in MacPhail's path on the baseball field and in his bank statements. The 1946 Dodgers drew 1,796,824 paying customers to lead the league in attendance. The club made a net profit of almost half a million dollars. Rickey's contract called for a share of the profits, and he padded these profits by selling $239,000 worth of surplus players to other teams.

On October 26, 1950, after a series of behind-closed-doors maneuvers at 215 Montague Street, much enmity, two pennants and one near-miss, the man they called "The Mahatma" was eased out as Dodger general manager and president by the man they called "The O'Malley."

Walter Francis O'Malley had first become involved with the Dodgers in the 1930s when he discovered it was good business practice to take clients to Ebbets Field. In 1932, he became a director of the team and purchased a block of stock. In 1943, O'Malley became the legal representative for the Dodgers. Then together with Rickey, he was part of a syndicate that purchased the team from Larry Mac-Phail.

O'Malley and Rickey contrasted sharply. "The Mahatma" and his Anthony and Cleopatra cigars versus "The O'Malley" and the twenty or so expensive cigars he smoked each day (one wit cracked that "O'Malley spends more on cigars than most people spend on food") symbolized just part of their differences. In the last year of a five-year contract, Rickey's $50,000 per annum salary plus bonuses based on attendance provided him with a great deal of money. O'Malley thought that perhaps it was too much money.

At a press conference at the Hotel Bossert, the atmosphere was relaxed. All the fighting had apparently been concluded behind closed doors.

"Comest thou here," Rickey began addressing reporters, "to see the reed driven in the wind?" Then he resigned and explained that it was his "duty and privilege to introduce the new president of the Dodgers, a man of youth [O'Malley was forty-seven], courage, enterprise and desire . . . Walter O'Malley."

The new Dodger president and 60-percent stockholder was equally gracious. "I would like to say that for the past seven years that I have been associated with Mr. Rickey, I have developed the warmest possible feelings for him as a man. I do not know of anyone who can approach Mr. Rickey in the realm of executive baseball ability. I am terribly sorry and hurt personally that we will now have to face his resignation."

"The whole thing was a matter of finances and ego," said Stan Lomax. "O'Malley and Rickey were two dynamic people in one organization. You can only have one. And it had to be O'Malley."

The last general manager the Dodgers ever had, Rickey moved on to Pittsburgh, attempting to build a third National League power. With his departure the title of general manager ceased to exist in the Dodger organization. Buzzy Bavasi, general manager at Montreal from 1948 to 1950, joined the Dodgers in 1951, inheriting Rickey's role but not his title. Bavasi was listed as executive vice president. The sagacious Bavasi and his Montreal teams had been the supplier of much Dodger talent. In 1948 all twenty-one Montreal players were promoted to the major leagues. Duke Snider, Carl Erskine and Don Newcombe were three of the players.

MacPhail had changed the Dodger image. Rickey had enhanced it. O'Malley embellished it, and Bavasi extended it.

The organization prided itself on "home-grown talent." Most of the players on the Dodgers were products of the farm system that Rickey had developed. The 1955 world championship team was assembled over the years for a total cash outlay of $118,388 in bonuses, drafts, and purchases. Only Pee Wee Reese and substitutes Rube Walker, Russ Meyer, and Frank Kellert were obtained in trades. The rest of the roster came through the farm system.

Johnny Podres, Roger Craig, and Clem Labine were responsible for all the Dodger wins in the 1955 World Series. The trio was acquired for a total expenditure of $10,500. The largest sum paid for any Dodger was $42,500—for Pee Wee Reese. Billy Loes cost $21,000.

"Back in 1940, the owner of the Reading Club in the Inter-State League got fed up and offered to sell out to Larry MacPhail for five thousand dollars," recalled Fresco Thompson, who headed the Dodger farm system and survived Rickey's purge of MacPhail's personnel and O'Malley's purge of Rickey's personnel. "That was dirt cheap for a franchise—twenty players and two full sets of uniforms

—but the thing that intrigued MacPhail was the new bus which the team used on road trips. This was a year before Pearl Harbor and most automobile production was earmarked for the armed forces.

"MacPhail figured the bus was worth twenty-five hundred dollars and forty uniforms cost at least ten bucks apiece . . . that meant Brooklyn was getting twenty players for twenty-one hundred dollars or one hundred five dollars apiece." One of the players was a solidly built, scatter-armed pitcher named Carl Furillo.

While he never made it as a pitcher, Furillo's arm became a Dodger trademark. Dubbed "The Reading Rifle," because of his uncanny ability to play the caroms off the right field wall, he had what Brooklyn fans were fond of calling "da best arm in da biznez." The eccentricities of right field at Ebbets Field frustrated most outfielders. For Furillo, it was a challenge and a joy. "I loved the game," he says, "I wanted to be there in right field. It was my job like someone goes to an office every day. It was my job to take care of right field and I tried to do my job with all the ability I had." The right field wall was uneven. Part of it included the scoreboard. Atop the scoreboard was a twenty-foot screen that stopped many balls from landing on Bedford Avenue, which was behind the scoreboard and the screen. The lower portion of the wall was padded with foam rubber. "They put it in," Furillo recalls, "all over the outfield after Pete Reiser screwed himself up by banging into a wall." There was a sharp corner in right field created by the connection of the scoreboard to the wall. Balls batted against the wall, the screen, the scoreboard rebounded unpredictably. But predictably, Furillo, who knew at least seventeen different angles at which the ball could rebound off the eccentric contours, made the plays. "Right field was my home; I was comfortable there." The powerfully built Dodger was more than just an outfielder with homing pigeon instincts and a bazooka for an arm. He could also hit. Eight times he batted .295 or better. Six times he drove in more than ninety runs. In 1953 he won the National League batting title.

The black stars on the Dodgers, like those on other teams, were acquired for incredibly low prices. The grand total of $4,700 made Robinson and Campanella Dodgers. Newcombe was acquired for $1,500. Brooklyn records list the cost of obtaining Junior Gilliam and

Joe Black at $6,666. And even that price was exaggerated. In 1951, the Dodgers were interested in obtaining pitcher Leroy Farrell of the Baltimore Elite Giants. The asking price for Farrell, who was in the Army, was $10,000. Thompson balked at the price, which he thought was too high, but he wanted to make the deal and suggested that the Elite Giants toss in a couple of other players. The deal was made. Farrell never become a Brooklyn Dodger. He came out of the service overweight and never regained his previous form. The couple of other players were Joe Black and Junior Gilliam. Cost-conscious Dodger accountants divided the $10,000 purchase price into three. The cost for Gilliam and Black was $6,666.

Sandy Amoros cost the Dodgers $1,300; George Shuba was picked up for $150. Pitcher Clem Labine was acquired for $500. The "Dook of Flatbush" (Edwin Snider) was signed for $800.

Strong, steady Gil Hodges, the heartthrob of so many Brooklyn teenage girls in that era, cost the Dodgers $1,500. Indiana-born Hodges adopted the Borough of Churches as his home just as the Borough of Churches adopted him. A powerful right-handed batter, from 1949 to 1955 Hodges recorded one hundred or more RBIs a season and more than thirty-two home runs each year.

Hodges was unable to "buy" a hit in twenty-one at-bats in the 1952 World Series. The strange slump, in the view of many Dodger fans, was the reason for the Bums' loss to the Yankees. When the 1953 season started, Hodges still was afflicted with a case of batting anemia. In his first seventy-five official plate appearances in 1953, the man they called "Gillie" had managed to hit but thirteen singles and one home run. On May 16, Hodges was benched for the first time in his career. At St. Francis Xavier Church in Brooklyn, the May 17 10:00 A.M. mass was concluded with these words by Father Herbert Redmond: "Go home, keep the Commandments, and say a prayer for Gil Hodges to help him out of his slump." Soon after Hodges snapped out of his slump. There were those in Brooklyn who truly believed in the power of prayer. A few skeptics, though (it was always suspected they were closet Giant fans), claimed the whole Hodges situation was rigged.

"Nothing was ever rigged with Gil Hodges," insists Irving Rudd. "That came spontaneously from the church. Gil got a lot of publicity and a lot of sympathy, and he could have capitalized on it. I had two speaking engagements at seven hundred fifty dollars each for Gil. 'I'm not a public speaker,' Gil told me. 'I don't go in for those things.' I really wanted him to do it. I think I was down for one hundred fifty bucks to introduce him. But he turned the whole thing down. Gil was a very, very honorable man. Every bit as clean and decent as everybody said he was."

Sandy Koufax won only nine games for the Brooklyn Dodgers. And there were those who said that the $14,000 he was given in bonus money in 1954 was a waste of money. Sandy Koufax didn't do too much to distinguish himself as a Brooklyn Dodger, for his days of glory came after 1957—as a member of the Dodgers of Los Angeles.

A product of Lafayette High School (he wrote in that Bensonhurst school's yearbook that his ambition was to "be successful and make my parents proud of me"), Koufax was signed off the campus of the University of Cincinnati. He had gone to the midwestern college on a basketball scholarship, and was talked into pitching for the baseball team after the basketball season ended. He struck out fifty-eight men in thirty-eight innings. Back in Brooklyn with his freshman year concluded, he joined the sandlot team, Nathan's Famous, a club sponsored by the Coney Island frankfurter institution. *Brooklyn Eagle* school sports writer Jimmy Murphy watched the intense left-hander pitch and was impressed. Scout Al Campanis of the Dodgers was tipped off and was impressed; Koufax became a Dodger. Signed as a 'bonus baby,' the major league rules of the time mandated that he stay with the Dodgers for two years and that he could not be sent to the minors.

"He couldn't hit the side of a barn door at sixty feet," recalls Tom Lasorda, who was sent down to the minors to make room on the Dodger roster for Koufax. "But he had that burning desire to whip control problems."

Lee Scott recealls, "The catcher in the bull pen wore all the equipment to catch Sandy, he was so wild in those early Brooklyn years; he was so bad, so out of control in one stretch, that there was a lot of talk about trading him."

A 6-foot 2-inch, 210-pound southpaw, born on December 30, 1935, the sensitive Koufax was embarrassed by his control problems but determined to succeed. "He used to work out behind the Vero Beach playing field barracks," said Scott. "He didn't want anyone to see him."

Duke Snider in those early years was one player who didn't even want to bat against Koufax. "It was like playing a game of Russian roulette," said Snider. "And most of the time the choices were he'd strike you out or come close to killing you."

In his second major league start on August 27, 1955, Koufax pitched a fourteen-strikeout, two-hitter against the Cincinnati Reds. That outing and a few others in his three years as a Brooklyn Dodger revealed the potential of the shy man who retired from baseball after a dozen seasons at age thirty-one.

"Koufax got so good," says Tom Lasorda, "that there were games when he was pitching to just half the plate, busting off the dropping curve and rising fast ball." Five times he led the league in ERA. Four times he pitched no-hitters. Three times he struck out three hundred or more batters in a season. He posted a ninety-seven–twenty-seven record his last four years and a fifteen strikeout victory over the Yankees in the World Series. Old Dodger fans groused. Not only did they lose their team to L.A., they also lost one of their native sons and perhaps the greatest Dodger pitcher ever.

Like Sandy Koufax, Don Drysdale's years of pitching greatness were with the Dodgers of Los Angeles. A six-foot six-inch sidearming fastballer, "Big D" was given sage advice from Sal Maglie when he arrived at the Brooklyn Dodger spring training camp as a nineteen-year-old in 1956.

"Every time a batter gets a hit off you," The Barber told him, "it's like he picked your pocket for a dollar." Drysdale remembered. Astride the mound, he was an intimidating figure who resented any batter who attempted to crowd the plate or "pick his pocket."

Six times he struck out two hundred or more batters in a fourteen-year career that saw him win, lose, and start more games; strike out more batters; shut out more teams, than any other pitcher in Dodger history.

When the bargain basement route of the farm system or the "bonus baby" still left a gap on the Dodgers, a major trade filled the gap. After the 1947 season the only missing link in what was to be an all-star infield was at third base. Rickey shipped Dixie Walker, Hal Gregg, and Vic Lombardi to Pittsburgh. Preacher Roe and Billy Cox became Dodgers.

"Billy was a sad man," recalls Irving Rudd, "a dear person. He looked like a plucked chicken when he stripped down . . . it always amazed everyone how he could go into the hole and get all that power into his throws." Cox was listed at 5-feet 10-inches, 150 pounds. There were those who said most of his weight was all heart. A Dodger from 1948 to 1954, he played third base with a magnet in his glove and a catapult in his arm.

Throughout the era, Dodger fans experienced moments of extreme frustration, The "Brooks" inability to beat the Yankees in the World Series caused depression in the heart of Flatbush. Even worse, for some, were the catastrophic last-minute pennant losses in 1950 and 1951.

Cal Abrams remembers 1950 and the Phillies. "We could've won it in the eighth inning of the last game. I was on second base. There was a hit to short center field. Catcher Stan Lopata had called for a pitch out and Robin Roberts had taken something off the pitch. The third base coach Milt Stock had one hand waving me in and the other in his mouth—he was biting his nails. Richie Ashburn probably had the worst arm in baseball; it was a short throw and I was out at the plate."

In the ninth inning, Philadelphia's Dick Sisler hit a three-run homer to win the game and the pennant for the Phillies. "I won't ever forget that moment in my life," said Sisler. "We had to win it or else we would've gone into a play-off. I don't think we woulda won the play-off. Our pitching was shot. I just happened to be up at the right time. Newcombe tried to get me to go for a bad ball with two strikes on me. The next pitch was a high fast ball—away. I put the wood to it. I didn't know it was gone until I rounded first base."

Duke Snider recalls, "I was chasing the ball that Sisler hit and just ran out of baseball field. I was groping at the wall wishing I could move it back. I kid Dick all the time when I see him. I tell him it was a windblown home run. He says it may have been windblown but that the only way I could have caught the ball was to have bought a ticket and been in the stands to catch the ball. It is more or less our hello whenever we meet—our moment in history."

Throughout the era, the only unsettled position in the Brooklyn lineup was left field. Pete Reiser played there in 1947, Marv Rackley in 1948; Gene Hermanski was the "other outfielder" along with Snider and Furillo in 1949 and 1950. At the trading deadline in 1951, Buzzy Bavasi moved to fill the left field spot. Eddie Miksis, Joe Hatten, and Hermanski were shipped to the Cubs. The Dodgers received catcher Rube Walker, infielder Wayne Terwilliger, pitcher Johnny Schmitz, and outfielder Andy Pafko. Dubbed "Handy Andy," the native of Boyceville, Wisconsin, helped the Dodgers in 1951, and his nineteen homers and eighty-five RBIs contributed some fire-power to the 1952 pennant-winning Brooks. By 1953, Pafko was gone. "Shotgun" George Shuba alternated with Jackie Robinson in left field. During the next three years Sandy Amoros played there most of the time. Gino Cimoli was the 1957 regular left fielder for the Dodgers. The position may have been unsettled, but the players who came and went had such varying images and personalities that Brooklyn fans had a ready-made topic of conversation.

Some took a fancy to the part-time (1949–1952) streakhitting Cal Abrams, Brooklyn born and Jewish. Others sighed about what could have been had handsome "Pistol Pete" Reiser stayed healthy. Pafko, the veteran, was solid and reliable. Shuba had the alliterative nickname and a fine arm, but he lacked power as a batter. Amoros could not speak English but he could run, run, run. His slight size and World Series catch were endearing qualities. Gino Cimoli, a native of San Francisco, was hailed by some Brooklyn rooters as the second coming of Joe DiMaggio when he joined the Dodgers in 1956. Brooklyn fans saw him at his batting best. In 1957 he batted .293 but then he, like the team, went west.

The team was blueprinted for Ebbets Field. A collection of powerful right-handed sluggers plus southpaw Duke Snider, it seemed at times cramped in the small confines of the little ball park. Nineteen times in the years from 1947–1957, a Dodger recorded one hundred RBIs. The awesome scoring power of the Dodgers erupted time after time.

On August 31, 1950, sparking a 19–3 romp over Boston, Hodges slashed four home runs and a single, driving in nine of the nineteen runs.

On August 31, 1952, the Dodgers scored fifteen runs against the Cincinnati Reds in the first inning:

Billy Cox grounded out. Reese walked. Snider cracked a home run to right field. Jackie Robinson doubled. Andy Pafko walked. George Shuba singled. Robinson scored. Pafko wound up on second base. Bud Byerly replaced Cincinnati pitcher Ewell Blackwell. The Reds got the second out when Pafko was thrown out attempting to steal. Shuba took second base. And then the Dodgers really began to hit. Hodges walked. Shuba was singled home by Rube Walker. Dodger pitcher Chris Van Cuyk singled Hodges home. Cox drove in Walker with a single. Reese's single brought Van Cuyk in and made the score 7–0. Herman Wehmeier became the third pitcher for the Reds. He walked Snider, loading the bases. Robinson was hit by a pitch. Cox scored. Pafko singled home Reese and Snider. The score was 10–0. Frank Smith replaced Wehmeier. Smith walked Shuba, loading the bases once again. Hodges walked. Robinson was forced in with another run. Walker singled, bringing home Pafko and Shuba. Van Cuyk singled. Hodges scored the fourteenth run. The bases were loaded again when Cox was hit by a pitch. The fifteenth run came in when Reese walked, scoring Walker. Snider made the final out—lunging at a pitch and striking out. The Dodgers collected fifteen runs, ten hits, seven walks, and had three batters hit by pitches. The batting fireworks resulted in the following records: most runs in an inning, most runs scored with two outs (twelve), most batters to reach base safely in a row (nineteen), most batters to come up and hit in one inning (twenty-one).

On June 25, 1953, they pounded five home runs in a 12–3 shelling of the Reds. On July 10, 1953, a Dodger homered for the twenty-fourth straight game. Especially pleasing for Brooklyn fans was the fact that the Dodger homer was blasted by Campanella off Sal Maglie.

On August 20, 1953, Carl Erskine shut out the Giants, 10–0, for the thirteenth consecutive Brooklyn win.

On August 30, 1953, they slaughtered the St. Louis Cardinals, 20–4. In the seventh inning a dozen Dodgers scored.

On June 16, 1956, Snider stroked four home runs as the Dodgers won their sixth straight.

The pulverizing power, their crushing of the opposition, their come-from-behind victories just seemed to whet their fans' appetites. The Dodgers had pride in what they were doing. Their fans were uncontrolled in their bragging, rooting passion for the team. Adolescents filled brown paper bags with water and threw them out of apartment house windows, joyous after a Dodger romp. Adults on the job or the subway the day after a win cheered and congratulated each other. "That was some game we won . . . How did you like what Robby did? . . . Ain't Newk somethin'? . . . That Cox is magic . . . What a glove . . . What an arm . . ." If one were a Dodger fan, and his or her co-worker were a Giant fan, so much the better. "Didja hear what the Bums did yesterday? . . . What'd you think of their pitching last night? . . . Why don't you give up on the Jints and root for a real ball club? . . . Wait'll we get at the Yanks in the series this year . . . We're ready this time, we are."

Power, speed, daring, drive, verve, clutch performance, bigger-than-life personalities, all shaped the Dodgers. As each new component fitted inself onto the team throughout that era, as each new season brought victories and pennants, the pride of the players increased. "We had such talent," said Pee Wee Reese, who once had balked at joining the Dodgers because of their "loser" image, "that it was tough for anyone to break into the starting lineup, to make the team."

"They were all-stars, the Dodgers, at every position," said Jerry Coleman, who envied them from inside his Yankee uniform. "With a couple of more starting pitchers—they would have been completely unbeatable."

Year after year, Reese would bring the lineup card out to home plate, would raise the right arm and lead the Dodgers out onto the playing field. "Being captain of the Dodgers was much more than those things," said Reese. "It meant representing an organization committed to winning and trying to keep it going. We could have won every year if the breaks went right."

All the moments of the Brooklyn Dodgers now belong to history. "We knew we were good," muses Carl Furillo. "Our fans knew we were good. You couldn't do anything wrong for the Brooklyn fans. They were hungry for baseball, and we were hungry to win for them."

The Yankees

The New York Yankees came into existence in 1903 and shared the Polo Grounds as tenants of the New York Giants. In 1920, the Yankees acquired Babe Ruth from the Boston Red Sox. His gate appeal enabled the tenant Yankees to outdraw the landlord Giants in their own ball park. The Yankees were told to find a new home. Yankee owner, beer baron Jacob Ruppert, acquired the land across the Harlem River from the Polo Grounds at the mouth of a stream called Crowell's Creek and planned his new stadium. "It was all farm-land," recalled Giant ticket taker Joe Flynn. "It was beautiful, you could get fresh milk and vegetables there." On May 22, 1922, the White Construction Company was given the contract to build the new home of the Yankees.

In less than nine months, on two hundred forty thousand square feet of land, over the completely filled-in bed of Crowell's Creek, the stadium was constructed of reinforced concrete and steel. Grandstand seats were produced on the site; one hundred thirty-five thousand individual steel castings were used and four hundred thousand pieces of maple lumber were fastened to the castings by over a million brass screws. Over nine hundred fifty thousand board feet of Pacific Coast fir were brought through the Panama Canal for the erection of the bleachers.

Dubbed the "House that Ruth Built," constructed at a cost of $2,500,000, the park stretched from 157th to 161st streets, River Avenue to Doughty Avenue. The first game at Yankee Stadium took place on April 18, 1923. The National Anthem was played by John

Philip Sousa's band. New York State Governor Al Smith threw out the first ball. And Babe Ruth hit a home run.

Yankee Stadium was the first triple-decked structure of its kind, an oval-shaped, dull green, cathedral-like edifice in which autumn's afternoon sun created strange mosaic designs on the center field grass and interfered with outfielders' vision.

It seated 67,224. Thousands more came in as standees. Hundreds would watch the game from the 161st Street elevated subway line platform and the neighboring apartment houses. The park had 13,378 bleacher seats, 4,857 upper boxes, 10,459 lower boxes, 8,785 reserved mezzanine seats. There were 10,712 seats in the upper grandstand and 14,543 in the lower grandstand. Mezzanine boxes totaled 3,995. The loge section seated 135.

The triple-decked grandstands arched into foul territory off the line of left field behind home plate and out to the right field line, shaping the playing field into a gigantic horseshoe. It was not only the "House that Ruth Built" but a park built for left-handed sluggers like Ruth. Thus it was easiest to hit home runs in right field and right center field. Straightaway center field was dubbed "Death Valley." At its deepest part, it was 461 feet from home plate. The monuments to Miller Huggins and Ed Barrow, to Babe Ruth and Lou Gehrig—the tradition that all opponents battled against, the legends that supported the Yankees—were on the playing field more than 450 feet from home plate.

Down the line, it was 296 feet in right field and 301 in left field. Pull hitters would consciously aim for home runs. The dimensions and the triple decking and the tradition made Yankee Stadium—the home of champions—into an asymmetrical ascendant ball park.

East 157th Street was behind first base and Ruppert Place was located behind third base. Beyond right field was River Avenue, and 161st Street was in back of left field.

It was a park of pigeons, vast numbers of them, fat from the popcorn and peanuts of stadium fans, lodged in the beams and rafters and fluttered about when the huge crowd rose to its feet cheering a big hit or a spectacular play.

On this playing field and throughout baseball, the Yankees were viewed as aristocrats, winners. Under manager Miller Huggins

(1921–1928), they racked up six straight pennants and two world championships. In 1932, 1936, 1937, 1938, 1939, and 1941, Joe Mc-Carthy piloted them to World Series victories. They won the pennant in 1942 but lost to St. Louis in the World Series; the next year there was another pennant and this time a World Series victory over the Cardinals.

When Larry MacPhail teamed with Dan Topping and Del Webb on January 25, 1945, to purchase the Yankees for $2.8 million, tradition, attitude, keen baseball minds, and a glorious history of nine world championships and fourteen pennants came along with the purchase.

MacPhail's innovations further added to the image of the Yankees. In 1946, MacPhail removed the flagpoles that protruded from the stadium roof and replaced them with structures to hold hundreds of electric lights. There was now night baseball at Yankee Stadium. The first night game was May 28, 1946. He originated the Stadium Club and season box seats. Individualized dining and seating increased corporate patronage. Companies began to reserve season boxes for the entertainment of clients, for the rewarding of loyal employees. Under MacPhail, the Yankees became the first team in history to draw over two million in home attendance. The 1946 club packed 2,265,512 into the stadium.

In the 1947–1957 era, the Yankees topped the American League in attendance each season except for 1948. They became the first team in history to record two million or more in home attendance for five straight years.

Yankee fans contrasted sharply in vocation and image with those of the Dodgers, and to some degree with the supporters of the Giants. Geographically a great many Yankee patrons came from affluent communities in the Bronx, Westchester, Queens, and suburban centers in New Jersey. "They were refined people for the most part," said Eddie Lopat. "You'd hear the cheering, but they were kind of sedate, generally people with character." The team had high-class standards and the audiences at the stadium generally had high-class behavior. "The fans were controlled," continued Lopat. "And there was control in the ball park."

The individual especially responsible for the control and the success of the team was George Weiss, master builder. A short, rotund, drab, flannel-clad man, Weiss personified the Yankee quest for and attainment of excellence. He also symbolized the machinelike efficiency that produced the phrase: "Rooting for the Yankees is like rooting for General Motors."

A Yalie of German descent, Weiss was brought to the Yankees in 1932 by Ed Barrow, general manager of the Bronx Bombers since October 29, 1920. Weiss had begun his career as a baseball executive at New Haven in the Eastern League in 1919, four years before pinstripes first appeared on Yankee uniforms.

During the roaring twenties, the Yanks won six pennants. Player purchases contributed a great deal to the team's success. Several of these deals were with the Boston Red Sox. One of them took place on the third day of the new decade—a player named George Herman Ruth came over to the Yanks from Boston.

The depression years and tight money prompted another approach to the construction of winning Yankee teams. Weiss emulated—some say surpassed—the farm system concept pioneered by Branch Rickey. He planted teams in Newark; Kansas City; Butler, Pennsylvania; Norfolk, Virginia; Springfield, Mass.; Akron, Ohio; Augusta, Georgia; Bassett, Virginia; Beaumont, Texas; Portland, Binghamton, and other cities north and south, east and west. Rickey built and observed. Weiss built, observed, and personally supervised every detail of the Yankee operation—major league and minor league.

"Weiss was a quiet man who did not like to get into crowds," said Jim Thomson, who worked under the Yankee general manager as plant supervisor of Yankee Stadium. "But how he could pay attention to details."

One of the details Weiss kept track of was player performance, and he used these details in salary negotiations. "My first year," former Yankee hurler Eddie Lopat recalls, "I won seventeen and lost eleven. I had to battle like heck to get a twenty-five-hundred-dollar raise. The next year I was fifteen and ten. I didn't pitch quite as well as the year before. Deep down, deep, I knew it. I didn't get a raise. I was told I wasn't pitching against contending clubs. I said that was no choice of mine. 'I pitch against whom you tell me to,' I said. I pitched against Cleveland a lot; that was a contending club. Then in 1950 I was eighteen and eight and second or third in ERA. I got twelve of my eighteen wins against contending clubs. I had to tell him, 'You can't tell me nothing now about contending clubs.' I had to fight like hell to get a fifteen-hundred or two-thousand-dollar raise. The next year I was twenty-one and nine. I had to fight like hell to get a six-thousand-dollar raise. The following year, 1952, I hurt my arm and was out for three months. I finished at ten and five and won five games down the stretch. I had to take a cut—all that and an ERA of 2.53, and I had to take a cut. In 1953, I was sixteen and four and led the league in ERA. And I didn't even get a raise. My top salary was thirty-five thousand dollars—there were only three players making a hundred thousand dollars: Williams, DiMag, Musial."

Weiss was the Yankee inspector-general. The quality of toilet paper, the garb and look of athletes, the style of the team, lockers, stands, positions players were slotted for—over all of these and more, Weiss prevailed. He was a tireless, careful, introverted individual who hated to make mistakes. He would weigh his options sometimes for months before making a decision.

Those who came into conflict with Weiss usually lost. In 1948, Bucky Harris began his twenty-second year as a major league manager, his second with the Yankees. Harris was an easygoing, carefree type. He believed in putting in his hours at the ball park and not taking the game home with him. Dubbed "the four-hour manager," he even had an unlisted phone number as a screen against his professional life intruding on his private life. Weiss was just the opposite. The two men clashed over life-styles, over the Yankee GM's habit of placing private detectives on the payroll to check on the leisure-hour activities of players. They also were in open conflict over the relationship of minor league farm teams to the "big club," the Yankees.

The Newark Bears, number-one farm team of the Yankees, had Bob Porterfield pitching like a major leaguer. Harris insisted that he be promoted to the Yankees. Weiss insisted that Porterfield remain in the minors, arguing that he did not wish to disturb the routine and success of the Newark team. Porterfield was finally brought up in August and won five of eight decisions. The White Sox defeated the Yankees in the last two games of the season, knocking them out of the pennant and setting up a one game play-off with Cleveland. An October 6 Indian victory over Chicago gave Cleveland the pennant. That was the last day of Bucky Harris as Yankee manager. Weiss had waited and acted.

The man Weiss chose to replace Harris was a picturesque character, a man whose roots went all the way back with the Yankee general manager to the Eastern League of the 1920s—Casey Stengel. It was perhaps the most unpredictable but most intelligent of all the moves Weiss made during his long administrative career. Stengel was officially introduced as Yankee manager on October 12, 1948, six days after Harris was removed and just two months after Babe Ruth had died at age fifty-three.

"It was a shock," Eddie Lopat remembers his reaction and that of the other Yankees when Stengel was announced as the new manager. "We thought we got us a clown. When spring training started in 1949, we just sat back and watched his reaction. He never said too much about anything to anyone. It was a treat for him to be with us after all the donkey clubs he had. He was something. He didn't need notes. He knew what every hitter or pinch hitter could do against certain pitchers. He could make the moves."

Stan Lomax recalls, "There was no doubt that Casey was a newspaperman's best friend. He only used 'Stengelese' [his own special version of double-talk] when he didn't want to say anything," Lomax continued. "He would talk about how he met the King of England when he and George Kelly made a 'round-the-world tour. Case would talk you 'round the world in his talks, but if you were honest with Case . . . Case would be honest with you."

If Casey did not want to reveal anything, he lapsed into Stengelese. Mickey Mantle remembers a classic example of his former manager's superconvoluted syntax. Mantle, along with Ted Williams, Stan Musial, and Stengel, was summoned to Washington to testify during Senator Estes Kefauver's baseball reserve clause hearings.

"I was scared to death," recalls Mantle. "I didn't have any idea about what to do; I thought we were going to jail or something. Casey, he loved it.

"They asked him one question and he spoke for an hour and a half. He started off: 'In 1900, in Wakakkee, Illinois, or someplace like that, I tore my suit sitting in the stands . . . now they've got high seats.' He then told about how good the railroads were getting and that planes were fast. He was going on. They said, 'Mr. Stengel, would you please excuse yourself?' They dismissed him. They couldn't get him out of there fast enough. Then they called me up. I said, 'I agree completely with everything Casey said.' "

Charles Dillon Stengel, born July 30, 1890, in Kansas City, Missouri, was an original, a complex character. "There was Casey Stengel of the huge ego," said former Yankee Tony Kubek. "There was the Casey Stengel of the public relations image, there was the Casey Stengle who could talk for hours on the long thirty-six hours of train trips to Kansas City, there was the sensitive Casey Stengel . . . there was the Casey Stengel of the Yankee pride."

Pride was part of Casey and part of the Yankee way. A feeling about their craft and a sense of their relationship to the opposition contributed a great deal to the special makeup of the team. "When we won the pennant and the World Series in 1949 and came to spring training the next year, Stengel told us, 'Last year is past history'," said Lopat. " 'We never look back. We gotta go back out and beat 'em again this year.' He did it every spring."

"When we played the other teams," continued Lopat, "we never underestimated them or ourselves. We only played the Giants in the 1951 World Series. We were told by the newspapermen that the Giants would run us off the field, that they were hot and that they had won all those games down the stretch. Our attitude was that they would have to run us off the field, not in the newspapers. In 1949, we played the Dodgers in the Series. We knew they were all young fellows without that much experience and that we could beat them. In 1952, however, we knew they were a tough club, but we were prepared. We never underestimated an opponent, no matter what anybody ever said about them."

In four October days in 1950, the Yankees took the zip out of the Whiz Kids of Philadelphia, a team that had come out of nowhere to snatch the 1950 pennant from the Dodgers. As Eddie Lopat recalls, "We knew they were a bunch of young kids—not like the Dodgers. We knew we could handle the Phillies, but we didn't expect to do it in four straight games."

Bespectacled Jim Konstanty was the Phillies' starting pitcher in the first World Series game in Philadelphia. The National League's top relief pitcher that season with sixteen wins, all of Konstanty's record seventy-four appearances had been as a result of his coming out of the bull pen. Konstanty was a desperation choice as a starter, for the Philadelphia staff had ended the season in a state of exhaustion. The Yankees managed just five hits and one run off Konstanty, but it was enough. Vic Raschi allowed only two hits and no runs. "Raschi wins because he pitches here, here, and there," said Stengel, pointing to his arm, his heart, and his head.

Two of the game's premier right-handers opposed each other in the second game. Through nine innings, Allie Reynolds and Robin Roberts matched each other almost pitch for pitch. Going into the tenth inning the score was tied, 1–1. A second inning single by Gene Woodling accounted for the Yankee run. A fifth-inning fly ball by Richie Ashburn scored the Philadelphia run. The only other scoring of the game came in the top of the tenth. DiMaggio drilled one of Roberts' pitches into the stands for a home run. "God bless DiMag," Reynolds told reporters. "If he hadn't hit it, I'd still be pitching."

Through seven and two-thirds innings of game three the Phillies were leading, 2–1. Kenny Heintzelman, a relief pitcher who had won only three games all year, had yielded just three hits. Perhaps it was the monuments in deep center field or New York City or the buzz of the huge stadium crowd, for from that point on the Phillies collapsed. Heintzelman walked three batters and was taken out. Eddie Sawyer, the Philadelphia manager, brought back Konstanty. Stengel sent Bobby Brown in to hit for Bauer. Brown bounced the ball to rookie shortstop Granny Hamner. He juggled the ball. The score was tied.

In the ninth inning Russ Meyer, loser of more games than he won in 1950, was the Philadelphia pitcher. Gene Woodling, who had popped up as a pinch hitter for Lopat in the eighth inning, slammed a grounder to Jim Bloodworth. The veteran infielder could not find the handle on the ball. Woodling was safe at first. It was Rizzuto's turn to hit to Bloodworth. Flagging the ball down in midair, Bloodworth dropped it. Rizzuto was now on base. Both Woodling and "The Scooter" were credited with hits. Choking up on the bat, Jerry Coleman came to the plate. He blooped the ball into left field. Woodling scored; the Yanks won, 3–2.

Whitey Ford, who posted a 9-1 record after being promoted from Kansas City in June, started the fourth game for New York. He would go into the Army after the series and not pitch again for the Bombers until 1953. The slick left-hander left something for everyone to remember him by.

Ford had a 5-0 shutout going into the ninth inning. The game would probably have ended that way had it not been for the late afternoon autumn haze and stadium shadows. Gene Woodling, the leading Yankee batter in the series and a normally dependable left fielder, lost a fly ball. Instead of it landing in his glove, it struck his leg. A run scored. Ford, rattled, gave up another run. Stengel grew restless. Ford had finessed the Phillies; Casey brought in Reynolds to finish them off. The "Super Chief" fanned hitter Stan Lopata and the Yankees had their sixth World Series sweep.

"We really clobbered them," Jerry Coleman would joke later. "They were a young club, a one year team. They couldn't match our depth and our pitching." Very few organizations could.

"We had guys on the bench," said Lopat, "who could play as good as the starters. They hated to get on the bench because they knew they might not get back for three or four weeks. Snuffy Stirnweiss was a regular in 1948. The next year he slipped a little, and he got hurt, and in came Jerry Coleman. Stirnweiss never came back. He played seven games in 1950 and they traded him off."

The Yankees had three Triple-A farm teams—Kansas City, Newark, and Oakland. These provided organizational depth and a strong bargaining hand for George Weiss. "He told young players," noted Stan Lomax, " 'It might be four years before the Yankees will need you. However you'll have good food, a good bed to sleep in and when you come up, you'll be coming up to the Yankees.' They called Joe McCarthy a push-button manager. Weiss was a push-button executive. He might have four players ready to play in the majors, but there was no room for them to come up. But all he had to do was push a button when he needed them."

With Weiss and Stengel in charge, the Yankees reeled off an unprecedented string of pennants: 1949, 1950, 1951, 1952, 1953, 1955, 1956, 1957. Talent gravitated to the roster. Allie Reynolds, Yogi Berra, and Vic Raschi in 1947; Lopat, Joe Collins, and Hank Bauer in

1948; Coleman and Gene Woodling in 1949. The supply kept coming. Whitey Ford and Billy Martin in 1950; Tom Morgan, Gil McDougald, Bob Cerv, Mickey Mantle in 1951; Andy Carey in 1952. Bill Skowron and Bob Grim joined the club in 1954, Johnny Kucks, Elston Howard, Don Larsen, Bob Turley, Bobby Richardson, Tom Sturdivant in 1955. In 1956, Ralph Terry was a newcomer and in 1957, there was Tony Kubek.

These lines from Casey Stengel, vintage spring training 1955, provide insight into Yankee personnel and depth:

"And now we come to Collins which may be an outfielder. He played center field in Newark and also played right field for me in the World Series. You can look it up but he had Novikoff on one side of him and some one else whose name I've forgotten on the other but you can look it up. That should prove he's a great outfielder in order to be able to do it with them guys on either side of him.

"There's a kid infielder named Richardson who was in our rookie camp which he don't look like he can play because he's stiff as a stick —but whoost!—and the ball's there and he does it so fast it would take some of them Sunshine Park race track handicappers with the field glasses to see him do it so fast does he do it. He never misses. As soon as he misses a ball we'll send him home.

"We start out to get us a shortstop and now we got eight of them. We don't fool we don't. I ain't yet found a way to play more than one man in each position although we can shift them around and maybe make outfielders outta them or put 'em all at ketch like we done with Howard..."

Despite the surfeit of players, the competition for jobs, the almost annual certainty of a postseason paycheck, a selflessness existed on the part of virtually all the players on the roster. "We all had a loyalty to the organization," said Lopat. "It was part of the Yankee way. There was always a personal responsibility to new players coming up. If there was some technique we could teach the young players to improve, we did it and they learned it, if they didn't—they were gone."

A couple of Yankees who benefited from the instruction of veterans were Bobby Richardson and Tony Kubek. "Bobby and I were astonished," said Kubek, "that Jerry Coleman and Gil McDougald went out of their way to help us, for we were to ultimately take their jobs. It was typical of Yankee pinstripe loyalty. There was such an atmosphere of helping on the club—the Mantles, the McDougalds, the Careys, the Colemans, were eager to help out. They had been through it and were there to show us the way."

When a spare part was needed, a pinch hitter, a crafty pitcher who could be used for specialty roles, Weiss sought out veterans and made his own deals with them. He picked up Johnny Mize, a ten year man most baseball people thought had his glory days behind him. Recycled with the Yankees, the "Big Cat" came off the bench and time after time delivered important hits. Johnny Sain, former star right-hander of the Boston Braves, won thirty-one games as a part-time performer for the Yankees in 1952-54. Enos "Country" Slaughter, former St. Louis Cardinal star, was another warhorse who in 1954 was rejuvenated through the Weiss recycling program. Other veterans picked up by Weiss included Johnny Hopp (1950–52), Ewell Blackwell and Johnny Schmitz (1952–1953), Jim Konstanty (1954-56), Gerry Staley (1955-56), Mickey McDermott (1956), Bobby Shantz (1957), Sal Maglie (1957).

When it was time to get rid of a veteran, Weiss did not hesitate. On August 25, 1956, Old Timer's Day at Yankee Stadium, Weiss conferred with Phil Rizzuto in Stengel's office. A fixture at shortstop since 1941, a veteran of nine World Series, "The Scooter" seemed to fans to have always been a Yankee. Now he was expendable. Gil McDougald, Jerry Coleman, and Billy Martin all could play shortstop. Rizzuto became an ex-Yankee.

Just about a year before Rizzuto's departure on July 30, 1955, Weiss waived Eddie Lopat to the Baltimore Orioles. A winner of 4 of 5 World Series games, and 113 regular season contests against just 59 defeats, Lopat was let go to make room on the Yankee roster for Don Larsen.

Actions such as these—the unceremonious release of Yankee legends—earned for the organization its reputation as a callous, calculating, cold corporate entity. The endless stream of spare parts and new parts from the highly productive farm system created an atmosphere for stunts like the flagpole sitting of Cleveland fan Charlie Lupcia in 1949. Lupcia ascended a flagpole. There he sat perched and vowed he would not come down until the Indians knocked the Yankees out of first place. Lupcia came down 117 days later. But the Yankees were still in first place. Phrases like "Rooting for the Yankees is like cheering for U. S. Steel" became popular. Feature articles and editorials that focused on Yankee success appeared regularly. "We honestly feel it would be better for baseball if the Yankees lost once in a while," an editorial in the March 1953 *Sport Magazine* explained, "but the resentment against their astounding success is both silly and petty."

Jerry Coleman, the gentlemanly second baseman who starred for the Yankees for nine years and played in six World Series, felt the resentment first hand. "People watched the Yankees," he said, "and admired the pride of the Yankees, but unfortunately, the Yankees became so successful, people hated them for their success."

It wasn't just their success year after year that rankled Yankee haters. It was the way they achieved success. With machinelike efficiency, with methodical consistency, their pursuit and attainment of excellence became boring stuff, especially for the fans of the Dodgers and the Giants. In those years the Giants were unpredictable. Twice they finished first; once they finished second; twice they finished third; there was a fourth place finish, a fifth place, and twice they finished sixth. The Dodgers were consistently potent, but last-minute losses in 1950 and 1951 and an inability to defeat the Yankees in the World Series frustrated Brooklyn fans. The Bronx Bombers just grooved along.

In the years 1947 to 1957 the Yankees averaged almost ninety-eight victories each season, and compiled an overall winning percentage of .634. Nine times they finished first; once second; once third. Their composite team batting average for those years was .270. Nine of those eleven years they ranked one, two in team batting. Periodically they took off on long winning streaks. In 1947, nineteen in a row; in 1953, eighteen in a row; in 1954, thirteen in a row. The Lopats, the Fords, the Colemans, the Rizzutos, the Mantles, and the others and their pride in their craft pushed them to excel.

"As a kid growing up in New York City, I was always a Yankee fan," said Eddie Lopat. "I wondered what made them tick. Even when I was with the White Sox, I wondered." In 1948, Lopat was traded to the Yankees for catcher Aaron Robinson and rookie pitchers Fred Bradley and Bill Wight. "After two or three months with them, I knew," he noted.

"One day, we were playing Detroit at the stadium. We were behind, four to three, in the seventh inning. Yogi [Berra] hit a short pop fly to center. It dropped in. He half trotted to first and got a single. The next man up grounded out. Yog was forced to second. Then there were two fly balls that ended the inning. Yog started to put on his catching gear. Charlie Keller looked at Yog and said 'You feelin' all right?'

"Yogi said 'Yeah, Why?'

" 'Hell, you didn't run the ball out. If you had, you would've been on second and a ground ball and a fly ball would've brought you in.'

"Then Tommy Henrich and Johnny Lindell jumped on Yogi with more intensity. Yogi looked over at DiMag and DiMag just gave him that icy stare.

"Another time we played a doubleheader in Washington," said Lopat. "We won the first game; the second ended after ten innings in a three to three tie," the former star southpaw recalls. "Yogi didn't catch the second game. Charlie Silvera caught and when he walked up to the plate he was like a battleship in a canoe. He came up three times with the bases loaded and made out three times. You know Yogi, three times with the bases loaded something would've popped. After the second game was called, DiMag was in the clubhouse about to fall down he was so exhausted from the heat and the strain of playing both games. Yogi was jumping around. 'What in the world are you so happy about?' DiMag asked Yogi. 'We didn't do so bad today,' Yogi said. 'You're twenty-one years old and you can't catch a doubleheader," DiMag lit into him. You could hear a pin drop. Then two or three other fellows started with Yogi. The next few years Yogi caught one hundred fifty-two, one hundred fifty-three games a season. He was afraid to ask Stengel to get out. He knew we'd ask him 'what's the story?' That was part of the Yankee way and what they tried to instill in the young fellows coming up. This is a twenty-five man operation. If there's something wrong with you, you don't play, but if you play, you give it one hundred five percent."

Lopat not only understood but personified Yankee dedication to excellence. Mel Allen gave him the nickname "Steady Eddie." Five years in a row he paced Yankee pitchers in ERA. Five years in a row, he started thirty or more games. Five years in a row his winning percentage was between .667 and .800.

Lopat and the others played as a team. But as individuals they churned out award after award. Joe DiMaggio was the MVP in 1947, Rizzuto in 1950, Berra in 1951, 1954, 1955, and Mantle in 1956 and 1957. Gil McDougald, playing second base and third base and batting out of his unorthodox right-handed stance, hit .306 to win the 1951 American League Rookie of the Year Award. Twenty-four-year-old Bob Grim won twenty and lost just six in 1954 to give the Yankees another Rookie of the Year. All purpose Tony Kubek won the Rookie of the Year Award in 1957. The handsome Milwaukee native played outfield, shortstop, third base, second base, and batted just three points below .300 despite the fact that with Stengel's juggling he didn't know day to day where he would be positioned in the field or in the lineup.

Five times Yankee pitchers won ERA titles. Six times the staff produced a twenty-game winner. Four times Yankee hurlers paced the league in games saved. The overriding image of the team was power. Sluggers like Mantle, Bauer, DiMaggio, Mize, Berra enhanced the image. "There was the spontaneous power," notes Lopat. "But we didn't just bowl them over with power. They all overlooked our speed. The Yankees could run. Berra could run. Collins could run. Bauer could run. Woodling could run. Mantle could fly."

"And we won so many games with our defense," continued Lopat. In 1947, DiMaggio led all center fielders in fielding. Stirnweiss was the top fielding second baseman in 1948, Coleman in 1949, McDougald in 1955. Rizzuto topped all American League shortstops in 1949 and 1950, and Gene Woodling had the best fielding percentage among left fielders in 1952 and 1953. Berra, a masterful handler of pitchers, led all catchers in fielding percentage in 1957.

The public image of the Yankees was one of corporate efficiency and expertise, where all the individual stars blended in the pursuit of victory. Off the field, however, it was quite often a different story. "We had a loose clubhouse," recalls Lopat, "and there were a lot of shenanigans and horsing around even though on the field it was strictly business."

Mickey Mantle remembers the atmosphere: "Casey was an easy-going guy as long as things were going well and we were winning, we could do whatever we wanted. If we lost four or five in a row he'd say, 'Cool it. Get in the room tonight by midnight.' . . . We were in Boston and that night me and Billy [Martin] didn't make it back by twelve o'clock. And we're coming back to the Kenmore Hotel and there's not very many ways to get in the Kenmore.

"We went around to the back door and it's locked. Billy sees a window right over the back door that's open. 'Get me up on your shoulders,' he says, 'and I'll get up there and unlock the door and let you in.' We were dressed pretty nice. Billy gets up on my shoulders and disappears. Then he comes back to the window and says, 'I can't unlock the door, I'll see you tomorrow.' "

Mantle explained that he saw a batch of garbage cans and decided to stack them up to climb into the window. 'I woulda been better off just to go through the lobby and take my fine, but I tried the trash cans. I climbed upon them and fell off. I tried again and again and kept falling off. I ruined my suit and both my knees were bleeding until I finally got in."

The most famous off-the-field "explosion" of excess Yankee energy took place at the Copacabana nightclub in May 1957. Mickey Mantle, Hank Bauer, Yogi Berra, and some other Yankees went to the Copa to celebrate Billy Martin's birthday. Mantle remembers what happened. "Two bowling teams came in to celebrate their victories. Sammy Davis, Jr., was the entertainer. They kept calling him 'little black Sambo' and stuff like that. Hank [Bauer] and Billy [Martin] asked them to sit down a couple of times. They kept standing up . . . the first thing I knew the cloak room was full of people swinging. I was so drunk I don't know who threw the first punch. I seen one guy laying there. It scared the hell out of me. His face was pretty well smashed . . . that guy sued each of us for five thousand dollars and the Yankees for somethin' too. They found out in the end that it was one of the bouncers in the Copa that hit him with a blackjack in the face or somethin'. I think that's what they found out.

"At that time I was hitting pretty good. They couldn't get rid of me so they got rid of Billy. Mr. Weiss said he was a bad influence on the club. Mr. Weiss sent him to Kansas City. Billy thought that Casey got rid of him. I never thought that. It was the farthest thing from the truth. Casey loved Billy. A manager would love to have a guy like Billy on his team. I remember a lot of times when we'd lose four or five straight games, Casey would say, 'We're gettin' in a rut. Martin get out there and start a fight today.' Just as soon as Billy would get on the field, he'd start a fight. Casey loved him for that. . . ."

What Yankee fans loved was the organization's ability to create almost effortlessly a situation in which a coming superstar was poised to replace a departing superstar.

The Yankee many called the best player of his generation was replaced in 1951 by the Yankee many would call the best player of *his* generation. It was a scene out of Hollywood Central Casting—one Yankee legend replacing another. Nineteen-year-old Mickey Mantle came up from Joplin, Missouri, in the Class C league to succeed thirty-six-year-old Joe DiMaggio, just as DiMag in 1936 had stepped into the spotlight that once had shone on Babe Ruth. Joseph Paul DiMaggio was purchased from the San Francisco Seals in 1934 for $25,000 and five minor league players. The purchase had one condition—that DiMaggio be allowed to play one more season in San Francisco. Batting .398, rapping out 270 hits, driving in 154 runs, he gave the city of San Francisco something to remember him by. And from 1936 to 1951, the flawless, stoical DiMaggio became perhaps the most dominant force in New York City baseball. In 1941, he hit in a record fifty-six consecutive games. He recorded 361 career home runs, 8 World Series homers, a lifetime batting average of .325. Three times he was voted American League MVP; three times he pounded three home runs in one game.

Writers overreached struggling for nicknames, for adjectives, for quotations to characterize the six-foot two-inch, two-hundred-pound center fielder. "Joltin' Joe," "The Yankee Clipper," "DiMag," all became his nicknames. He had the eye, the arm, the intellect and the desire for greatness. He roamed center field with an almost poetic nobility. He played when he was hurt, when he was tired, when it mattered a great deal, and when it didn't matter at all.

He played with bone chips in his heel, ulcers in his stomach, and the tension in his heart of a private life rent with divorce. He carried the Yankees on his back most of those years, and when things did not go the way he wanted them to, he sulked in silence and sometimes snapped out his rage. Most of the time he presented to the world an undemonstrative silent pursuit of excellence that deservedly placed him in the Hall of Fame in 1955.

Eddie Lopat recalls what it was like to have DiMaggio as an opponent and as a teammate:

"In 1947, I got him out most of the year when I was a White Sox pitcher with slow curves and a screwball. In a game at the stadium, I walked Johnny Lindell. DiMag was in the circle watching me. He came up to the plate. I busted him with a fastball down the pipe. He never flinched, which showed me that he was looking for that other stuff. I said, 'You're getting another one.' I threw it right down the pipe. I saw the nerves stand out on his neck. He was madder 'n hell. He had taken two fat fastballs. Now I said, 'You belong to me. Here comes that scroogie.' And it's bing, bing, bing, down to short and he is raving mad now. Finally, in the seventh inning, we're leading nine to one. I said to myself, 'I'm going to test him out. If he hits one, I'm up nine to two.' I threw him a change—one of my best changes. And he hit that thing like a bullet into the left field seats. It just screamed in there. And I said to myself. 'That's all I want to know.' He was looking for that ball and he got it.

"When I first joined the Yankees, I was pitching one day against Cleveland in the stadium. Lou Boudreau was the hitter. It was a late inning. DiMag was playing him straight away center field. My first pitch was a ball. I turned around a bit and rubbed up the ball. I threw and the next pitch was also a ball. I was real upset with myself. The next pitch he hit a line drive that went over Rizzuto's head. When my eyes got to the ball, I saw that DiMag was there catching it for an out. When we got into the dugout, I said, 'How in the world did you get over there, Joe? I noticed you were playing him dead center field the first two pitches and then you're standing there in the gap for the third pitch.'

"He said, 'I have seen you pitch often enough to know that with two balls and no strikes, if you were even up or ahead of him you wouldn't let him pull the ball—but you were behind. I moved over in the hole—seventy, eighty feet.' That was why the man was so great. That was his perfectionism. Many times if he went zero and four, he would sit in the clubhouse and brood. He would feel that he let the club down."

Joe DiMaggio's "comeback year" of 1949 clearly demonstrated why he was the leader of the Yankees. "I think I overworked every nerve in my body, making it to that last game." That was how "Joltin' Joe" characterized the 1948 season, a year during which he played with painful calcium-deposit bone chips in his right heel. "Each time I took a step on the field," he said, "it was like someone was driving an ice pick into my heel."

Cushions and padding placed in the shoe helped little. A hurting DiMag was still a force. He batted .320 and led the American League in home runs and RBIs. Only his normally flawless play in the field showed the effects of the pain. In 1947, he made just one error and recorded a .997 fielding percentage; in 1948, DiMag committed thirteen errors and fielded .972. It was his worst defensive year in a decade. The Yankees ended up the season in third place, two and a half games in back of pennant-winning Cleveland. There are those who still say had DiMaggio been healthy, there would have been another pennant for the Bronx Bombers.

In November 1948, the heel was operated on. The cast was removed from DiMaggio's foot on New Year's Day, 1949. DiMaggio missed all of spring training. The season began—April, May, June. He still was unable to play. He would get up every morning and put pressure on the heel. There was still pain. He lost weight, lost sleep, sulked. He carried the burden of pride and not playing deep inside himself. During his career, DiMag was always a relatively slow healer and he missed about an average of twenty games a year because of injuries. Now he had missed almost half a season.

One morning he got out of bed, stood up and put pressure on the heel. The pain had vanished. DiMaggio told Stengel that he was ready to come back, that he needed a week or so to toughen his hands and tone his muscles.

On June 27, exactly one year and fourteen days after Babe Ruth's final stadium appearance, the Yankees and Giants were scheduled to play in the Mayor's Trophy exhibition game. Stengel planned to have DiMaggio play four innings. It was to be a test of the Yankee Clipper's stamina and a trial for the heel. DiMag played nine innings. He didn't get a hit, but he evoked a standing ovation from the thirty thousand plus New York City baseball fans.

The Yankees left for Boston after the game for a three-game series with the Boston Red Sox on June 28–30. The 1949 BoSox had a powerful club. First baseman Billy Goodman batted .298 that year. Bobby Doerr, the second baseman, hit .309. The .290-hitting Vern Stephens, with 159 RBIs, played shortstop and Johnny Pesky, the third baseman, batted .309. Joe's younger brother, Dom DiMaggio, clicked off a thirty-nine-game hitting streak during the season and was a virtual mirror image of Joe as far as fielding went. Tempestuous Ted Williams won the MVP award and was a one-man batting range. Southpaw pitchers Mel Parnell and Ellie Kinder recorded forty-eight wins between them.

When the Yankees came into Boston for the late June series, the Red Sox were confident and surging. Winners of ten of their last eleven games, they were in second place and closing fast on the league-leading Yankees.

Wearing an orthopedic shoe without spikes which was elevated at the heel, DiMag was ready. He had missed sixty-six games, and it had been eight months since his last official American League at-bat, but when the first game of the series started before 36,228 at Fenway Park, the Yankee Clipper was back.

His first time up he singled off southpaw Mickey McDermott. His second time up in the third inning with Rizzuto on base, he homered over the left field wall. Rising as one, the Yankee and Boston benches and the partisan Red Sox crowd stood and watched the Yankee Clipper circle the bases, trotting out his two-run homer. The four-bagger proved the margin of victory in the 5–4 Yankee win. They were still buzzing in the stands about what kind of man Joe DiMaggio was when he loped into deep center field in the bottom of the ninth inning and effortlessly took away a bid by Ted Williams for an extra base hit.

The second game of the series was again the Joe DiMaggio show. With the Yankees losing 7–1 in the fifth inning, he homered with two on to help his teammates tie the score. In the eighth inning he slammed a two-run home run to give the Yankees a 9–7 triumph.

In the final game of the series, Vic Raschi was matched against

March 1949: Jackie Robinson and Branch Rickey relaxing in the Florida sunshine at the Dodger training camp in Vero Beach. (PHOTOWORLD)

October 1, 1952: Charlie Dressen (center) in the locker room at Ebbets Field with four of his top stars—Joe Black (top left), Pee Wee Reese (top right), Duke Snider (bottom left), Jackie Robinson (bottom right). (PHOTOWORLD)

April 1947: Members of the Dodger Sym-phoney musically protesting Commissioner A.B. Chandler's suspension of manager Leo Durocher. (PHOTOWORLD)

April 1947: One of the millions who was for Jackie Robinson, selling mementoes off Empire Boulevard near Ebbets Field. (PHOTOWORLD)

A very young Red Barber doing what he did best, broadcasting Brooklyn Dodger baseball at Ebbets Field. (PHOTOWORLD)

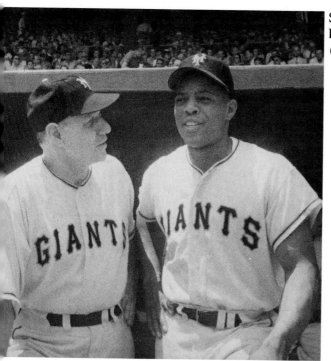

Summer 1954: Leo Durocher and Willie Mays. (PHOTOWORLD)

On the set of the TV show "Day with the Giants," Laraine Day (Mrs. Leo Durocher) chats with bespectacled Jim Konstanty and Bobby Thomson. Announcer Kevin Kennedy looks on. (PHOTOWORLD)

The cobblestones, the trolley tracks, the familiar expectant walk to the home of "Dem Bums"—Ebbets Field. (PHOTOWORLD)

Subway Series time—October 6, 1949. The Dodgers defeated the Yankees
1–0, to tie up the series 1–1, before a packed house at Yankee Stadium.
(PHOTOWORLD)

Autumn 1955: Allie Reynolds (left) and Vic
Raschi (right), two of the greatest pitchers in
New York Yankee history. (NEW YORK YANKEES)

October 8, 1951: Joltin' Joe DiMaggio (#5)
entering the Yankee dugout after hitting a
two-run homer in the fourth game of the 1951
World Series. It was the Yankee Clipper's final
major league home run. (NEW YORK YANKEES)

April 1951: A familiar scene—Casey Stengel (left) disagreeing with an umpire, and Leo Durocher (right) registering his 'beef.'
(NEW YORK YANKEES)

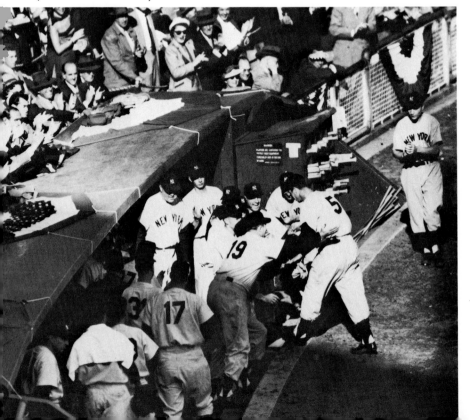

April 18, 1947: President Harry S Truman, Washington pitcher Bobo Newsom, and Yankee pitcher Allie Reynolds. Newsom would become a Yankee teammate of Reynolds later that year. (NEW YORK YANKEES)

"The Ol' Perfessor," Casey Stengel, with the cake presented to him for his sixty-fifth birthday by reporters whom he called "my writers." (NEW YORK YANKEES)

A 1957 look at three significant figures of the era: (from left to right) Casey Stengel, former Mayor Robert F. Wagner, and Charlie Dressen (former Brooklyn Dodger manager, here as pilot of the Washington Senators). (NEW YORK YANKEES)

January 23, 1950: New York Yankee general manager George Weiss looks on approvingly as Phil Rizzuto (left) and Allie Reynolds (right) prepare to sign their 1950 contracts. (NEW YORK YANKEES)

October 5, 1952: "The Commerce Comet" (Mickey Mantle) and "The Captain" (Pee Wee Reese) at Yankee Stadium for another Subway Series. (NEW YORK YANKEES)

Sal "The Barber" Maglie in Yankee pinstripes— just one of the three New York City baseball team uniforms he wore. (NEW YORK YANKEES)

August 13, 1951: "Music Appreciation Night" at Ebbets Field. More than two thousand "musicians" assaulted eardrums serenading "Dem Bums." Charlie Dressen (left) blows a trumpet. Plugging their ears are New York City Council President Joseph Sharkey, Brooklyn Borough President John Cashmore, Mayor Vincent Impellitteri, and Bronx Borough President James J. Lyons. Walter O'Malley (right) holds a tiny saxophone.
(NEW YORK YANKEES)

October 1, 1949: "Joe DiMaggio Day" at Yankee Stadium. Mel Allen, master of ceremonies, stands near the Yankee Clipper.
(NEW YORK YANKEES)

April 15, 1947: The start of the 1947–1957
era. Yankee manager Bucky Harris and
coach Charlie Dressen (right) plot strategy.
(NEW YORK YANKEES)

May 16, 1951: Fans in the bleachers taking
in the sun and the action at Yankee Stadium.
(NEW YORK YANKEES)

From 1949 to 1957, a New York City baseball team was the World Champion. The '57 season saw the Yankees dethroned and the Dodgers and Giants depart for California. (NEW YORK YANKEES)

October 9, 1951: Steady Eddie
Lopat being congratulated by
Gil McDougald (left) and
Phil Rizzuto (right). Lopat
had just pitched the Yankees
to a 13–1 victory over the
New York Giants in the fifth
game of the World Series at
the Polo Grounds.
(NEW YORK YANKEES)

October 8, 1956: Don
Larsen's final pitch of the
first perfect game in World
Series history.
(NEW YORK YANKEES)

Mel Parnell. The Yankees led 3–2 after seven innings. With George Stirnweiss and Tommy Henrich on base, DiMag slugged a 3–2 pitch by Parnell to the top of the bleachers in center field. Everyone except for the most fanatic of Red Sox fans stood up and cheered as the Yankee Clipper trotted out his three-run home run.

"Those three days in Boston," said DiMaggio, "were the most satisfying of my life." In the three-game series with their traditional American League rivals, DiMag batted .455 and collected nine RBIs and five hits—four home runs and a single.

Autumn in New York in 1949 was once again a time of baseball fever. The Red Sox had won fifty-nine of their last seventy-eight games and came into Yankee Stadium for the last two games of the season. Boston was in first place, a game ahead of the Yankees. The two games were scheduled for a weekend, October 1 and October 2.

October 1 was "Joe DiMaggio Day." The Yankee Clipper was eulogized and presented with dozens of gifts. The crowd was most taken with the brand-new automobile he received and the three hundred quarts of ice cream. Mrs. Rosalie DiMaggio, Joe's and Dom's mother, flew in from California.

"Which team and which center fielder are you rooting for, Mrs. DiMaggio?" a reporter asked.

"Mother is impartial," her son Dom interrupted.

Probably the only ones aside from the mother of the ballplaying DiMaggios who were impartial at Yankee Stadium that weekend were the umpires. And there were Red Sox fans who thought they too were rooting. Almost one hundred forty thousand attended the two games; thousands were turned away from "the house that Ruth built." A few hundred of them remained on the sidewalks around the stadium listening to the game on big, bulky portable radios.

Joe McCarthy, the old Yankee "push-button" manager, now Red Sox pilot, started Mel Parnell. Stengel countered with Allie Reynolds. DiMaggio, enervated from viral pneumonia, started too. The Red Sox jumped out to a 4–0 lead. Stengel removed Reynolds and brought in Joe Page. The talented, hard-throwing left-hander appeared in sixty games in 1949, saving twenty-seven and winning thirteen more. Never was he in better form than on that first day of October. The "Fireman" allowed just one hit and no runs in six and two-thirds innings.

The Yankees pulled the game out on an eighth-inning home run by Johnny Lindell. It was the first homer for Lindell, a .229 hitter, since July 31. DiMag contributed once again with his bat, stroking a single and a double.

The season came down to the final game on October 2. It was just the fifteenth time all year that DiMaggio, Henrich, and Berra had played together in the same lineup. Stengel had juggled, manipulated, and patched the pieces together in his injured squad all year.

Eighteen hours before game time the line for bleacher seats was more than a block long. Rizzuto tripled off Ellis Kinder to start the game and scored on an infield out. DiMaggio tripled to right but did not score. Vic Raschi made the one Yankee run stand up as the game moved to the top of the eighth; McCarthy pinch hit for Kinder but the Red Sox did not score. Parnell was brought in to pitch to the Yankees in the bottom of the eighth. The Bronx Bombers scored four times. "If the old man had let me stay in," said a dejected Kinder later, "we would've won the game."

Boston came close, scoring three runs in the top of the ninth; two of the runs came in on a triple over DiMaggio's head by Bobby Doerr. The Yankee Clipper, exhausted, removed himself from the game. He had gone as far as he could. It was far enough. The Boston rally fell two runs short, as the Yankees won 5–3 for the first of Stengel's five straight pennants and world championships.

The statistics of DiMaggio's comeback season of seventy-six games were these: fourteen home runs, sixty-seven RBIs, a .346 batting average. Two years later he would retire. Four years later he would marry Marilyn Monroe and crack, "It's better than rooming with Joe Page." Five years later he would be voted into the Hall of Fame. But on that October day—with the Yankees poised to face the Dodgers in the World Series—anywhere that anyone went in New York City the talk was about what DiMag had done for the Bombers during the 1949 season.

The dark-haired, long, lean DiMaggio and the blond, more heavily muscled Mantle were opposites. DiMaggio husbanded his ability. Mantle just let it explode. DiMag was a loner. Mantle liked convivial companions. They were very different types of men, but they were both stamped out of the same Yankee mold, which forged them into superstars for their generations.

Born October 20, 1931, in Commerce, Oklahoma, Mickey Charles Mantle was named Mickey after his father's favorite ballplayer—Mickey Cochrane. His .383 batting average and 136 RBIs powered his 1950 Joplin team to the Western League title and earned him a trip to the Yankee spring training camp in 1951. George Weiss insisted that Mantle needed more seasoning and should be sent out to play for Kansas City in Triple A ball. But Mantle batted .402 in Florida, slammed gigantic home runs, and was clocked in just a shade over three seconds going from home to first base.

At Joplin, Mantle had been a shortstop. The Yankees already had one of the best shortstops in baseball—Phil Rizzuto—so DiMaggio and Henrich schooled Mantle in the intricacies of outfielding. By mid-July of 1951, the super potential of the player they were all calling "The Commerce Comet" was clear, but so were his deficiencies. The speed was there, the power was there. "If that kid only hit right-handed," the "Old Perfessor" Stengel said, "he'd be *tree*-mendous. If he only hit left-handed, he'd be *tree*-mendous. But since he does his hittin' both ways, he's just tremendous. He kin drag bunt with two strikes on him. He kin hit with power to all fields. He's just tremendous." Mantle was tremendous but also young and very inexperienced. "I don't think I will ever experience a day like Opening Day 1951," Mantle said. "It was the worst day of my life. I don't think I slept a wink the night before, and I was trembling all over from the moment I reached the Yankee Stadium . . . I was so scared."

Scared, overeager, a bit too green, Mantle was toyed with by veteran pitchers in the first few months he was in the major leagues. He chased bad pitches. He tried to win games all by himself. Failure brought unhappiness. He sulked.

Stengel reluctantly admitted that Weiss had been right. The "Commerce Comet" was sent down to Kansas City to gain more experience. He batted .361 at Kansas City. In mid-September he returned to the Yankees to star for eighteen years and 2,401 games, more years (along with Berra) and more games than any other player in Yankee history.

A shade under six feet tall and two hundred pounds, Mantle was a switch-hitter. And on the streets of the city of New York, whenever they argued about Mays versus Mantle versus Snider, fans of the Bronx Bombers would "stick it" to Giant and Dodger rooters: "Snider's a lefty; Mays a righty. Mantle can do it both ways, and he hits a ball harder and further than both of them. Some of the shots he hit are still going."

A new term crept into sports lingo because of the awesome power of Mantle: the tape-measure home run. Yankee publicists, tape measure in hand, would trudge to the outer reaches of ball parks to calculate just how far the mighty wallops traveled. In 1953, in Washington, one of Mantle's clouts was alleged to have traveled an estimated 565 feet.

DiMaggio retired at age thirty-six. The Yankees attempted to woo him into playing just one more year. He had too much pride to continue. Perhaps a scouting report that appeared in *Life* magazine around the time of the 1951 World Series had something to do with his decision. It was prepared by a Dodger scout, for Brooklyn had expected to face the Yankees in the series, but Bobby Thomson had his own plans. "He can't stop quickly," the report said. "He can't throw real hard. You can take an extra base on him if he is in motion away from the line of the throw. He won't throw on questionable plays, and I would challenge him even if he did throw a man or so out. He can't run and he can't pull the ball at all."

Mantle retired at age thirty-five. "I would have played to age forty," he jokes, "if it weren't for Whitey [Ford] and Billy [Martin]," a pointed reference to the trio's off-the-field escapades. If anything shortened Mantle's career it was the day-by-day, season-by-season pounding for eighteen years of knees made fragile by a chronic case of osteomyelitis.

To New York City's National League fans, DiMaggio and Mantle and the Yankees were in another league. Most of the players on the other teams in the American League felt that way too. "The Yankee clubhouse had a bell," Lopat recalls. "It rang five minutes before a game started. We went through the door. We were ready. The Yankees were always ready."

There was a contest among the three teams, a rivalry to be the best team in New York City.
— CARL FURILLO

The Rivalry

The competition among the Dodgers and their fans, the Giants and their supporters, and to an extent, the Yankees and their followers, went beyond mere sports competition. It was a contest among the boroughs and those who lived and worked in those boroughs. It was a pitting of New York City baseball teams against each other and against the rest of the world.

Whom you rooted for provided an identity. It usually began when parents brought a child to a game and created a new Dodger or Giant or Yankee fan. Loyalty to the team became virtue. Hatred of the opposition was expected. Whole families rooted for one club. A nonconformist who switched allegiance provoked family rifts and worse. A resident of one borough who mistakenly displayed fondness and affection for a team from another borough courted ostracism, even violence. The tradition of standing up for the home team in the bottom of the seventh inning was done with a flourish, especially at Ebbets Field. There was an expansive exaggeration to the act of stretching hands and arms. Those who stood up at the Polo Grounds or Yankee Stadium or Ebbets Field in the top of the seventh inning were cursed at or tugged back to their seats. Sometimes they were knocked down.

"In public school in Brooklyn going on a bus on class trips," recalls Ron Gabriel, "everyone would start singing 'Take Me Out To The Ballgame.' Instead of singing 'Let's, root, root, root for the home team,' they would scream, 'Let's root, root, root for the Dodgers.' The Yankee fans would sing, 'Let's root, root, root for the Yankees.'

149

They would practically get torn apart on the bus. . . . I never even met any Giant fans who lived in Brooklyn."

A litany of the times was the language describing the competition between and among the New York City baseball teams: SUBWAY SERIES, WAIT 'TIL NEXT YEAR, ARE THE DODGERS STILL IN THE LEAGUE? THE GIANTS IS DEAD, CREEPING TERROR, LEAVE US GO ROOT FOR THE DODGERS, ROGERS, DAT DAY, SHOT HEARD 'ROUND THE WORLD, MIRACLE AT COOGAN'S BLUFF, NICE GUYS FINISH LAST, JINTS, BUMS, FLOCK, BROOKS, BOMBERS, WALT, WHO? There are hundreds of thousands of people who can still identify the meaning of all those special phrases.

An independent city until 1898, when an act of the State Legislature made it part of the city of New York, Brooklyn fueled the rivalry. A borough of neighborhoods with strange-sounding names— Canarsie, Gowanus, Red Hook, Flatbush—Brooklyn was a land and a life-style removed from the mainstream of metropolitan ways. Some people who lived in Brooklyn had never ventured across the river to Manhattan. "Only the dead know Brooklyn," Thomas Wolfe had observed. Others were fond of relating humorous anecdotes of how they got lost attempting to find Ebbets Field.

During World War II, more Brooklyn men served in the Armed Forces than the total of men from thirty-eight states. War movies capitalized on this. Brooklyn was William Bendix. Brooklyn was 'dese, dem and dose.'

The Dodgers of Brooklyn evoked images of Babe Herman, who once attempted to steal third base with the bases loaded, of chubby manager Wilbert Robinson (1914–1931), who once meaning to submit a lineup card to the umpire handed him a laundry list instead, of Charles Dillon Stengel, who once doffed his cap allowing a little bird to fly away. The Giants and the Yankees were the franchises of stars —the glamour teams. Brooklyn inspired among players the phrase: "If at first you don't succeed—try the Dodgers."

The rivalry between the two New York National League teams was intensified in 1934. The Dodgers of Brooklyn were a weak and disorganized club. The Giants of Manhattan were a strong and efficient organization. During the season, with the Dodgers struggling to stay out of last place and the Giants fighting for the pennant, Bill Terry, "Jint" manager, responded to a question as to how the Dodgers might do that season with—"Are the Dodgers still in the league?"

Van Lingle Mungo, who pitched for Brooklyn from 1931 to 1941 and the Giants from 1942 to 1945, recalled, "Because of what Terry said, we wanted to win just a little more each time we played them that year. The fans in Brooklyn were even more so; they'd boo Terry each time he'd stick his head out of the dugout."

Going into the last two games of the season, the Dodgers were still in the league, in sixth place. The Giants were tied for first place with St. Louis. The two New York City teams met for their final two games at the Polo Grounds. Thousands of Flatbush Faithful traveled across the river uptown to the ball park of the Giants. They came with cowbells, horns, whistles; they came to cheer on their "Beloved Bums." "No matter where we stood in the standings," recalled Mungo, "you could count on a big crowd when we played New York. They usually had much better teams than we did, but we came up for a game with them."

The din and the racket the Dodger fans made reduced the home field edge at the Polo Grounds for the Giants. The Dodgers won both games and the pennant. Mungo, who pitched more innings than any other hurler in 1934, especially remembered his last nine innings against the Giants. "It was like a World Series to me. I never wanted to win a game as much. I think it was one of the best games I ever pitched."

"Well Brooklyn got sore," wrote Dan Daniel in the *Sporting News*. "It took umbrage. When Brooklyn takes umbrage it takes it heavier than any other center in baseball."

Umbrage, rancor, histrionics, pride, all characterized the interplay between the New York City teams and their fans.

"When the Dodgers played the Giants," said Pee Wee Reese, "it was the most important game in your life. There will never be a rivalry like that again."

The rivalry was further intensified by the strange inbreeding and odd crossovers that were grist for newspapers, gossip for fans.

Casey Stengel played the outfield for the Brooklyn Dodgers in the first game ever staged at Ebbets Field. He piloted the "Bums" from 1934 to 1936. In 1937, he was paid not to manage the team. A bandy-legged man, viewed as a good-natured clown by many, he surfaced in 1949 as manager of the New York Yankees, the class team of baseball.

The most hated rival the Giants ever had was five-foot nine-inch, one-hundred-seventy-five-pound Leo Ernest "The Lip" Durocher. A lavish user of cologne, a wearer of one-hundred-seventy-five-dollar suits crafted by actor George Raft's tailor, a dandy who lived in a Park Avenue apartment during the baseball season and in posh Beverly Hills in the off-season, Durocher was fired as Dodger manager on July 16, 1948—in his ninth season as Brooklyn field boss. Laraine Day, Durocher's actress wife, had tastefully decorated his Ebbets Field office with rugs and photographs. She removed all the decorations except for one—an autographed picture of the man who released Durocher, Branch Rickey, remained, hanging over the toilet.

Incredibly, with both the Dodgers and Giants tied for fourth place, Durocher crossed the river to become manager of the Polo Grounders. The absurdity of the crossover was further accentuated by the man Durocher replaced as Giant field boss. Mel Ott was a Giant tradition. He had been with the team since 1926 when he arrived as a sixteen-year-old and earned the nickname, "John McGraw's Baby."

In the spring of 1948, Durocher had insulted Giant fans by remarking that Ott was a gentleman—but "nice guys finish last." Thus it was clear why Giant rooters had difficulty adjusting to the new manager of the team. Dodger fans proved resilient. They turned their infatuation and admiration for "The Lip" into invective. They referred to him in quickened Brooklynese as "Da-ROACH-a." In 1948, Durocher was about equally effective managing on either side. As Dodger manager, he won eight of twelve games against the Giants. As manager of the Giants, he was the victor in seven of ten games played across Brooklyn.

"It didn't matter who I pitched for," Sal Maglie says. "I want to be remembered as someone who tried to win all the time, as someone who tried to keep his team in the ball game." Salvatore Anthony

Maglie, better known as "The Barber," pitched for all three New York City baseball teams. He won ninety-four games for the Giants, twenty-six for the Dodgers and pitched them to the 1956 pennant, three for the Yankees at the very end of his career.

He is best remembered wearing a Giant uniform, a swarthy, stern figure, glowering at some Dodger batter. Brooklyn fans still recall him pitching and winning the tension-filled games in the painfully close arena that was Ebbets Field sweltering in pennant fever on a summer's day.

Maglie was the most hated and the most respected of all "enemy" pitchers who came into the little Bedford Avenue ball park. "I pitched better at Ebbets Field," he says. "The fans there made a lot of noise, but I didn't hear what they said. It just kept me awake. I was more careful and deliberate pitching there. I made sure I kept the ball down and had them hit it on the ground."

His nickname originated because of his appearance and his ability to nick the corner of the plate or thread a pitch under a batter's chin. "I didn't shave the day of a game because when you perspire your face burns," says Maglie. "I didn't know how I looked out there. I knew I had a dark beard. When I went out there I stared the batter down. It was him or me."

A newspaper photo of that time shows Carl Furillo pressed close to Maglie with a razor in hand, attempting to shave "The Barber," promising the razor won't slip. "Although there were players on the Dodgers who were bitter enemies," Maglie commented on the photo, "there was no trouble when I joined them. It's your job as a pitcher to win the game and all the players have to go with you. Furillo and I got along real well when I became a Dodger. But the rivalry was good. The rivalry between the boroughs was baseball."

Another fierce personality on the baseball field who made the crossover from one New York City baseball team to another was Eddie Stanky. A Dodger from 1944 to 1947, a Brave in 1948, in the winter of 1949 Stanky's former mentor Durocher traded for him. "The Lip" and "The Brat" drove the Giants and tormented their former team, the Dodgers. "Stanky was a mediocre player," says

Bavasi, "your average everything, but he made himself an all-star, a great player because of desire. He gave the Dodgers and their fans fits."

Larry MacPhail was the only club president to win pennants with two different New York City baseball teams. As general manager of the Dodgers, he wheeled and dealed, enabling Brooklyn to win its first pennant in two decades in 1941. He was an Army major during World War II. He joined with Del Webb and Dan Topping to purchase the New York Yankees for $2.6 million on January 25, 1945. MacPhail had brought Durocher to the Dodgers. When "The Lip" was suspended by Commissioner Chandler for the 1947 season, MacPhail was quoted as saying he believed Branch Rickey wanted it that way. "The odds are a hundred to one," MacPhail allegedly said, "that Durocher gets his job back." The Dodgers competed against the Yankees in the 1947 World Series. When the series was concluded, MacPhail attempted to apologize to Rickey. "Never speak to me again," said Rickey. It has been assumed that the two strong-willed men never spoke to each other again. MacPhail's last hurrah in baseball was the 1947 season.

A man who did a lot of talking was Charlie Dressen. "Jolly Cholly" loved to talk baseball and loved to brag that he never read a book in his life. He spent time with all three New York City baseball teams, as did Casey Stengel. He was an infielder for the Giants of McGraw in 1933. Larry MacPhail brought him in as an aide and coach for Durocher. "The Lip" found out that Dressen was coming when he arrived. In 1947, MacPhail summoned Dressen from the Dodgers and gave him a coaching job under Bucky Harris. When MacPhail left the Yankees and baseball after the 1947 World Series, George Weiss dropped Dressen. When Stengel became Yankee manager in 1949, Dressen took over as Oakland manager in the Pacific Coast League, replacing Stengel. In 1951, still recycling, Dressen returned to New York City baseball as manager of the Dodgers. He confronted Leo Durocher, manager of the Giants, and Casey Stengel, manager of the Yankees. It was an incestuous cycle of events.

Johnny Mize played for 15 years in the major leagues, recorded 359 home runs and a .312 lifetime batting average. He played five years for the Cardinals, five years for the Giants, and performed for five years as a pinch hitter deluxe for the Yankees. The Georgia strong boy led the American League in pinch hits in 1951, 1952, and 1953. The Giants played the Yankees in the 1951 World Series. The man they called "The Big Cat" batted .286 against his former Giant teammates.

Storied Dodgers Ralph Branca and Hugh Casey were also part of the odd crossover of players that existed in those years. Casey closed out his career by appearing in four games for the Yankees in 1949. Branca was near the very end when he appeared in five games for the Yankees in 1954.

There were even crossovers on the part of New York City baseball broadcasters. Russ Hodges went from the Yankees to the Giants; Ernie Harwell was a Dodger announcer in 1948 and 1949. In 1950, Harwell described Giant games. The most controversial switch of a broadcaster took place in 1954. Red Barber, after fifteen years as the "Voice of the Dodgers," crossed over to the American League to team up with the "Voice of the Yankees," Mel Allen, as a Yankee announcer. Brooklyn's beloved redhead lasted but three years with the O'Malley Dodgers and left "the Rhubarb Patch" in controversy by calling O'Malley " a devious man . . . the most devious man I ever met."

In 1950, even the head groundskeeper at Ebbets Field was persuaded to become a turncoat. Marty Schwab was asked by Horace Stoneham: "How'd you like to come to the Polo Grounds?" Schwab liked it. He and his family were provided with a rent-free, two-bedroom apartment under the grandstand in left field, and the new Polo Grounds groundskeeper just had to fall out of bed to be on the job.

Arguments characterized the rivalry. "Every game the Dodgers and Giants played against each other was a war," said New York-born sportswriter Jack Lang. "The writers would leave a night game at one or two in the morning after finishing up their work and there would be a dozen Giant and Dodger fans still arguing under the street lights at the corner of McKeever Place and Montgomery Street."

There were arguments on the street, in the subway, on the job, in the bars, and in the stands. There were quite a few arguments, or "rhubarbs" as Red Barber liked to refer to them, on the playing field. Sometimes it was Maglie versus Durocher. Furillo against Durocher. Maglie and Durocher versus Furillo. Dressen against Durocher.

Stanky versus Roe. Newcombe pitted against Durocher. Snider against Hearn. Martin versus Robinson. The combinations were limitless, always changing, but the arguments were constant. There were always arguments. Sometimes they got violent.

Monte Irvin said, "No matter when we met, if the Dodgers were on top and we were in fifth, it didn't matter. We looked forward to the game. We always played hard. At times you'd play over your head. You never knew what the outcome of a game between those two teams would be."

Through most of those years the Dodgers were always the team to beat for the National League pennant. And the Giants, when they were not involved in the heat of the race for the flag, seemed to always hunger for the chance to knock the Dodgers out of contention.

One of those incidents took place in a game where Sal Maglie was skillfully "barbering" the Brooks. "We've got to do something about that guy throwing at us," Reese told Robinson. "If we don't, somebody's going to get hurt," continued the only captain the Brooklyn Dodgers ever had. "When you come up this inning, drop one down the first base line and try to dump Maglie on his butt."

Robinson deftly dropped a perfect bunt down the first base line. The shrewd and experienced Maglie stayed on the pitcher's mound. He was not going to plant his body in front of an impassioned Robinson barreling head-down to first base. Giant second baseman Davey Williams covered first base and Robinson's body almost covered him up as he sent the smaller player sprawling onto his back.

"You asked for it," some of the Giants screamed from the dugout. "We're going to give it back to you." Robinson was surprised that it was Williams he had bowled over and not Maglie, but running head down, Jackie would have gone through any obstacle to reach base.

The Giants came to bat the next inning and Alvin Dark slugged the ball up the alley in left field. Dark rounded second and was racing for third on his way to a triple. Robinson was playing third base that day. Reese's relay throw hit the dirt in front of third base just about the same time as Dark left his feet launching into a slide. Robinson fielded the throw after it bounced once and positioned himself as if ready to absorb Dark's sliding body. Then Robinson stepped back and slammed the ball against the Giant shortstop's nose. The ball bounced off Dark, and he was safe at third.

Maglie threw at no more Dodger batters that day. The Dodgers won the game. In their dressing room afterward, there was a great deal of celebrating. A victory over the Giants was sweet. A victory over the Giants and Sal Maglie was doubly sweet. Teammates came over to Robinson and congratulated him for ferociously physical play. "The only thing I hate about the deal," Robinson said, "is that I had to get involved with a nice guy like Al Dark. I really didn't mean to tag him in the nose even if it looked like I did."

The battle royal of the era took place in September 1953. Its roots went back to 1949 when a pitch by Giant hurler Sheldon Jones hit the side of Carl Furillo's head, sending the Dodger right fielder into the hospital with a concussion. Afterward, Jones apologized to Furillo. "I just threw what Durocher told me to," Furillo remembered. In the intervening years, the memory of that beaning returned every time the Dodgers played the Giants.

Furillo's hatred of Durocher and his dislike of the Giants surfaced in a game during which Maglie was shaving the corner of the plate just a bit too sharp. One of "The Barber's" pitches almost nicked Furillo. "You better watch the hell what you're doing," he screamed. Maglie threw again—this time a bit closer. And Furillo, enraged, threw a bat at Maglie. Players raced out on the field but there was no real violence.

These incidents were just warm-ups for the events of September 6, 1953. It was Giants versus Dodgers. Manhattan versus Brooklyn. Leo Durocher against Carl Furillo.

"The Lip" had cursed at and ranked out Furillo and the Dodger outfielder had returned the compliments. Then Giant pitcher Ruben Gomez hit Furillo with a pitch. Furillo remembered Sheldon Jones; he remembered Maglie. He wasn't interested in Gomez. Charging into the Giant dugout, his powerful body filled with rage, Furillo headed straight for Durocher. There were too many Giants performing as interference. Before Furillo could even reach the Giant manager, someone in the crowd of Giant blockers knocked him to the dugout floor. Someone stepped on his little finger and fractured it in two places. Furillo did not play again during the 1953 season; he left the game batting .344 but got consolation in that it was more than enough to give him his only National League batting crown.

The tempestuous antics of players was weak stuff compared with the frenzy of fans gripped by New York City postseason baseball fever.

Thousands camped out for ten, twenty, thirty hours before game time in front of Ebbets Field or the Polo Grounds or Yankee Stadium, hoping to purchase the precious seats, to root personally for their favorite team. Mounted police supervised the lines around the clock.

The Hotel Concourse Plaza at 161st Street and the Grand Concourse close to Yankee Stadium advertised pregame breakfasts and lunches for fans and rooms at "World Series" rates.

The telephone company advised fans who wanted the up to the minute score to dial N-E-R-V-O-U-S; the N-E-R- was the same as the telephone company exchange ME-7, and after that any four dialed digits made the connection.

The Transit Authority added more cars, extra personnel, special service, and reduced waiting time for trains. Hundreds of thousands of fans rode the BMT, the IRT, the IND—for although the competition and rivalry took place on the playing field, it was the subway that carried a good portion of the rooting sections of the teams, and even some of the players. The total phenomenon was called the "Subway Series."

Between 1947 and 1957, the Dodgers and Giants played 242 regular season games against each other, 22 contests each season—11 at Ebbets Field, 11 at the Polo Grounds. Only in 1952 and 1954 did the Giants win more games against the Dodgers. In 1948, the "Jints" and the "Bums" split their season series. Overall, the Dodgers recorded 136 wins to 109 for the Giants.

In 1947, 1949, 1952, 1953, 1955, and 1956 the Dodgers of Brooklyn opposed the Bronx Bombers in the World Series. It was Giants versus Yankees in 1951.

Intimate, dramatic, personal, unpredictable, baseball in New York City season after season was one of the most important things in the lives of many who lived in the Big Apple. And in the last weeks of September and the early days of October, baseball in New York City became for some the most important thing in their lives.

The ultimate, supercharged moment of all the electric instants of entanglement and confrontation was the last hit of the last half of the last inning of the last game of the 1951 National League play-off. . . .

Nineteen-fifty-one was the one hundredth anniversary year of the *New York Times* and the fiftieth anniversary of Oppenheim Collins. Mario Lanza, an ex-truck driver, was the most popular singer in the United States. Millions watched Senator Joe McCarthy's televised hearings on un-American activities and communism. The average salary of public school teachers was $3,000 a year. Children practiced air raid safety precautions in school class rooms. It was the 111th year of the *Brooklyn Eagle*, which sold for 5 cents. The rate for a room for a week at the Hotel St. George was $15.50, and the Breevort Savings Bank in Brooklyn advertised a 2 percent per annum interest rate.

It was the last season of Joe DiMaggio, the first season of Willie Mays and Mickey Mantle. Warren Giles was the new president of the National League and Walter O'Malley was the new president of the Brooklyn Dodgers. More than four and a half million tickets were sold to those who came to the New York City ball parks to watch the Dodgers, the Giants, and the Yankees.

The season began badly for the Giants. At one point they lost eleven games in a row. They were teased and taunted all over the league as "Durocher's kind of team." It was a pointed reference to all the trades, sales, and position changes "The Lip" had effected in attempting to create the right combination.

Charlie Dressen, Durocher's old sidekick and coach, had won the Pacific Coast League pennant with Oakland in 1950. He had replaced Shotton as manager of the Dodgers, a team so power-laden that at times during the 1951 season it was able to afford the luxury of batting Carl Furillo eighth. Furillo hit .295 for the year.

"Dressen was the supreme egotist," recalls Stan Lomax. "He was so damn honest about being egotistical that you had to like him. Once he said in the middle of a tough game, 'Just you fellows hold them and I'll think of somethin'.' He considered himself a great sign reader, which he wasn't."

Once Willie Mays made one of his incredible plays in the outfield.

The Dodgers on the bench marveled at what Willie had done. The man they called "Jolly Cholly" was not impressed. "I'd like," he said, "to see him do that again."

The animosity between the two teams was showcased in an early back-to-back series. The Dodgers swept three games from the Giants at the Polo Grounds. They made it five in a row with two more wins at Ebbets Field. Before a noisy crowd of 33,962, the Giants behind Sal Maglie managed an 8–5 win to salvage one game of the six played. In the third inning of that game, Robinson dumped a bunt down the first base line. When Maglie came over to field it, Robinson banged into the Giants' best pitcher. For the rest of the game—as it had been throughout the series—invective poured out from both dugouts. Dodger pitcher Don Newcombe kept screaming, "Eat your heart out, Leo." And Durocher continually taunted Robinson as a bush leaguer. Durocher's words only made Robinson intensify his efforts. He pounded three home runs and knocked in eight runs in the six games.

Durocher characterized Robinson's entanglement with Maglie as a "bush stunt." And Robinson told reporters after the game, "If it's a bush stunt, he ought to know. He taught me."

In July, Dressen looked down the standings at the Giants and announced: "The Giants is dead." It would be a quote to rank with Bill Terry's query: "Are the Dodgers still in the league?"

August 12, 1951, was Wes Westrum Day at the Polo Grounds. It was a day the affable Giant catcher was presented with a brand new Mercury automobile, a day the Giants trailed the Dodgers by thirteen and a half games. From that day on, the Giants locked into what has become known as the "Miracle Run." Winning thirty-seven of their remaining forty-four games, sixteen straight in one stretch, the Giants magically closed the gap.

In Boston, on the final day of the season behind Larry Jansen, they nipped southpaw Warren Spahn and the Braves, 3–2, for their seventh straight win to take over first place and clinch at least a tie for the pennant with the Dodgers.

"I was anxious to get something on tape for my WOR radio show," recalls Stan Lomax. "I went into the Giant dressing room. I tried to get one or two of them to say 'We won the pennant.' They were cautious. The Dodgers were still playing in Philadelphia."

The Giants hurried to the Boston railroad station to catch the 5:00 P.M. train. "The next train out was at midnight," says Lomax. "We still didn't know the final score of the Dodger-Philadelphia game. When we got to Providence—we learned the Dodgers had won."

The Brooklyn victory was a personal triumph for Jackie Robinson. On the playing field where four years earlier he had been racially abused by Philadelphia manager Ben Chapman, Robinson performed heroically. His twelfth-inning lunging grab of a drive by Eddie Waitkus which could have won the game for the Phillies was followed in the fourteenth inning by a tremendous home run off Robin Roberts which gave the Dodgers a 9–8 victory and set up the second National League play-off in history. Robinson's stop of the Waitkus smash forced Jackie's elbows into his chest, and he knocked himself unconscious for a few moments. A mere mortal would probably have been carried out on a stretcher. Robinson was carried out on the shoulders of his teammates after he pounded the game-winning home run. "That moment," Rachel Robinson notes, "always ranked as one of Jack's biggest thrills in baseball."

When the train carrying the Giants pulled into Grand Central Station in New York, "there was the God darnest collection of people you ever saw waiting," recalls Stan Lomax. "I was surprised. Giant people weren't those type of fans. They weren't that enthusiastic. Toots Shor, the big Giant fan, had lined up all the drunks, I guess, from his restaurant. And when the team came out of the train really expecting nothing—they got these tremendous cheers."

Monte Irvin brings back the feeling of that time: "It was a once-in-a-lifetime situation. How do you catch a team like the Dodgers in a matter of a month and a half? We never said we were going to win it. We said, 'Let's see how close we can get.' We kept on winning. The Dodgers kept on losing. It seemed like we beat everybody in the seventh, eighth, and ninth inning."

Durocher had manipulated, cajoled, pleaded with his "kind of team." He had prevailed on Horace Stoneham to bring Willie Mays up from Minneapolis where he was hitting .477. "The Lip" had moved Lockman from left field to first base. He gave the ball to Sal Maglie and Larry Jansen and told them to win—they responded with twenty-three victories each.

Durocher cared about every aspect of the game, especially team-work. "We had a team of specialists," said Monte Irvin, "but we worked as a team. Durocher taught us and emphasized how to get the job done. We pulled the ball. We hit behind the runners. We worked on advancing the runners. We had efficient hitters."

A key player for the Giants was the man they called "Mandrake the Magician." Don Mueller struck out only 13 times in 469 at-bats in 1951 while recording a .277 batting average and 16 homers. "One game," said Irvin, "he got five straight hits and the outfielders never touched the ball. His first hit was a squib past third base, then he got a hit off the shortstop's glove, a hit off the second base sack, a single off the pitcher's mound. Another hit was a shot past first that pulled the pitcher off to cover. He could find the holes with his bat. He was magic with that bat."

On the first day of October, 1951, the first game of the play-off took place at Ebbets Field before 30,707. New Yorkers were not only divided as to which team to root for, but selecting a radio station to listen to also posed a pleasant problem. The Dodger announcers were on WMGM. The Giant broadcasters were carried on WMCA. The Mutual network provided national coverage.

A two-run homer by Bobby Thomson and a solo shot by Irvin helped "Jumbo" Jim Hearn pitch the Giants to a 3–1 win. The Dodgers evened the series with a 10–0 romp on October 2, a cold, clammy day at the Polo Grounds. Clem Labine pitched a six-hitter for Brooklyn, and Rube Walker's home run cleared the right field roof.

Amidst overcast skies and a threat of rain, Tallulah Bankhead, the most famous of all Giant fans, arrived early at the Polo Grounds for the third and final game and predicted a home-team triumph. Don Newcombe of the Dodgers, a twenty-game winner, was pitted against Sal Maglie of the Giants, a twenty-three-game winner. "When Maglie was right," notes former Yankee Jerry Coleman, "he might've been as good as any pitcher that ever lived." Newk was an imposing man, a power pitcher at six feet four inches. "With his arms flying," said Monte Irvin, "he was tough to hit against." Dodger manager Charlie Dressen bragged that with the autumn shadows from the grandstand lengthening, "Newk would blind their eyes."

Each pitch, each out, each inning, was followed on the radio in

city prisons, school rooms, on the job. The Wall Street teletype inter-
mingled a play-by-play account of the game with the Dow Jones
averages. The General Electric Black Daylite seventeen-inch set had
been marked down from $379.95 to $299.95 and advertised in New
York City newspapers as a play-off special. Virtually all the Manhattan bars were jammed with TV watchers. Thousands took the day off
to watch the game at home on their black and white Philcos and
Motorolas.

The Dodgers scored a run in the first inning. Reese walked. Snider
walked. Robinson lined a single to left. Reese scored. In the third
inning, at 2:04 P.M., the lights were turned on. Newcombe was over-
powering. He was rocketing the ball to the plate. "He was blinding
us," said Monte Irvin. Maglie, swarthy, intense, unshaven, skillfully
spun out his web of off-speed pitches, varying his pace with an occasional fast ball.

In the bottom of the seventh, Irvin doubled. Lockman moved him
to third base with a bunt single. Thomson stroked the ball high and
deep to center field. Irvin tagged up and scored. The game was tied,
1–1.

Cal Abrams, who sat on the Dodger bench watching the drama
play out, recalls: "Newk came in after he got the side out and said he
was tired. Robinson got angry. He yelled at Newk, 'Don't give me
that shit. Go out there and pitch.'"

In the top of the eighth inning, the Dodgers scored three times.
"We thought that was it," said Jack Lang, who remembers making
the long walk around the horseshoe under the stands with the other
writers to the Dodger clubhouse to await the victory celebration.
"We thought Newk with that lead would just blow it by them."

Newcombe blew the ball past the Giants—striking out the side in
the bottom of the eighth inning. He did not want to pitch the ninth.
"It looks like I just don't have it anymore," he told Dressen. "Take
me out." Dressen did not agree.

"Durocher and we knew that Newcombe would make the wrong
pitch," recalls Irvin. "That was his history. In 1950, he made the bad
pitch to Sisler that lost the Dodgers the pennant. Durocher had told us
if you stay close to Don in the eighth or ninth, you can beat him . . .
but he had blinded us for eight innings."

With only three outs remaining to them, Durocher addressed the Giants in the dugout as the bottom of the ninth got underway. "You've had some kind of year," he remembers telling them. "You've got nothing to be ashamed of, boys. When you walk off this field, I want your head right up."

Throughout the game Durocher had coached at third base. "I'd look at Don Newcombe and I'd call him everything you could think of trying to get him mad so he'd get into a fight with me and we'd both get thrown out and we'd be rid of Newcombe. Now it was up to the players to get rid of him."

Alvin Dark opened the Giant ninth with a single through the right side of the infield. Mueller singled sharply to the right of Hodges, who was playing very close to first base. "Hodges was playing out of position," Irvin recalls. "He should not have been holding Dark on. That run meant nothing."

Irvin fouled out to Hodges in the coach's box at first, but Lockman sliced a double down the left field line, scoring Dark for the second Giant run. Mueller slid into third base and broke his ankle. He was taken out of the game and carried ceremoniously across the outfield to the center field clubhouse.

"I picked the biggest guy on my club," said Durocher, "for a pinch runner for Mueller. I wanted him to come stand over with me at third base. I knew when the game was over, Newk was coming for me. I picked Clint Hartung, the big Texan."

The most famous of the World War II serviceman ballplayers, Hartung came from Hondo, Texas, and was known as "The Hondo Hurricane." A six-foot five-inch, two-hundred-twenty-pounder, he was the super-phenom of his time. He attracted much newspaper space and fan devotion. In 1947, he played thirty-four games in the outfield and batted .309 while winning nine games and losing seven in his other role as a pitcher. He was 8–8, in 1948, 9–11 in 1949 with a 5.00 ERA. His final major league years of 1951 and 1952 saw him relegated to a utility role, and his batting average was about the same as his playing weight. "Hartung made one mistake," observed sportswriter Tom Meany. "He stopped at the Polo Grounds. He should not have stopped. He should have gone right to the Hall of Fame at Cooperstown." Hartung and Giant fans always mused about what he might have been.

"The Hondo Hurricane" stood on third base near "The Lip." Carl Erskine and Ralph Branca were warming up in the Dodger bull pen. Preacher Roe, possessor of a 22–3 record and probably the best pitcher in baseball in 1951, was being saved to open the World Series. Clyde Sukeforth, Dodger pitching coach, recommended that Branca come in to relieve Newcombe. Sukeforth would be fired that winter.

Newcombe started for Durocher as soon as Branca reached the mound. "I didn't say a word," said Durocher. "I didn't want him there. But Clint Hartung yelled, 'Just keep comin'.' Newk made a wide turn and walked down to the clubhouse. All the fans yelled at him and waved handkerchiefs."

There was a little window in the Dodger clubhouse in center field. John Griffin, three-hundred-fifty-pound Brooklyn clubhouse attendant, was seated in front of the window. "He covered up the view," recalls Jack Lang, who followed the events as New Yorker, fan, and reporter, "but we had the Dodger radio on."

"When they brought in Branca," said Cal Abrams, "I was expecting something. Thomson had hit a few homers off Ralph that year. Branca was tight. Thomson was loose."

The Giants had runners on second and third. "Willie Mays, who was in his rookie year, was the batter after Thomson," notes Durocher. "I didn't know if they'd pitch to Thomson or not. On Monday, Thomson had hit a homer off Branca in the upper deck in Ebbets Field to put us in front, two to one. I went up to Thomson and I told him 'Branca remembers that you hit a slider off him for a home run. He won't throw that today. He'll give you a fast ball—right there.' "

The precise moment was 3:58 P.M., October 3, 1951. Russ Hodges, in his twenty-second year of broadcasting, described what happened to the radio global village that linked Bensonhurst to Gowanus, to the Grand Concourse, to Washington Heights.

"Bobby Thomson up there swinging . . . He's had two out of three, a single and a double, and Billy Cox is playing him right on the third-base line . . . One out, last of the ninth . . . Branca pitches and Bobby takes a strike call on the inside corner . . ."

Durocher recalls, "Thomson looked at me and I yelled, 'C'mon, c'mon. He'll throw it again. If you ever hit one—hit one now.'"

Russ Hodges continued with the play-by-play; the sound of his voice mesmerized people all over the city. "Bobby batting at .292 . . . He's had a single and a double and he drove in the Giants' first run with a long fly to center. Brooklyn leads it, four to two . . . Hartung down the line at third not taking any chances . . . Lockman without too big of a lead at second, but he'll be running like the wind if Thomson hits one . . . Branca throws . . . there's a long drive . . . it's gonna be, I believe . . . THE GIANTS WIN THE PENNANT! THE GIANTS WIN THE PENNANT! THE GIANTS WIN THE PENNANT! . . . Bobby Thomson hits into the lower deck of the left-field stands . . . THE GIANTS WIN THE PENNANT! THE GIANTS WIN THE PENNANT AND THEY'RE GOING CRAZY! THE GIANTS WIN THE PENNANT! THE GIANTS WIN THE PENNANT! . . . YAAAAHOO! THE GIANTS WIN THE PENNANT!!!" Eight times Hodges screamed out the phrase "the Giants win the pennant!" and then he could speak no more and had to give up the microphone.

The Polo Grounds was agog. Dodgers stood trancelike for a few seconds in fixed positions on the field. Thomson ran out what would become known as "The Shot Heard 'Round the World."

"I really laid into the pitch," recalls Thomson. "But then as I got away from home plate, I began to wonder. It started out high and looked then as if it were sinking."

Ralph Branca remembers turning to look at Andy Pafko backed toward the left field wall. "I kept saying, 'Sink, sink, sink.' I knew he couldn't catch it."

Pafko would say later, "I thought all the time there was a chance I could get it."

"I figured it'd be off the wall," said Thomson, "enough to get Whitey [Lockman] in with the tying run." Sal Maglie, who had departed after the eighth inning and was replaced by Larry Jansen, who became the winning pitcher, was in the clubhouse with owner Horace Stoneham. "When Bobby hit that ball, I could not see the wall, but I knew the score was tied."

The ball went over the wall in left field less than 315 feet from home plate. "When the ball went into the stands," recalls Thomson, "I was more excited than I ever was in my life."

Ralph Branca remembers thinking, "Oh, God, why me, why was I the one?"

Jackie Robinson remained stolid and serious at his position in the field. His hands on his hips, he watched to make sure that the jubilant Thomson touched each base.

"Holy hell broke loose all over," said Westrum. "We could not believe what happened. Some Giant players bumped their heads on the roof of the dugout as they jumped up to watch the drive."

Ten feet in front of home plate, Thomson leaped into the air. He came down planting his right foot on the plate and fell into the arms of a dozen screaming, hysterical Giant teammates. "It was a real line drive home run," said Leo Durocher. "In any other park in the country, the left fielder would've probably had to come in four or five steps to catch it."

Sid Frigand was forced to leave the *Brooklyn Eagle* office as the bottom of the ninth inning got underway. He boarded the subway and rode to his graduate course at Brooklyn College. "When I got out of the train at Flatbush and Nostrand avenues," he recalls, "it was like an atomic bomb had hit. Except for the noise of vehicles, there was no noise, no talking, no movement. I walked over to a newsdealer and asked, 'Who won?' He got angry. 'Didn't you hear?' And when he told me, I walked like a zombie just like the rest."

At Ebbets Field, head groundskeeper Jimmy Esposito and his crew were taking up the lumber for the construction of the portable press box for the World Series they expected the Dodgers to play in. "One of my men had a portable radio. When Thomson hit the home run everybody's heart just fell apart."

Former Mayor Wagner was then Manhattan borough president. "I had attended the first two games," he says. "When the Dodgers murdered the Giants in the second game I thought I had placed the whammy on them. I decided to listen to the third game on the radio in my office. When Thomson hit the home run, all of us there were hysterical."

The Dodger Sym-phoney had managed to obtain seats for the historic play-off game. "When the ball went in for the home run,"

Brother Lou Soriano recalls, "we folded up fast and got the hell out of there. We were in enemy territory."

Mrs. Valeda Stoneham, wife of the owner of the Giants, was at home with her first granddaughter. "I had the radio on throughout the house. She was a toddler. I had jumped up to rescue her from some predicament, and then I heard the screaming on the radio. It took me some time to realize that Bobby had hit the home run."

"Bang! Bang! Bang!" Lee Scott, traveling secretary of the Dodgers recalls. "The roof fell in." Scott had left his press box position in the eighth inning to sit with Walter O'Malley and his daughter Terry. "She kept crying," says Scott, "Oh, daddy, oh, daddy, oh, daddy!"

"Home plate was a mob scene," remembers Thomson. "People were trying to rip pieces off my uniform. I thought I could get killed out there. The fans were out of their minds. I took off for the clubhouse weaving through all those people who were trying to get a piece of me."

Eddie Stanky sprinted all the way from the Giant dugout to third base. He leaped onto Durocher's back. Thinking Stanky was a fan, Durocher readied himself to punch the monkey on his back. "When he saw it was Stanky," says Scott, "he was speechless. A speechless Durocher, that's something."

Tom Ryley was an undergraduate student at Rutgers University. "I had a religion class and when I entered the classroom, the Giants were losing and seemed out of it," he recalls. "Someone had a radio. He did not play it, fearing the chaplain would not appreciate it. We were halfway through the class when there was a tremendous roar. We all yelled at the guy with the radio: 'Turn it on, turn it on.' And all we could hear was Russ Hodges screaming, 'THE GIANTS WIN THE PENNANT! THE GIANTS WIN THE PENNANT!' . . . People wandered about the campus—stunned. That night, my mother, who knew nothing about baseball said, 'I feel so sorry for Mr. Branca.'"

In Manhattan, thousands of automobile horns honked simultaneously at two minutes to four P.M. The honking continued intermittently for the next hour and a half. At the Theresa Hotel in Harlem on Seventh Avenue and 125th Street, three TV sets had been the messengers that had brought the astounding news. The sets were still on hours after the game. No one looked at them. Instead glasses kept being lifted in praise of the Giants. In Staten Island, the home borough of Bobby Thomson, the blasts of automobile horns mixed with the throatier sounds of factory whistles and tugboats. In Brooklyn, there was quiet.

It took O'Malley and Scott and Abrams and Irvin and the others —players and executives—a very long time to make their way across the field swarming with thousands of fans exhibiting different stages of emotional reaction. The clubhouses of the Giants and the Dodgers were a few feet apart. "One place was like a morgue," said Jack Lang. "And in the other it was New Year's Eve."

In the Dodger clubhouse, "Ralph Branca was crying and leaning on the staircase with his arms back like Jesus on the Cross. And he was crying to beat the band," Scott remembers. "And some of the players kept saying, 'It's over, it's over.' "

"What happened really affected Branca," said Stan Lomax. "For a while he became almost a recluse."

The New York Telephone Company reported that from 4:00 P.M. to 4:25 P.M., so many people in Manhattan and parts of Brooklyn were on the phone that some businesses were cut off from the outside world.

For hours after the game, Giant fans were still celebrating the "Miracle at Coogan's Bluff." They screamed, cheered, danced, hugged each other and raised their fists toward the sky as darkness enveloped New York City. They clustered about the steps leading to the center field clubhouse and cheered the Giant players who came to the top of the steps and waved and bowed. "Bobby Thomson had to come out," former New York Giant publicist Garry Schumacher recalls. "It was like he was giving them the Papal blessing."

After all the ballplayers had left, hundreds of fans remained clutching the moment. A drunk circled the bases. A couple made love. A group danced a polka. Finally, the lights were turned out at the Polo Grounds and the remaining celebrants grudgingly departed.

New York City was a house divided. The Giants called their pennant drive "the Creeping Terror" and the Thomson home run was known to Giant players and their fans as "The Miracle at Coogan's Bluff." The Yankees and their supporters were reserved and ready for another "Subway Series." But in Brooklyn, October 3, 1951, is still remembered (as comedian Phil Foster put it) as D-Day: "Dat Day." "The bombing of Pearl Harbor was less of a shock to some fans," recalls Sid Frigand, the former *Brooklyn Eagle* writer. Bronx Borough President James J. Lyons phoned condolences to Brooklyn Borough President John Cashmore and suggested that he fly flags at half mast.

Bad news for Brooklyn did not end with "Dat Day." On October 4, 1951, the first parking meters were installed on the streets of the Borough of Churches and a Brooklynite received a parking ticket in his own borough for the first time. The Dodgers announced they would begin redeeming World Series tickets at any branch of the Manufacturers' Trust Company.

About a week after the tumultuous and historic final play-off game, Walter O'Malley entered an elevator in a Manhattan office building. "There were a few people in the elevator," O'Malley recalled, "and one of them was Bobby Thomson. I said, 'Hello Bobby,' and one of the men on the elevator said, 'You talk to that bum, he cost me a hundred dollars.' I smiled and said, 'He must have cost me half a million dollars.'

"The man looked at me wide-eyed. 'You bet that kind of money, Mister?' he asked."

On September 30, 1947, the Yankees faced the Dodgers in the World Series. It was the first time since 1941 that the teams had met in the fall classic. Burt Shotton's Dodgers had won the National League pennant by five games over the Cardinals. The Yankees, managed by Bucky Harris, finished a dozen games ahead of Detroit. It was the first World Series to be televised. Hundreds sat in the auditorium of Wanamaker's department store, a few blocks from Washington Square Park, and watched the action on the store's four giant TV sets. Many New York University professors cancelled classes and went with their students to watch the Bums battle the Bombers. The most boos and cheers would be directed at Jackie Robinson, the first black man ever to play in the World Series.

Twenty-one-game-winner Ralph Branca was fifteen years old the last time the two teams had met in 1941. He retired the first twelve Yankee batters. Then they battered him, scoring five times in the fifth inning to clinch the opening-game victory before 73,365. Rookie Jackie Robinson rattled Yankee pitcher Spec Shea as he had rattled National League hurlers all season long. Robinson walked in the first inning and then stole second base. In the third, he walked again. His dancing, darting lead so upset Shea that the Yankee pitcher balked Robinson to second.

Allie Reynolds won the second game. The big Yankee right-hander struck out a dozen batters and spaced nine hits in his complete game victory.

The series moved to Ebbets Field for the next three games. Much-traveled, forty-year-old Bobo Newsom faced his two-time former Dodger teammates. Southpaw Joe Hatten started for Brooklyn. Newsom began his baseball career in 1929 with the Dodgers. He then criss-crossed the majors, pitching for the Cubs, the Browns, the Senators, the Red Sox, the Tigers. In 1942, he was a Dodger again. In 1943, he pitched for Brooklyn, the St. Louis Browns, and the Washington Senators. Then he pitched for the Athletics of Philadelphia for a couple of years before moving back to Washington. The Yankees obtained him in 1947. The Dodgers shelled Bobo and his successor, Vic Raschi, for six runs in the second inning of the third game. Then they held on to win, 9–8. Hugh Casey in relief of Ralph Branca, who had taken over for Hatten, saved the game for Brooklyn. Casey had saved eighteen games to pace the National League during the season. Joe DiMaggio pounded a two-run homer for the losers, and Yogi Berra recorded the first pinch-hit home run ever in the World Series.

Bill Bevens and Harry "Cookie" Lavagetto ended their careers in 1947. They will always be remembered for what they did in the fourth game of the World Series on the second day of October before 33,443 raucous fans. In the bottom of the ninth inning the Yankees were winning, 2–1. Bevens was on his way to pitching the first no-hitter in World Series history. Much would later be made of the fact that Red Barber had told the listening audience that the no-hitter was in progress. Dodger fans would claim that it was good reporting; Yankee zealots would cry that Bevens was "jinxed."

Catcher Bruce Edwards led off the Dodger ninth by flying out deep to Johnny Lindell in left field. Furillo walked. It was the ninth walk issued by Bevens, whose wildness had enabled the Dodgers to score their run in the fifth inning. Al Gionfriddo came in to run for Furillo. Spider Jorgensen fouled out. Pete Reiser had not started the game because of an injured ankle. Burt Shotton sent him up as a pinch hitter. Reiser worked the count to 2–1. On the next pitch, which was high and wide, Gionfriddo stole second. With the count now 3–1 on Reiser, Yankee manager Bucky Harris ordered him intentionally passed. Eddie Miksis came in to run for Reiser. Now the Dodgers had two swift pinch runners on first and second. Shotton inserted "Cookie" Lavagetto, age thirty-five, to pinch hit for Eddie Stanky. Ebbets Field was bedlam. So what if Lavagetto has batted just .261, played but forty-one games, collected just eighteen hits during the season. "Cookie, Cookie, Cookie!" the screams shook Ebbets Field.

Bevens got one quick strike on Lavagetto. The next pitch was a high fastball on the outside corner. Lavagetto swung and lifted a fly ball toward the concrete wall in right field. Henrich went back, back, back—the ball hit the wall and the Yankee outfielder had to play the carom. Gionfriddo and Miksis took off the instant Lavagetto's bat contacted the ball. Gionfriddo rounded third and slid across the plate in a cloud of dust. Seconds later Miksis scored. Bevens had incredibly lost the no-hitter and the game. He had pitched a one-hitter and been defeated, 3–2. He stood dumbfounded on the mound. Lavagetto was lifted onto the shoulders of ecstatic Brooklyn fans. His pinch-double was his first hit to right field in 1947 and it was to be his last major league hit. Gladys Gooding played "I'm Just Wild about Harry."

Later Tommy Henrich said, "I just knew that ball would hit the wall. Those were five seconds I could have lived without." The *Brooklyn Eagle* headlines exclaimed: "We're Cookin' Today," and "More Miracles Tomorrow."

Cookie Lavagetto came up again as a pinch hitter in the ninth inning of the fifth game. The Dodgers trailed Spec Shea, 2–1. Gladys Gooding played "Lookie, Lookie, Here Comes Cookie." And thousands cheered for lightning to strike again. This time Cookie struck out. Shotton used eighteen players, but Shea, who yielded just five hits and helped himself at bat with two singles and an RBI, proved equal to the test. A fifth-inning home run—DiMaggio's second of the series—was the Yankee winning margin.

The series shifted to Yankee Stadium for the sixth and seventh games. "We said our farewell to Brooklyn yesterday," said Tommy Henrich, "now we'll give them something to remember in the Bronx."

The sixth game was the wildest and most memorable of the 1947 series. More than 74,000 attended. A record thirty-eight players were used by both teams, including ten pitchers.

In the bottom of the sixth inning, the Dodgers had an 8–5 lead. In May, Branch Rickey had engineered with Pittsburgh what many thought was an astonishing deal motivated solely by cash considerations. The Mahatma sent Kirby Higbe, Hank Behrman, Gene Mauch, and Dixie Howell to the Pirates. In return, the Dodgers received $300,000 plus a tiny, left-handed throwing reserve outfielder named Albert Francis Gionfriddo. "Al was obtained to carry the money," was the big joke of the time in the streets of Brooklyn. Gionfriddo batted .177 for the Dodgers in thirty-seven regular season games.

Shotton inserted him into left field for defensive purposes as Snuffy Stirnweiss came up to bat for the Yankees as the home half of the sixth got underway.

Stirnweiss walked. Berra singled. With two men on base and the Yankees trailing by three, the stadium crowd screamed as DiMaggio came up to the plate.

DiMag poled Joe Hatten's first pitch toward the low bull pen barrier in left field. "Back . . . back . . . back goes Gionfriddo," shouted Red Barber. "It may be out of here! No! Gionfriddo makes a one-handed catch against the bull pen fence. Ohhhhhh doctor!!" Gionfriddo never gave up on the ball, and his last-second leaping stab enabled him to catch it at the 415-foot marker. The five-foot six-inch, one hundred-sixty-five-pound utility outfielder never had a more glorious moment. Like Bevens and Lavagetto, 1947 was his last major league season.

The catch in itself was spectacular. But the drama of the moment was that Joe DiMaggio, the Yankee Clipper, had hit the ball that

Gionfriddo caught. The great DiMag, 1947's Most Valuable Player, had also kicked at the dirt at second base raising a cloud of dust when Gionfriddo made his impossible play. It was a rare display of emotion for the stoical DiMaggio.

Joe Page saved sixty games for the Yankees in 1947–49 regular season play. And his five scoreless innings of relief work in the seventh game of the series preserved the 5–2 Yankee victory. Once again, it was Brooklyn's turn to "Wait 'til next year."

In the festive Yankee clubhouse, Larry MacPhail, a bottle of beer in one hand and a cigarette in the other, screamed out, "My heart can't stand it anymore. I'm through. I'm through." He had ranted and raved and berated Yankee players throughout the season, and there was disbelief at his announcement. But MacPhail truly was through. He resigned as club president, selling his one-third interest in the team to Del Webb and Dan Topping. MacPhail exited with a $2-million profit on his Yankee investment. And New York City baseball lost one of its most colorful and creative characters. He would never return to participate in the sport he had done so much to promote.

In 1948, there was no World Series schedule for the subways of New York City. Cleveland faced the Boston Braves in the Series that year. The Dodgers and the Yankees finished in third place and the Giants wound up the season thirteen and a half games out, in fifth.

In 1949, the minimum wage was 40 cents an hour, and the average family income after taxes was $4,000—twice that of 1941. Industry was engaged in full-scale conversion to peacetime products: plastics, automobiles, frozen foods, TVs. Christian Dior's "New Look" showcased narrow shoulders, a cinched waist, plunging neckline, and long skirts with wide hems. *Kiss Me Kate* was a new hit Broadway musical. Ezio Pinza starred in *South Pacific*. Once again the New York City subways ran on World Series schedules. Winning pennants on the final day of the 1949 season, the Dodgers and Yankees wound up with identical 97–57 records.

Brooklyn celebrated its pennant with wild abandon. The highlight of the celebration was a Dodger motorcade down Flatbush Avenue and Fulton Street to Borough Hall. Players sat on the back seats of open convertibles, waving to hysterical fans. The names of the players were listed on the side of the automobiles they rode in. Just in case

anyone had difficulty deciphering the names, Tex Rickards made generous use of a loudspeaker to announce which Dodgers occupied each
car.

Confetti, streamers, rolls of toilet paper fell from the windows of
tall buildings along the parade route. Scarecrow figures of Yankees
were mounted on long poles and held up as the Dodger caravan
passed. Signs announced: "Moider the Yanks," "Tear Out Their
Hearts," "Reese for Mayor," "God Help Da Yanks," "Brooklyn Has
Those Atomic Bums," "Robby Will Steal the Series." At Fulton and
Willoughby Streets, the location of the Spanish newspaper *El Diario*, a
huge banner was displayed. "El Diario Felicita a Olmo. Estamos Con-
tigo." (*El Diario* congratulates Olmo.) A part-time outfielder on the
Dodgers, Luis Olmo was of Spanish descent.

During the final part of the motorcade, the procession passed
shoppers on Flatbush Avenue. Women doffed their hats. The biggest
show of affection was directed at Duke Snider. He covered his ears to
protect them against the screams of thousands of passionate fans.

The motorcade ended near the Hall of Records in Borough Hall.
Police held back the screaming, shoving mob that was lined up fifty
to sixty deep behind barricades. American flags vied for air space with
Dodger banners and pennants. Vendors competed enthusiastically
with each other peddling Dodger pins, buttons, yearbooks, pens.

Brooklyn Borough President John Cashmore telegraphed Bronx
Borough President James J. Lyons:

"Bring on the Bombers. Know they are good especially Joe
DiMaggio, but our Dodgers are better. You may have reputation as
'bombers' but we have radar and Ebbets Field arsenal is well stocked
with secret weapons. Greatest City's Greatest Borough (Brooklyn)
obviously welcomes meeting with so called Borough of Universities
(The Bronx). Before culture is possible, there must be three R's and
we have the gentlemen who will provide first lessons—Robinson,
Reese, Roe, and whole Dodger team . . ."

Not only the borough president but all of Brooklyn bragged about
Robinson, Reese, and Roe. Robinson had the best year of his career in
1949. Playing in 156 games at second base, he batted a league-leading
.342, recorded 142 RBIs and pounded sixteen home runs. Reese also
had his best year as a Dodger, teaming with Robinson as the second

half of the best keystone combination in baseball. The "Louisville Colonel" played in 155 games at shortstop, hit as many home runs as Robby and drove in 73 runs while notching a .279 batting average. Preacher Roe kept denying that he was wetting the baseball in racking up his fifteen wins against just six defeats to pace all National League pitchers in winning percentage.

It was estimated that if the World Series went seven games, $12 million would be spent on baseball-related goods and services in New York City. The biggest shortage of hotel rooms since the days of World War II existed as thousands checked into New York City for another Dodger-Yankee World Series. Hundreds of police officers were stationed around the clock at Yankee Stadium and Ebbets Field to guard the facilities and prevent incidents. Hundreds more would ride the subways, monitoring the fans who rode the trains to the ball parks.

The first game was a classic pitcher's duel before 66,224 at Yankee Stadium. Don Newcombe became the first black pitcher to start a World Series game. He pitched brilliantly. He struck out eleven batters, yielded no walks, and just five hits. The fifth hit, unfortunately for Dodger fans, was a lead-off ninth-inning home run by Old Reliable Tommy Henrich. Reynolds gave up only two hits in posting the 1-0 shutout. Asked later what kind of pitch he threw Henrich, Newcombe joked: "A change of space."

The score of the second game was the same as the first game, only this time the Dodgers had the one run. Preacher Roe, who was accused of throwing a spitball, scattered six hits and Gil Hodges batted in the Dodger run in the second inning. The headline on the back page of the October 7 bulldog edition of the *Daily Mirror* that sold for three cents read:

"DODGERS WIN, IT WAS
ROOO–OOO–OOO E"

The third game was another low-scoring contest for eight innings. Tied 1–1 in the top of the ninth, the Yankees scored three times. Two of their runs came in on a pinch single by Johnny Mize. The Dodgers had scored more runs than any other National League team in 1949. As they came to bat in the bottom of the ninth inning, the twelve thousand who had paid a dollar each for bleacher seats were pleading for home runs. Luis Olmo, the pride of *El Diario*, was sent up as a pinch hitter. He cracked a home run. Ebbets Field rocked. Roy Campanella followed with a home run and the Dodgers trailed by just one run. That was as close as they got. Pinch hitter Bruce Edwards struck out. The Yankees won, 4–3.

On October 8, the first front-page British newspaper coverage of a World Series took place. A two-hundred-fifty-word story appeared in the *London Daily Telegraph*. On that day the Yankees moved to within one game of the World Championship. Allie Reynolds relieved Eddie Lopat after the Dodgers had scored four runs in the sixth inning and preserved the 6–4 Yankee win.

The Dodgers used six pitchers in the fifth and final game in a losing cause as the Yankees again with strong relief pitching—this time by Joe Page—won 10–6, for the first of what would be five straight world championships.

The biggest disappointment in the 1949 World Series for Dodger fans was Duke Snider. The handsome center fielder views the Series as a turning point in his career. "I struck out eight times in five games to tie a record and batted just .143," notes Snider. "In those first years I was moody and kept everything in. When I went home that winter, I changed. From then on when things went bad, I thought of the 1949 World Series and how things could be worse."

In 1951, the Yankees confronted the Giants in the World Series for the first time since 1937. "All the reporters told us to watch out," said Lopat. " 'The Giants are hot,' they said. 'They beat the Dodgers coming out of nowhere.' We didn't believe what anybody told us or what they printed in the newspapers. The other teams had to beat us on the field. That was where it counted."

When the first game of the series was concluded, Giant fans bragged that the "Miracle Run" of the regular season was going to continue through the postseason competition. Durocher, unable to start either of his arm-weary twenty-three-game winners, Maglie and Jansen, chose ten-game winner Dave Koslo. The Giant southpaw spaced seven hits and Monte Irvin supplied the power in the 5–1 opening game victory. Irvin stroked four hits including a triple. "I really wanted five," he said. "No one in World Series history ever went 5–5." The Hall of Famer also stole home—he had accomplished the feat five times during the season. The starting and losing pitcher for the Yankees was Allie Reynolds. The Super Chief had won seventeen games in 1951.

Irvin continued his torrid hitting on his way to a .458 batting average in the Series. He collected three hits, but his Giant teammates could manage only two more. Eddie Lopat coasted to a 3–1 win. The most frightening moment of the Series took place when Mickey Mantle, going after a fly ball, tripped and fell over a drainpipe that protruded from the outfield grass. Playing in his first World Series, just three weeks away from his twentieth birthday, Mantle lay motionless. There were many in Yankee Stadium who thought he might be dead. Mantle was just stunned by the fear that his career might have been over, and he remained still, seized with fright. What had happened was that his right knee snapped, and Mantle was lost to the Yankees for the rest of the series.

The Giants won the third game of the series powered by a five-run fifth inning triggered by Eddie Stanky's kicking of the ball out of Phil Rizzuto's glove and capped by Whitey Lockman's three-run homer. Jim Hearn was the winning pitcher in the 6–2 Giant victory.

It rained on October 7 and the fourth game was postponed. Giant fans claimed the extra day of rest helped out Allie Reynolds and the Yankees and helped cool off the surging Giants. In 1951 the Super Chief became only the second man in history to pitch two no-hitters. He didn't have no-hit form in the fourth game, but he had enough. He spaced eight hits, and he even spaced the two runs the Giants scored, yielding one run in the first and the other in the ninth inning. Joe DiMaggio collected his first hits of the Series, a single and a home run in the 6–2 Yankee win.

The fifth game personified Yankee power and pitching. Junkman Eddie Lopat coasted to a 13–1 triumph, yielding but five hits. The Yankees pounded five Giant pitchers for a dozen hits, including a grand-slam homer by Gil McDougald. Phil Rizzuto, who topped Yankee batters in the Series with a .320 average, chipped in a two-run homer. Leo Durocher used sixteen players, scrambling to get back into the game. Hank Bauer was the key figure as the Yankees won the sixth game 4–3, recording their third straight world championship.

The ex-Marine tripled in a trio of runs in the sixth inning and made a spectacular diving catch in the ninth, aborting a Giant rally.

Mantle and Durocher would joke with each other years afterward. "We had a fine time with you and DiMaggio and Lopat and Rizzuto. We couldn't find the ball," said "The Lip."

"Ah Leo, we thought the Giants were lucky to win just one game," joked "The Commerce Comet."

Dick Sisler's home run in the final game of the 1950 season denied the Dodgers the pennant. Bobby Thomson's home run in the final game of the 1951 play-off denied the Dodgers the pennant. In 1952—scoring more runs, stealing more bases, blasting more home runs than any other team in the league—they won the National League pennant by four and a half games over the Giants. The Dodgers were confident they could beat the Yankees in the World Series *this time*. The Brooklyn set lineup was supported by stronger pitching since they had last faced the Yankees. Billy Loes, Carl Erskine, Joe Black, and Clem Labine had collectively won fifty-four games in 1952 against twenty-two losses. The Bronx Bombers had struggled to win their pennant. Casey Stengel had constantly juggled the lineup. Joe DiMaggio was gone. Whitey Ford was in the Army. Eddie Lopat had been injured a good part of the season. It was true that the Yankees had Allie Reynolds, but how many games could he pitch?

In 1952, the Yankee Super Chief topped the American League in earned run average, in shutouts, in strikeouts. He won twenty games and saved six more. "He was some pitcher," recalls his former roommate Eddie Lopat, but he developed into it.

"My first year with the Yankees in 1948, he was strictly a hard-baller. The first couple of batters used to get on and then he worked on the next batters as if they were Babe Ruth. I explained to him, 'Why not work on the first pitch of the first batter with some thought, a plan.' He got huffy. We almost had a brawl, but he was twice my size. We never discussed pitching again that year. Two years later, he brought it up. 'You throw those big curves that far outside and they jump across the plate swinging at them in the dirt. I miss the plate that far (he held his fingers close together) and they take it —how come?'

"I told him that when his express train came in there, they took it because they did not have time to swing the bat. 'With mine,' I told him, 'it comes up there bigger 'n a balloon and they chase it.' Hard throwers can't fathom that, but in 1952, he started with a change and he understood my pitching pattern and he started getting the results he wanted."

In game one of the World Series, Reynolds did not quite get the results he wanted. The Dodgers for the first time in their history won the opening game of the series, 4–2. Robinson, Snider, and Reese homered to pace the Brooklyn win. Rookie of the Year, Joe Black, hurled a six-hitter.

A three-run Billy Martin homer highlighted the Yankee five-run fifth inning in the second game. Vic Raschi went the distance in the 7–1 Yankee victory.

The series moved to Yankee Stadium for the third, fourth, and fifth games. Two crafty pitchers, Preacher Roe of the Dodgers and Eddie Lopat of the Yankees, provided an interesting matchup. The Dodgers won 5–3. It was the first time since 1920 that Brooklyn led after three series games. Berra's passed ball in the top of the ninth allowed two runs to score and lessened the impact of Johnny Mize's pinch-hit home run in the bottom of the ninth inning. Berra's error triggered renewed subway and sidewalk debates between Dodger and Yankee rooters about the relative fielding merits of the catchers on both teams.

"Yog got too much criticism for that passed ball," said Lopat. "Back in '48, he couldn't throw anybody out. You could not win a close game with him catching. He could not block the ball in the dirt. Bucky Harris put him in the outfield. You could not take him out of the lineup. He was hitting a ton.

"Yog had a real good arm. He could throw a man out from the outfield. Bill Dickey trained him all the next spring teaching him how to throw, to block the plate, to position himself to help the pitchers. Yogi had good baseball instinct. He worked at it. By 1951, 1952, he was a complete catcher . . . anyone could make an error."

Born Lawrence Peter Berra on May 12, 1925, in St. Louis, Missouri, he didn't look like a Yankee, he didn't walk like a Yankee, he didn't talk like a Yankee—but he sure played like a Yankee. The name "Yogi" came from his boyhood friends on the hill in St. Louis where he played soccer and baseball. The word denoted an odd character. And Yogi was odd and original.

At the start of his career in 1946–47, he was an overanxious batter. Pitchers soon learned that he came up to the plate ready to swing at the first pitch. And they made it a bad one.

"You can't do that, Yog," said Yankee manager Bucky Harris one day. "Think, wait for your pitch. If you think when you're up there, you'll do better." Harris slapped Berra on the back and shouted: "Now get up there and do exactly as I told you."

The short-armed, short-legged, swarthy Berra sauntered into the batter's box. He took the first pitch. "Strike one," bellowed the umpire. The next pitch was a fastball right down the center of the plate. Berra watched it go by. "Strike two," shouted the umpire. Berra tugged at his cap and concentrated. The third pitch was right in there. "Strike three, yee're out," shouted the umpire.

Yogi did not argue. He carried his bat back with him to the dugout. "What where you doing up there?" Harris was livid. "It's all your fault," Yogi said angrily. "How do you expect a guy to think and hit at the same time?"

Through eighteen illustrious years with the Yankees, Berra learned to hit and think at the same time, to hit and think three pitches ahead of most any hurler he faced.

He recorded a lifetime .989 fielding average. Between July 27, 1947, and May 10, 1949, he performed in 148 games without once committing an error—an all-time record. The Hall of Famer three times won the American League's Most Valuable Player award. A squat, left-handed batter, the vision of him slugging one of his 358 career home runs or blasting in one of his 1,430 lifetime RBIs is what made Yankee fans rank Campanella and Westrum far behind their clutch-hitting catcher.

Over the years, Berra's one-liners helped earn him the affection of millions and his reputation as a character. One night he accepted an award and told the audience, "I want you to thank me for making this award possible."

"I never meant to be funny," he says. "It just seemed to come out that way." Berra was the comic relief that softened the Yankee image even for Dodger and Giant fans.

Joe Black and Allie Reynolds were rematched in game five. This time the powerful Yankee right-hander got the results he wanted. Reynolds fanned ten and allowed four hits in the 2–0 Yankee victory. A Mize home run and a Mantle triple accounted for the two runs.

The fifth game went eleven innings and Carl Erskine pitched every one of them for the Dodgers, retiring the final nineteen batters. Former National Leaguers Johnny Sain and Ewell Blackwell hurled for the Yankees. Another ex-National League star, Johnny Mize, cracked his third home run of the series for the Yankees. Snider's single drove in the winning run as the 6–5 Dodger victory gave them a 3–2 lead in the series.

Casey Stengel used Lopat, Reynolds, and Raschi in the seventh game, but it was southpaw Bob Kuzava who retired the last eight Dodger batters and insured the Yankee's fourth straight world championship. The year before, Kuzava had closed out the Giants in the final game of the World Series. Only 8–8 with a 3.45 ERA during the regular season, Kuzava came in to face Snider and Robinson with the bases loaded and one out in the seventh inning. Both Dodger sluggers popped up on 3–2 counts. The 4–2 victory made it six straight world championships for the American League, four in a row for Casey Stengel, and sixteen triumphs in nineteen attempts for the Yankees.

In 1953, the start of the baseball season was marked by the death of famed athlete Jim Thorpe. He died penniless. Ninety-two-year-old Abner C. Powell died in August. He was the originator of Ladies' Day and the rain check. That summer thousands were entertained by the twenty-eight-foot-high, seventy-foot-long movie screen that was introduced at Radio City Music Hall in Manhattan. Thousands more flocked to see Danny Kaye perform in a one-man vaudeville show at the Palace on Broadway. In fourteen weeks, he grossed three-quarters of a million dollars. The big news story of the year was the signing of an armistice on July 27 that concluded the Korean

War. The United States spent $20 billion on the conflict that killed 54,246 servicemen and wounded 103,284. New York City baseball players drafted into the war included Whitey Ford, Bobby Brown, and Jerry Coleman of the Yankees, Don Newcombe of the Dodgers, and Willie Mays of the Giants.

The Milwaukee Braves, a seventh-place team in 1952, finished in second place behind the Dodgers in 1953. Playing in a city with a population of just 600,000, in a ball park that seated but 35,000, the Braves recorded a season attendance of 1,826,397—more than half a million more fans than the Dodgers, almost a quarter of a million more fans than the world-champion Yankees, who played in a park twice the size of Milwaukee's. The Braves notched the largest National League home attendance to that point in history. Though Milwaukee won the battle at the box office, once again the Dodgers and Yankees met in a subway World Series.

"The 1953 Dodgers were the best team of that era," notes Jack Lang. They had clubbed 208 home runs, won 105 games. They had taken over first place on June 28, demolishing the Braves 11–1, and had gone on to clinch the pennant at the earliest date in National League history, thirteen games ahead of Milwaukee. Snider topped the league with a .627 slugging percentage. Campanella, Snider, and Hodges all drove in more than one hundred runs. Campanella's 142 RBIs led the league; Furillo's .344 batting average led the league; Snider scored more runs and recorded more total bases than any other National Leaguer. Five Dodgers in the solid, set lineup batted .300 or better. Carl Erskine won twenty of twenty-six decisions. Russ Meyer, acquired from Philadelphia, won fifteen of twenty decisions. Billy Loes, a product of the New York City sandlots, chipped in with fourteen wins.

The Yankees had only two .300 hitters and no twenty-game winners, but sixty-three-year-old Casey Stengel had constantly tinkered with and juggled his lineup. When the stats were added up at the end of the season the Bombers once again were in first place, and as a team their hitters paced the American League in batting average and their pitchers led all staffs in earned run average.

The fiftieth anniversary World Series followed a familiar pattern. The Dodgers won two games at Ebbets Field. The Yankees won two games at their stadium and then went on to win the series, once more intensifying the frustration of the Dodgers and their "faithful."

Five home runs were hit in the first game. The decisive one was pounded by Joe Collins of the Yankees in the seventh inning. It broke a 5–5 tie. The Yankees added three more runs in the eighth inning to lock up their 9–5 win. Another George Weiss "pick-up," former National League star Johnny Sain known as "The Man of a Thousand Curves," relieved Allie Reynolds and was credited with the victory.

Eddie Lopat outpitched Preacher Roe as the Yankees won the second game, 4–2. Billy Martin, who would bat .500 during the series and collect a dozen hits, eight RBIs, and twenty-three total bases, blasted a home run. Martin had batted .257 during the 1953 season. Mickey Mantle's eighth-inning home run won the game for the Yankees.

Carl Erskine was racked up by the Yankees in the first game's first inning but came back in game three to pitch one of the finest games of his career. He struck out fourteen batters—Mantle and Collins, the heroes of the first two games, each struck out four times. Despite Erskine's splendid performance, he was just barely able to win. Vic Raschi matched him virtually pitch for pitch. The score was tied 2–2 in the eighth when Campanella homered to give the Dodgers a 3–2 win.

Dodger power in game four deadlocked the series. Snider drove in four runs with two doubles and a homer. Jim Gilliam, 1953 Rookie of the Year, cracked three doubles. Clem Labine relieved Dodger starter Billy Loes to choke off a bases-loaded Yankee threat and preserve the 7–3 Dodger victory.

The fifth game was a slugging competition. The two teams collected twenty-five hits and forty-seven total bases. Mantle, Woodling, Martin, McDougald, Cox, and Gilliam all homered. Mantle's shot was the key blow. It came with the bases loaded and capped the 11–7 Yankee triumph.

Some Dodger rooters complained that Stengel's choice of nine-game winner "Hot Rod" Jim McDonald was an insult. It turned out to be a clever move by "The Old Perfesser." The Yankees staked McDonald to an early lead with a five-run third inning, and he clung on until the eighth, when the Dodgers scored four times. McDonald's performance provided respite for the tired Yankee pitching staff and set it up for the sixth and if necessary the seventh game.

In the top of the ninth inning of the sixth game, Carl Furillo's "opposite field" home run tied the score. Billy Martin's twelfth hit of the series—a single in the bottom of the ninth inning—made the seventh game unnecessary. Martin's hit scored Hank Bauer, giving the Yankees a 4–3 victory.

Casey Stengel's 1953 Yankees posted a new World Series record —five straight championships. They also came away with $8,240 per player, a record winner's share. The Dodgers would be back—not "next year" but in 1955—but Dressen would not be back.

The feisty and jovial Dressen had boasted in the summer of 1951, "The Giants is dead." That year Durocher's players battled back from the dead to win the second play-off in National League history and snatch the pennant from Dressen's Dodgers. In 1952, Dressen wrote a magazine article: "It Won't Happen Again." He said, "The three grand I've made for this article is found money. If we lose, I'll be fired anyway." In 1953, Dressen's Dodgers won 105 games, finished the season with a .682 percentage, 13 games ahead of the second-place Braves. After losing the World Series to the Yankees, Dressen said, "If I had had Newcombe, I could've won this." Newcombe was in the Army.

After the 1953 series, Dressen demanded a two-year contract. Winner of two straight pennants, 298 games in three seasons for a .642 percentage, he had, he reasoned, earned what he was asking for. Dressen argued that his record was better than Durocher's and Leo had just signed a three-year contract with the Giants. Walter O'Malley listened to Dressen's arguments and responded by hiring Walter Alston, who would remain with the Dodgers through twenty-three years of one-year contracts.

When Alston was announced as the new Dodger manager, the headline in the *New York Daily News* asked: "WHO, HE?" Walter Emmons Alston was forty-two years old when he came to the Dodgers. A minor league manager for thirteen years before he came to the Dodgers, Alston was the strong, silent force who contrasted sharply with the flamboyant Durocher and the egocentric Dressen. "Walt was miscast," said Dodger announcer Vin

Scully. "He should have been born in another time period; he would have been comfortable back in the days of the old west riding shotgun on a stagecoach."

A championship pocket billiards player, a man comfortable with his woodworking hobby, Alston at six feet two inches and two hundred ten pounds quietly and methodically learned when to exert pressure and when to leave his players alone. His great skill was in getting the most out of his material. Through the years he won with teams built on power, teams built on speed, teams built on pitching. The one constant was that he won.

Junior Gilliam came to the Dodgers a year before Alston. "A lot of the players knew him because they had played for him in the minors," said Gilliam. "He didn't have a major league reputation but he had a background and with the Dodgers he had a bunch of stars who knew how to win. His chief assets were knowing his personnel, knowing how to talk to them, getting all he could out of them every day, every game, every season."

Duke Snider admitted that he missed Dressen. "I never played for Alston in the minors. Dressen got the most out of me. We were used to a fiery guy and all of a sudden we got a quiet guy. It took us a year to get used to it. The next year Walt knew the league better, and we knew him better, and we won it all."

On September 8, 1955, the Dodgers clinched the pennant, setting a new record for the earliest clinching date in National League history. Karl Spooner pitched five and two-thirds hitless innings against the Braves in the 10–2 Dodger win.

"This Is Next Year" was the headline in the *Daily News*. The second-place Milwaukee Braves finished thirteen and a half games back; the Giants ended the season in third place, eighteen and a half games out. The Dodgers scored more runs (857), recorded more doubles (230), more home runs (201), more stolen bases (79) than any other team in the National League. Brooklyn's team batting average and slugging percentage paced the league. Its pitching staff had the best ERA, the most saves, the most strikeouts. Newcombe was the league leader in winning percentage with a 20–5 record. He was second in ERA and complete games. Snider, Furillo, and Campanella all batted over .300. Snider, Hodges, and Campanella all drove in more than one hundred runs each.

"It was an awesome collection of talent," said Jack Lang. "They knew they were good, but they just could not beat the Yankees in the World Series. It was something they felt about themselves."

Everyone including Stengel knew the Dodgers destroyed left-handed pitchers. But ol' Case started southpaws Whitey Ford and Tommy Byrne anyway in the first two games at Yankee Stadium. Two two-run homers by Joe Collins and another by rookie Elston Howard enabled Whitey Ford to post the Yankee 6–5 opening game victory. Jackie Robinson stole home in the eighth inning, and Snider and Furillo hit home runs for the Dodgers.

Veteran southpaw Tommy Byrne allowed only five hits and drove in two runs with a fourth-inning single as the Yankees won the second game 4–2. Byrne's route-going performance was the first by a left-handed pitcher in 1955 against the Dodgers. Billy Loes, rookies Fred Bessent and Karl Spooner, and veteran Clem Labine pitched for Brooklyn.

The series moved to Ebbets Field for the third, fourth, and fifth games. The "Faithful" wondered if there would be a fifth game. The Yankee machine was operating at maximum efficiency.

Pitching on the last day of September, on his twenty-third birthday, Johnny Podres got the job done for Brooklyn. The stylish south-paw, using a deceptive change of pace, kept the Yankee sluggers off balance. They kept lunging at his pitches and popping up. He spaced seven hits, struck out six. The Dodgers won, 8–3. It was the first complete game Podres had pitched since June 14. Campy paced the Brooklyn eleven-hit attack with three hits, one of them a two-run home run, and three RBIs.

Fourteen hits, including home runs by Hodges, Campanella, and Snider, gave the Dodgers an 8–5 victory in game four, evening the series. Clem Labine was the winning pitcher. Don Larsen was the loser.

The largest crowd ever to see a World Series game at Ebbets Field, 36,796, was in attendance for game five on October 2. Sophomore manager Walt Alston started slim rookie Roger Craig, who had but a half year of major league experience. Stengel countered with 1954 Rookie of the Year Bob Grim. Three home runs in the first five innings, two by Snider, one by Sandy Amoros, built the early Dodger lead. Craig held the Yankees to only three hits until the seventh inning. Bob Cerv slammed a pinch-hit home run. Elston Howard walked. Berra homered off reliever Clem Labine, but the Yankees came up short. The Dodgers won 5–3.

Southpaw Whitey Ford started against southpaw Karl Spooner in the sixth game at Yankee Stadium. Tom Lasorda, who was his team-mate, remembers Spooner's major league debut:

"September 28, 1954, was my twenty-eighth birthday. The Giants had clinched the pennant the day before. Manager Walt Alston was undecided whether to pitch me or Karl. At the last minute, he went with Karl, since it was my birthday. Spooner had the bases loaded and no out. He had three balls and no strikes on Bobby Hoffman. I was warming up in the bull pen and knew if he walked Hoffman I would come in. On three and zero, Hoffman swung at a pitch over his head. Then Spooner struck him out."

Spooner struck out six in a row to start the game—a major league record. "He went on to fan fifteen for the whole game," continued Lasorda. "That was some debut. Four days later he pitched against Pittsburgh and struck out twelve. Everybody was excited about him. The Brooklyn fans had the slogan: "Sooner With Spooner." He had the ability to be another Koufax, but he hurt his arm. The thing that will always be on Spooner's mind is how far, how far he coulda gone . . ."

Spooner went only as far as the first inning of the sixth game of the 1955 World Series. He gave up two walks, singles to Berra and Bauer, and a two-run homer to Bill Skowron—five runs in all. He never pitched in the major leagues again. Ford, in the fourth year of what would be a sixteen-year Hall of Fame career, yielded just four hits going the distance in the 5–1 Yankee win. His disdainful toying with Dodger batters was reflected in this exchange he had with Berra:

"Your slider ain't workin' good, Whitey. Don't throw no more," Berra told him after one of Ford's sliders had been slammed for a base hit.

"Aw, Yog," grinned Ford. "Say, don't be a spoil-sport. I need the practice. Let me throw it to this guy."

"No more," snapped Berra. "Do your practicin' when we get to Japan. The World Series ain't the right time to horse around."

Sandy-haired Johnny Podres, twenty-three, of Witherbee, New York, opposed Tommy Byrne, thirty-five, of Baltimore, Maryland, in the final game. Podres had won nine and lost ten during the regular season. "He was a boy who never grew up," said Lee Scott. "He was my personal favorite. He'd give you the shirt off his back. Johnny loved to have a good time." Byrne had won sixteen and lost five and led the American League in winning percentage. Each southpaw had won once in the series.

The Dodgers scored in the fourth inning when Hodges singled to drive in a run. They scored again in the sixth inning—again Hodges got the RBI. Alston, scrambling for more runs, sent up George "Shot-gun" Shuba as a pinch hitter for Don Zimmer. Shuba grounded out. As the bottom of the sixth began, Alston made a couple of defensive changes. Gilliam moved from left field to second base, replacing Zimmer. Speedy Sandy Amoros came in to take Gilliam's place in left field.

Mantle walked to start the inning for the Yanks. McDougald reached base on a bunt single. Berra came to bat with his teammates straining to run off first and second base. What happened next would be debated for years afterward. Berra sliced a long, high fly ball down the left field line. The ball seemed headed into the left field corner— far enough and deep enough at least to tie the game. Yankee coach Frank Crosetti, screamed at Mantle and McDougald to tear around the bases at full speed. Amoros was also running at full speed—streaking toward the ball that was just about a foot inside fair territory.

Amoros raced toward the stands, his body straining, his right arm extended. He caught the ball in the pocket of his glove and his running momentum carried him into the railing of the left field stands near the "301" marker. He recovered. Almost bouncing off the railing, he fired the ball to the relay man Reese who pivoted and threw to Hodges who stepped on first, doubling up McDougald who was scrambling to get back.

"I run and run and run," was the explanation the Cuban-born

Amoros offered for the play that would be discussed for years to come. There are still those who argue that had Gilliam been in left field he would never have caught the ball There are others who claim that only a left-hander could have made the play—that a right-handed player would have been unable to backhand the ball. Perhaps the explanation offered the next day in the *New York Times* by Arthur Daley is the most acceptable: "Conscience-stricken by the many shabby tricks she'd played on the Brooks throughout the years . . . lady luck put wings on the feet of Sandy Amoros and glue in his glove."

Jerry Coleman is still a little bitter: "It wasn't so much that Amoros made a great catch," he says. "It was the way he went after it in the sun. A better fielder would have made it easier . . . the circumstance was that we may have had a tie ball game . . . as it turned out, that was our last shot."

The Yankees tried to get back, but the play by Amoros *was* their last shot. Dodger announcer Vin Scully had described the first half of the game; Mel Allen, the "Voice of the Yankees," was announcing the last four and a half innings. With two Yankees retired in the bottom of the ninth, Allen surrendered the microphone to Scully, who said: "Howard hits a ground ball to Reese. He throws to Hodges . . . the Brooklyn Dodgers are World Champions." The time was 3:43 P.M., the fifth day of October, 1955.

It was the first time since 1921 that a team had won the series after having lost the first two games. "It was the first and only world championship Brooklyn ever had," said Duke Snider. "You had to pinch yourself. We finally had done it."

Between 3:44 P.M. and 4:01 P.M., New York City experienced the greatest flood of phone calls since V-J Day. Anyone attempting to place a business call received a no dial response. A total of 1,075,847 calls were made for the series—226,866 took place on the day of the seventh game.

Brooklyn had eight colleges, more than six thousand acres of parks, twelve hundred houses of worship, almost eight thousand factories—and now finally, it had a world championship baseball team. The Yankee jinx had been broken. *This was next year!*

Brooklyn became a carnival of noise. "On the trip back on the bus from Yankee Stadium to Brooklyn," recalls Snider, "everyone must have known our route. Everyone had a sign and the streets were packed with people making noise. I'll never forget it. We had the greatest fans in the world. They lived and died with us and this was their moment," continued Snider, who had his moments in the series with four home runs, seven RBIs, and eight hits.

Motorcades clogged Flatbush Avenue, Fourth Avenue, 86th Street, Ocean Parkway, and other major Brooklyn arteries. Effigies of Yankees were slung over lamp posts. The sound of automobile horns, clanging cowbells, popping toy cannons, and firecrackers continued through the night and into the next day. Joe's Delicatessen on Utica Avenue near Ebbets Field set up a sidewalk stand and dispensed free frankfurters. At 24 DeKalb Avenue in downtown Brooklyn not too far from the main offices of the team, hundreds danced in front of the Dodger Café. "Yea, Bums, Dodgers, Champs," they screamed. A baby was born in Ciudad Trujillo, Dominican Republic. He was named Podres Garcia. Intoxicated with liquor and the moment, fans of the "Bums" toured bar after bar throughout Manhattan and made their way to the outer reaches of the Bronx.

On South Second Street in Williamsburg, Brooklyn, a neighborhood not far from the Dodger offices on 215 Montague Street, a freckle-faced eighteen-year-old named Ira Schneider was happier than he had ever been in his entire life. Ira was a Dodger fan's **Dodger fan.** In his room on the fourth floor of one of the sagging tenement buildings on South Second Street were dozens of loose-leaf books devoted to his "Beloved Bums." Since the age of eight, he had clipped any article or photograph having to do with the Dodgers and neatly pasted them into the blue loose-leafs.

He attended ten, twenty, thirty Dodger games a year—as many as the money from his job as a supermarket delivery boy enabled him to. A tall, thin, pale youth, he was a veritable storehouse of records and anecdotes about the team he loved.

Ira had gone to the first game of the 1955 World Series and made a decision on his way home. "If I go to any more," he told his friends, "the Dodgers'll lose. I'll listen to the games . . . that'll help them win."

When Podres retired Howard for the final out, Ira raced out his bedroom, down the four flights of stairs, and took up a position against the black wrought-iron stoop railing. He had his stage. Through the darkening afternoon hours and through the night, Ira addressed all those in the neighborhood who would come and listen. The stoop was his stage; every passerby became part of his audience. He spoke in long, full sentences about the greatness of the Dodgers, their commitment to excellence, how much the victory meant to the borough, to the neighborhood, to the street. At about 1:00 A.M., when he finally retired, he could not sleep but lovingly looked through his scrapbooks, anticipating all the new additions.

Duke Snider was given the privilege of blowing out the candles at the Dodger victory party at the Hotel Bossert. "There were tons of grapes," recalls Sid Frigand, "big wedges of cheese, booze flowing like water. They had to carry out Johnny Podres. He got drunk. Everybody got drunk. It was wild there."

The victory of the Dodgers of Brooklyn over the Yankees of New York was the triumph of the underdog over the fat cat, the people over the corporation, Brooklyn over the rest of the world. In Flatbush, Bensonhurst, Bay Ridge, Greenpoint, the citizens of Brooklyn were triggered into wild tribal jubilation: bonfires in the streets, prideful speeches from the top of stoops by fans like Ira Schneider to other fans, noisy and impromptu parties. Thousands were content just to gather on sidewalks and porches and bang spoons against pots and pans. It was the happiest time in the long history of Brooklyn.

In a bar in Queens, on October 8, three days after Brooklyn had won its first and only World Series, William Christman, an off-duty detective, and Robert Thomson, Dodger and Yankee fans respectively, got into an argument about their favorite teams. The two men got angrier and angrier; they left the bar but continued their argument in the street. Thomson got so frenzied that he took out a gun and shot and killed Christman. Thomson was arrested for manslaughter.

Mickey Mantle and Whitey Ford were in the prime of their baseball lives as they led the Yankees to the 1956 nine-game pennant romp over the Cleveland Indians. Mantle paced the league's batters in homers (52), runs scored (132), runs batted in (130), batting average (.353), slugging percentage (.705), and total bases (376). He won the

Most Valuable Player award and became the first Yankee since Lou Gehrig in 1934 to win the Triple Crown. Ford won nineteen games and lost but six. He topped the American League in winning percentage and earned run average. Mickey and Whitey and the other Yankees were looking for revenge for 1955 as they again faced the Dodgers in the 1956 World Series.

The first two games were played in Brooklyn. President Dwight D. Eisenhower attended the first game. Looking strange in a Dodger uniform pitching against the Yankees, thirty-nine-year-old Sal Maglie struck out ten batters and spaced nine hits in the 6–3 Brooklyn opening game victory. He had triumphed in thirteen of eighteen decisions for the Dodgers during the regular season and seemed to be just the addition needed to give the men from Flatbush their second straight World Series victory. Dodger fans who once cursed at the very mention of his name now cheered him on. Jackie Robinson, once a confirmed Maglie-hater, homered in support of his old enemy. A three-run homer by Gil Hodges in the third inning broke a 2–2 tie and eased the former Giant's pitching load. Whitey Ford was charged with the loss, and Dodger fans crowed: "Even a good lefty like Ford gets 'rooned' at Ebbets Field."

The second game lasted three hours and twenty-six minutes, the longest nine-inning game in the history of the World Series. Don Larsen, Johnny Kucks, Tom Morgan, Bob Turley, and Mickey McDermott all hurled for the Yankees—a series record of seven pitchers for one team. Larsen, Kucks, and Turley would do much better later on. Berra pounded a grand-slam homer for the losers. Snider contributed a two-run homer for the victors as the Dodgers won, 13–8. "Murder At Ebbets Field," headlined the *Daily News*.

The Yankees recorded their first win of the series in game three in the familiar surroundings of the stadium. Former St. Louis Cardinal star Enos Slaughter hit a three-run home run and Whitey Ford came back from his game-one defeat and went the distance in the 6–3 win. The Yankees tied the series with a fourth-game victory. Mantle homered in the sixth. Hank Bauer belted his first World Series home run in the seventh off a twenty-year-old Californian. It was the first World Series appearance for Don Drysdale. Tom Sturdivant scattered six hits going the distance in the 6–2 Yankee victory.

There were 64,619 in attendance at game five in Yankee Stadium. They stayed through all nine innings, witnesses to one of the great moments in sports history—Don Larsen's pitching of the only perfect game in all the years of the World Series.

A six-foot four-inch, two-hundred-fifteen-pound rangy athlete, Larsen had won seven games and lost twelve in 1953 when he was a member of the St. Louis Browns. In 1954, the Browns became the Baltimore Orioles. Larsen won three games and lost twenty-one. In 1955, he was acquired by the Yankees and reborn. That year he won nine and lost two, and in 1956, Larsen was the victor in eleven of sixteen decisions.

In the second game of the World Series, Larsen had yielded four runs to the Dodgers in less than two innings. On October 8, 1956, the date of the fifth game, he was untouchable—he gave up no runs, no hits, no walks. He struck out seven batters. He was perfect.

The haze and the shadows of the stadium in autumn, the railings along the first and third base lines adorned with World Series buntings, Larsen almost nonchalantly pitching to Yogi Berra from a no-stretch windup, the scoreboard stretching out the zeroes—the images forever remain in the mind's eye. How he did it and against whom he did it further accentuated Larsen's incredible feat. This was not just another baseball team—this was the Dodgers of Snider, Hodges, Furillo, Campanella, Robinson, Reese, Gilliam . . . digging in, waving the bats, trying for the long ball, the seeing-eye single, straining to make contact. Snider had led the National League in slugging percentage, in walks, in home runs, and finished second in total bases and runs scored. Hodges had pounded thirty-two home runs, Furillo, twenty-one, and Campanella, twenty. The team had gotten older but it could still hit.

Five times Larsen's perfection was threatened. A screaming liner by Jackie Robinson in the second inning was knocked down by third baseman Andy Carey. Gil McDougald backed up the play and fired the ball to first base, just nipping the straining Robinson. In the fifth inning, Hodges clobbered the ball to deep left-center field. Mantle raced after the ball and made a spectacular backhanded catch. That same inning, Sandy Amoros rapped the ball into the seats—foul. Larsen got stronger and stronger, pitching toward immortality.

McDougald and Carey made neat fielding plays on balls hit by Gilliam and Hodges in the seventh and eighth innings.

By the seventh inning, the huge crowd cheered every out. The loud murmur of thousands of voices preceded and followed each pitch. Just before Larsen let the ball go, there was total silence. Fans stood or leaned forward in their seats.

"The last three outs were the toughest," said Larsen. "I was so weak in the knees I thought I was going to faint. I was so nervous, I almost fell down. My legs were rubbery, and my fingers didn't feel like they belonged to me. I said to myself, 'Please help me out, somebody.' "

The bottom third of the Dodger batting order was scheduled to hit in the ninth inning. Furillo led off. He flied out. Campanella was next. He bounced out. Former Cleveland Indian star Dale Mitchell, a lifetime .312 hitter, in his eleventh and final major league season, came up as a pinch hitter. There were those whose thoughts went back nine years to Bill Bevens and Cookie Lavagetto. Larsen turned his back on Mitchell and looked at center field for a moment or so. His first pitch was outside—ball one. A slider evened the count. Mitchell swung at and missed the third pitch. The count was one ball and two strikes. Each pitch tightened the tension, triggered the roar of the huge crowd. Larsen blazed in his fifth pitch. Mitchell hesitated and held back. The pitch caught the outside corner of the plate—strike three.

Pandemonium prevailed. Berra charged out to the mound and leaped into Larsen's arms. His Yankee teammates swarmed around Larsen. Thousands of fans broke past security personnel and swept out onto the field. The twenty-seven-year-old Larsen had not been touched by the Dodgers all day. Now he was being pummeled and pounded. He finally made it off the field into the relative sanctuary of the Yankee dugout.

Don Larsen and former sportswriter Arthur Richman were very good friends. "He came from the St. Louis Browns," said Richman, "that was one reason he was one of my favorites. The night before Don pitched the perfect game, I went out with him. He wasn't skunk drunk as many would have you believe. About midnight, Don took some money out of his pocket. 'I don't go to church,' he said. 'Why don't you give this to your mother and let her give it to her synagogue?' I gave the money to my mother and she gave it to the synagogue the next morning. And that day—lightning struck."

Sal Maglie had the misfortune to be the opposing pitcher on the day Larsen hurled his perfect game. Maglie yielded only five hits—one of them was a home run by Mantle, the other was a run-scoring single by Bauer. To this day Maglie says, "I don't want to talk about it. I don't want to think about it. I just want to forget it."

Mrs. Don Larsen, the estranged wife of the Yankee pitcher, had charged that he was delinquent in his support payments for her and their fourteen-month-old daughter and that they were subjected to a starvation diet. A court order issued to Baseball Commissioner Ford Frick asked why Larsen's World Series share should not be held for the payment of the support. After the game, Larsen was convinced to send his wife $420.00 and to pay her $60.00 a week for support.

The teams returned to Ebbets Field for game six. Again the Yankees pitched a no-windup hurler, Bob Turley. And again, the zeroes went up on the scoreboard—but this time they went up for both teams. At the end of nine innings, the game was scoreless. The Dodgers had managed just three hits off the man known as "Bullet Bob." The Yankees had collected four hits off Clem Labine. In the bottom of the tenth inning, Gilliam walked. It was the eighth base on balls issued by Turley, who was battling his control, the Dodgers, and most of the 33,224 iron-lunged zealots screaming for a Brooklyn rally. Snider was intentionally passed after Gilliam moved to second on a sacrifice. Robinson drove an inside pitch to left field over the leaping Enos Slaughter, who misjudged the ball. It sailed over his head, smacking against the outfield wall. The Dodgers won, 1–0. "I pitched the greatest game I ever pitched in my life," says Turley, "and I got beat."

The last World Series game ever played between the Brooklyn Dodgers and the Yankees was no contest. Berra blasted a two-run homer, and then another, knocking out Newcombe, the 1956 National League Most Valuable Player and Cy Young Award winner. Elston Howard whacked a fourth-inning home run and Bill Skowron whacked a grand slammer in the seventh. Allowing just three hits, Johnny Kucks coasted to his 9–0 win over the Dodgers. Never again would there be a Subway World Series.

Afterwards

There's silver in Duke Snider's hair. He is now a broadcaster and sometime batting coach for the Expos in a city that once hosted the top farm team of the Brooklyn Dodgers. Duke's first major league at-bat was April 15, 1947—as a pinch hitter in the first game Jackie Robinson ever played for the Dodgers.

Pee Wee Reese is back in Kentucky. From time to time he travels to banquets and muses about the other members of the Dodger infield. "Billy Cox is gone. Jim Gilliam. Gil Hodges is gone. Jackie Robinson . . . so I'm mighty glad to be here tonight," says the man who will always be number 1, the Captain.

Jerry Coleman is now the manager of the San Diego Padres, and Richie Ashburn is a broadcaster for the Phillies. Phil Rizzuto and his "Holy Cow!" add excitement to Yankee radio and TV broadcasts. Tony Kubek gets better and better each year as baseball's "Game of the Week" announcer.

Eddie Lopat still lives in the lovely home in New Jersey he purchased when he first joined the Yankees. He plays golf and does some scouting for the Expos. He is proud of the bats that were signed by his teammates that form the railing on his bar and the legs on his bar stools. "Steady Eddie" never paid too much attention to the attractions of New York City when he played there. "I knew it was a pleasant place to spend some time in," he says. "It was enjoyable because you did not have to worry about the things you have to worry about now. I wouldn't go in there now unless it was really important."

Johnny Podres is the new pitching coach for the Boston Red Sox, and he's once again battling Yankee batters.

Willie Mays is a designated legend for the Giants of San Francisco and the New York Mets. Old catchers Joe Pignatano and Rube Walker coach for the Mets; old catchers Elston Howard and Yogi Berra coach for the Yankees.

Joe DiMaggio makes a lot of money praising an automatic coffee maker and hyping the image of a New York savings bank by talking about the courage and grit of New York City—a place he rarely visits except for public appearances and the filming of commercials.

Red Barber writes a sports column for a Florida newspaper with the same style and flawless ability that he described those thousands of baseball games. He is still a gracious and gifted Southern gentleman. Mel Allen does cable TV for the Yankees and special appearances.

The Dodgers come into New York City with "L.A." on their caps. Walter O'Malley is dead. His son Peter, who used to play catch as a boy at Ebbets Field with Roy Campanella, is now the president of the Dodgers. Confined to the wheelchair the automobile accident put him into a couple of decades ago, Campy still smiles. He never complained.

Tex Rickards is dead. Shorty Laurice is dead. Garry Schumacher is dead. Hilda Chester is in a convalescent home. Irving Rudd's game now is boxing—he's a publicist for Top Rank, Inc.

Johnny Mize lives in Georgia and broods about not being elected to the Hall of Fame. Sal Maglie is settled in near Niagara Falls; Carl Furillo lives in Stony Creek Mills, Pennsylvania, and works as a night watchman. The sons of Maglie and Furillo wonder whether their fathers will ever be admitted to the Hall of Fame.

Old Dodgers Dick Williams, Tom Lasorda, Don Zimmer manage respectively the Montreal Expos, the Los Angeles Dodgers, the Boston Red Sox. Buzzy Bavasi is building a baseball powerhouse in the California Angels.

Most of the time the man they learned a lot of their trade from, Leo Durocher, is in Palm Springs, telling the old stories. Tommy Holmes works for the New York Mets. Holmes, suddenly remembered by so many fans when Pete Rose broke his consecutive game-hitting streak, is in charge of community relations. Cal Abrams works for Off Track Betting in Manhattan and lives in the suburbs outside New York City.

Billy Martin is still battling. Monte Irvin, stylish and serious, is an assistant to the Commissioner of Baseball; the old days come back easily.

Happy Felton is dead and Hank Thompson and George Weiss and Del Webb and Dan Topping and Snuffy Stirnweiss and Joe Collins and Charlie Dressen and Warren Giles. Casey Stengel and his beloved wife Edna are in Forest Lawn Cemetery. Arthur Richman, in charge of public relations for the Mets, still visits his grave. "We attempted to have Casey buried in Cooperstown," says Richman, "but it did not work out."

Stan Lomax calls himself a "professional old-timer" and feels the sorrow of the loss of old friends dying each year.

Ralph Branca and Bobby Thomson are still residents of the New York City area, linked, as Branca said, "like the Dolly sisters, forever." They have re-enacted the "Shot Heard 'Round the World" many times—they've even reversed roles.

Willy Brandt still mans a baseball switchboard. Nowadays she works only part-time at Shea Stadium where Jim Thomson is a vice-president and manager of all aspects of the ball park.

Joe Black works for the Greyhound Corporation out of Phoenix; Campy and Newk do community relations work with the Dodgers of Los Angeles; Allie Reynolds is back in Oklahoma.

Rachel Robinson heads the Jackie Robinson Foundation located on Court Street in downtown Brooklyn, a short walk from where the old Dodger offices used to be on Montague Street. The office is filled with memorabilia describing the black pioneer and the business of carrying forward the work for social causes that he was so much involved with.

Former Mayor Wagner sits in his beautifully appointed law offices on Park Avenue. The president's personal representative to the Vatican, Wagner is still a baseball fan "but I don't go to games nearly as much as I once used to."

Ebbets Field is now an apartment house complex and just beyond it is the Jackie Robinson Intermediate School. The Polo Grounds is a housing development with a playground named for Willie Mays. "I asked somebody once where the old Polo Grounds was," said Richie Ashburn. "I went there. It's sad. They were intimate, the old places.

Shea Stadium, for example, is like a cheap motel compared to the old ball parks. All the new stadiums are kind of alike."

Yankee Stadium is still there, but it's different, refurbished, remodeled. The playing field covers approximately 3.5 acres. The entire stadium area is on 11.6 acres. A combination of approximately 800 multi-vapor and incandescent lamps illuminate the field, projecting powers up to 1500 watts. The new scoreboard cost thirty times what the Yankees once spent for Babe Ruth. And its size and bulk eliminated the views from the rooftops of nearby apartment houses and the 161st Street station of the IRT where the fans used to watch games.

Dodger Stadium is the antithesis of Ebbets Field. The only privately financed park since Yankee Stadium was built in 1923, Walter O'Malley personally supervised every aspect of construction. "I learned a great deal at Ebbets Field," he said. "I made sure that the park would be beautiful and spacious."

Every one of the 55,000 seats in the column-free stadium has a completely unobstructed view of the symmetrical playing field. There was hardly any parking at Ebbets Field. Dodger Stadium has parking for sixteen thousand automobiles on twenty-one terraced lots adjacent to the five different seating levels. There are seven front rows in the park and no grandstand seat is deeper than twenty-odd rows. Dugout box seats, below ground level, provide a "player's eye view" of the happenings on the baseball field.

The first game in Dodger Stadium history took place on April 10, 1962. The Dodgers of Los Angeles have averaged two million or more fans each season. In 1978, they became the first team in history to draw more than three million.

Old New Yorkers, on vacation or business, go out of their way to attend a game at Dodger Stadium. Norman Bernstein, a retired furrier, who "lived and died with the Brooklyn Dodgers," went to Dodger Stadium once. "Once was enough," he said. "They weren't my Dodgers. Ebbets Field was more fun, much more fun."

The Giants are no longer owned by the Stoneham family, but some of the old-timers are still with the team. Jack Schwarz continues as director of scouting and minor league operations. Hank Sauer is minor league batting instructor. Carl Hubbell is a scout. The man who was so excited when he saw Willie Mays play for the first time,

Eddie Montague, is also still a scout for the Giants, looking for another Mays.

The team now plays in Candlestick Park, a windswept location on Candlestick Point east of the Bayshore Freeway. There are seventy-seven acres of parking that accommodate seven thousand cars and three hundred buses. Adjacent lots can handle another two thousand cars. Candlestick Park's first game was April 12, 1960. When the Giants first left New York they played for two seasons in the Seals' Stadium where Joe DiMaggio once starred. Candlestick Park is very much different from the odd-shaped Polo Grounds. It seats 58,000 and was built at a cost of $24.6 million. The foul lines extend 335 feet, the power alleys 365 feet, center field 410 feet. There are no more "Chinese home runs." The cheapest tickets cost three dollars for youth reserved seats and those who sit in the deluxe mezzanine boxes pay more than seven dollars—what a large family once spent to watch a game at the Polo Grounds.

Never again will there be a time like those eleven New York City baseball years from 1947 to 1957, the smallness and richness of eight teams in each league, the three distinctive teams in one city. The concentration of talent came from players returning from the war and blacks pioneering their way into the national game.

Keepsakes of that time still remain in attics, faded photograph albums, in the backs of closets or drawers: the Dodgerette jackets that teenaged girls purchased to wear when cheering at Ebbets Field, the blue and white buttons that still say, "Keep the Dodgers in Brooklyn," the white and black button made to look like a baseball—"I'm for Jackie," and the photographs of Jackie, at age twenty-eight, handsome, trim, determined.

The Hank Bauer bats and the Mickey Mantle gloves, the Dodger "line drives" publications, and the pennants of the New York Yankees, the Brooklyn Dodgers, the New York Giants—these are keepsakes of that other time still mellowing away in houses and apartments. Some still have the sheet music for a popular song of the time: "Keep the Dodgers in Brooklyn." Some have autographed pictures of Hodges, Reese, Mize, Thomson, Larsen, Ford.

The time comes back always in black and white, in baggy uniforms, in the numbers on the backs of the players. Gionfriddo's catch,

Larsen's perfect game, Robinson stealing home, Sid Gordon Night (the only night ever for a player on the opposition at Ebbets Field), Irvin breaking his ankle, Leo battling the umpires, Mantle smacking the tape measure home run, "This Is Next Year," the headline on the front page of the *Daily News*.

The look of the Schaefer beer sign atop the scoreboard at Ebbets Field and the sound of the train on the elevated line behind Yankee Stadium, these too are keepsakes.

The bleacher lines, the graduation presents that were tickets to a Yankee or Dodger or Giant game, form part of that era. When DiMag retired, when Koufax broke in, when Thomson hit the home run, when Lavagetto doubled, when Mays first came up—these are the markers and mementoes, too.

It will never be the same, but it will always be a time to remember.

NEW YORK GIANTS

POS	Player	AB	BA	HR	RBI	PO	A	E	DP	TC/G	FA	Pitcher	G	IP	W	L	SV	ERA

1947   W-81 L-73   Mel Ott

POS	Player	AB	BA	HR	RBI	PO	A	E	DP	TC/G	FA	Pitcher	G	IP	W	L	SV	ERA
1B	J. Mize	586	.302	**51**	**138**	**1380**	117	6	120	9.8	**.996**	L. Jansen	42	248	21	5	1	3.16
2B	B. Rigney	531	.267	17	59	184	229	11	41	5.9	.974	D. Koslo	39	217	15	10	0	4.39
SS	B. Kerr	547	.287	7	49	270	**460**	17	77	5.4	.977	M. Kennedy	34	148	9	12	0	4.85
3B	L. Lohrke	329	.240	11	35	118	187	20	20	2.9	.938	C. Hartung	23	138	9	7	0	4.57
RF	W. Marshall	587	.291	36	107	334	**19**	10	**6**	2.3	.972	K. Trinkle	**62**	94	8	4	10	3.75
CF	B. Thomson	545	.283	29	85	330	12	7	2	2.7	.980	H. Iott	20	71	3	8	0	5.93
LF	S. Gordon	437	.272	13	57	254	12	8	0	2.2	.971							
C	W. Cooper	515	.305	35	122	560	51	13	8	4.7	.979							
OF	L. Gearhart	179	.246	6	17	94	4	4	1	2.3	.961							
2B	M. Witek	160	.219	3	17	102	125	4	27	5.8	.983							
C	E. Lombardi	110	.282	4	21	86	11	2	2	4.1	.980							

1948   W-78 L-76   Mel Ott W-27 L-38   Leo Durocher W-51 L-38

POS	Player	AB	BA	HR	RBI	PO	A	E	DP	TC/G	FA	Pitcher	G	IP	W	L	SV	ERA
1B	J. Mize	560	.289	**40**	125	**1359**	111	13	**114**	9.8	.991	L. Jansen	42	277	18	12	2	3.61
2B	B. Rigney	424	.264	10	43	258	275	18	48	5.2	.967	S. Jones	55	201	16	8	5	3.35
SS	B. Kerr	496	.240	0	46	269	456	25	72	5.2	.967	R. Poat	39	158	11	10	0	4.34
3B	S. Gordon	521	.299	30	107	126	220	19	19	3.2	**.948**	C. Hartung	36	153	8	8	1	4.75
RF	W. Marshall	537	.272	14	86	266	**16**	5	2	2.0	.983	D. Koslo	35	149	8	10	3	3.87
CF	W. Lockman	584	.286	18	59	**388**	6	5	0	2.8	.987	M. Kennedy	25	114	3	9	0	4.01
LF	B. Thomson	471	.248	16	63	313	10	10	2	2.7	.970	A. Hansen	36	100	5	3	1	2.97
C	W. Cooper	290	.266	16	54	307	21	7	3	4.2	.979	K. Trinkle	53	71	4	5	7	3.18
32	L. Lohrke	280	.250	5	31	125	170	22	21		.931							

1949   W-73 L-81   Leo Durocher

POS	Player	AB	BA	HR	RBI	PO	A	E	DP	TC/G	FA	Pitcher	G	IP	W	L	SV	ERA
1B	J. Mize	388	.263	18	62	906	65	6	77	**9.7**	.994	L. Jansen	37	260	15	16	0	3.85
2B	H. Thompson	275	.280	9	34	197	175	15	44	5.6	.961	M. Kennedy	38	223	12	14	1	3.43
SS	B. Kerr	220	.209	0	19	125	224	15	33	4.1	.959	D. Koslo	38	212	11	14	4	**2.50**
3B	S. Gordon	489	.284	26	90	112	206	14	18	2.7	.958	S. Jones	42	207	15	12	0	3.34
RF	W. Marshall	499	.307	12	70	292	13	8	3	2.3	.974	C. Hartung	33	155	9	11	0	5.00
CF	B. Thomson	641	.309	27	109	488	10	9	4	3.3	.982							
LF	W. Lockman	617	.301	11	65	353	10	10	1	2.5	.973							
C	W. Westrum	169	.243	7	28	224	18	5	4	4.0	.980							
UT	B. Rigney	389	.278	6	47	185	317	32	46		.940							
UT	L. Lohrke	180	.267	5	22	86	143	9	13		.962							
C	R. Mueller	170	.224	5	23	197	21	4	2	4.0	.982							
C	W. Cooper	147	.211	4	21	148	18*	3	2	4.2	.982							

1950   W-86 L-68   Leo Durocher

POS	Player	AB	BA	HR	RBI	PO	A	E	DP	TC/G	FA	Pitcher	G	IP	W	L	SV	ERA
1B	T. Gilbert	322	.220	4	32	784	65	10	80	7.7	.988	L. Jansen	40	275	19	13	3	3.01
2B	E. Stanky	527	.300	8	51	**407**	**418**	20	128	5.6	.976	S. Maglie	47	206	18	4	1	2.71
SS	A. Dark	587	.279	16	67	288	465	30	101	5.1	.962	S. Jones	40	199	13	16	2	4.61
3B	H. Thompson	512	.289	20	91	136	303	**26**	**43**	3.4	.944	D. Koslo	40	187	13	15	2	3.91
RF	D. Mueller	525	.291	7	84	205	7	3	2	1.7	.986	J. Hearn	16	125	11	3	0	1.94*
CF	B. Thomson	563	.252	25	85	394	15	9	5	2.8	.978	M. Kennedy	36	114	5	4	2	4.72
LF	W. Lockman	532	.295	6	52	305	11	7	3	2.5	.978	J. Kramer	35	87	3	6	1	3.53
C	W. Westrum	437	.236	23	71	608	**71**	1	**21**	4.9	**.999**							
IO	M. Irvin	374	.299	15	66	568	50	12	62		.981							

* Numbers in boldface type indicate league-leading statistics.

1951 W-98 L-59 Leo Durocher

POS	Player	AB	BA	HR	RBI	PO	A	E	DP	TC/G	FA	Pitcher	G	IP	W	L	SV	ERA
1B	W. Lockman	614	.282	12	73	1045	89	16	113	9.7	.986	S. Maglie	42	298	23	6	4	2.93
2B	E. Stanky	515	.247	14	43	356	412	18	117	5.6	.977	L. Jansen	39	278	23	11	0	3.04
SS	A. Dark	646	.303	14	69	295	465	45	114	5.2	.944	J. Hearn	34	211	17	9	0	3.62
3B	H. Thompson	264	.235	8	33	64	120	15	16	2.8	.925	D. Koslo	39	150	10	9	3	3.31
RF	D. Mueller	469	.277	16	69	233	5	4	1	2.1	.983	G. Spencer	57	132	10	4	6	3.75
CF	W. Mays	464	.274	20	68	353	12	9	2	3.1	.976	S. Jones	41	120	6	11	4	4.26
LF	M. Irvin	558	.312	24	121	237	10	1	1	2.2	.996							
C	W. Westrum	361	.219	20	70	554	62	8	9	5.1	.987							
O3	B. Thomson	518	.293	32	101	258	139	20	14		.952							
C	R. Noble	141	.234	5	26	144	8	4	3	3.8	.974							

1952 W-92 L-62 Leo Durocher

POS	Player	AB	BA	HR	RBI	PO	A	E	DP	TC/G	FA	Pitcher	G	IP	W	L	SV	ERA
1B	W. Lockman	606	.290	13	58	1435	111	13	155	10.1	.992	J. Hearn	37	224	14	7	1	3.78
2B	D. Williams	540	.254	13	55	279	375	18	102	4.9	.973	S. Maglie	35	216	18	8	1	2.92
SS	A. Dark	589	.301	14	73	324	423	27	116	5.2	.965	L. Jansen	34	167	11	11	2	4.09
3B	B. Thomson	608	.270	24	108	82	184	17	13	3.1	.940	D. Koslo	41	166	10	7	5	3.19
RF	D. Mueller	456	.281	12	49	221	8	3	4	1.9	.987	H. Wilhelm	71	159	15	3	11	2.43
CF	H. Thompson	423	.260	17	67	182	5	4	1	2.7	.979	M. Lanier	37	137	7	12	5	3.94
LF	B. Elliott	272	.228	10	35	83	6	2	0	1.4	.978	G. Spencer	35	60	3	5	3	5.55
C	W. Westrum	322	.220	14	43	481	64	12	11	5.0	.978							
OF	D. Rhodes	176	.250	10	36	97	3	9	0	1.9	.917							
OF	W. Mays	127	.236	4	23	109	6	1	2	3.4	.991							
OF	M. Irvin	126	.310	4	21	44	3	0	1	1.5	1.000							

1953 W-70 L-84 Leo Durocher

POS	Player	AB	BA	HR	RBI	PO	A	E	DP	TC/G	FA	Pitcher	G	IP	W	L	SV	ERA
1B	W. Lockman	607	.295	9	61	1042	100	13	96	9.6	.989	R. Gomez	29	204	13	11	0	3.40
2B	D. Williams	340	.297	3	34	191	254	8	54	4.8	.982	J. Hearn	36	197	9	12	0	4.53
SS	A. Dark	647	.300	23	88	219	343	19	79	5.3	.967	L. Jansen	36	185	11	16	1	4.14
3B	H. Thompson	388	.302	24	74	90	194	13	18	2.9	.956	H. Wilhelm	68	145	7	8	15	3.04
RF	D. Mueller	480	.333	6	60	203	7	6	0	1.8	.972	S. Maglie	27	145	8	9	0	4.15
CF	B. Thomson	608	.288	26	106	391	16	7	0	2.7	.983	D. Koslo	37	112	6	12	2	4.76
LF	M. Irvin	444	.329	21	97	244	10	7	4	2.3	.973	A. Corwin	48	107	6	4	2	4.98
C	W. Westrum	290	.224	12	30	441	53	9	9	4.7	.982	Worthington	20	102	4	8	0	3.44
UT	D. Spencer	408	.208	20	56	179	269	32	52		.933							
32	B. Hofman	169	.266	12	34	55	83	7	18		.952							
OF	D. Rhodes	163	.233	11	30	76	6	3	4	1.8	.965							
1B	T. Gilbert	160	.169	3	16	381	26	2	34	9.3	.995							

1954 W-97 L-57 Leo Durocher

POS	Player	AB	BA	HR	RBI	PO	A	E	DP	TC/G	FA	Pitcher	G	IP	W	L	SV	ERA
1B	W. Lockman	570	.251	16	60	1261	88	18	122	9.4	.987	J. Antonelli	39	259	21	7	2	2.30
2B	D. Williams	544	.222	9	46	353	396	14	112	5.4	.982	R. Gomez	37	222	17	9	0	2.88
SS	A. Dark	644	.293	20	70	289	487	36	105	5.3	.956	S. Maglie	34	218	14	6	2	3.26
3B	H. Thompson	448	.263	26	86	125	267	23	27	3.2	.945	J. Hearn	29	130	8	8	1	4.15
RF	D. Mueller	619	.342	4	71	263	14	6	5	1.8	.979	D. Liddle	28	127	9	4	0	3.06
CF	W. Mays	565	.345	41	110	448	13	7	9	3.1	.985	M. Grissom	56	122	10	7	19	2.35
LF	M. Irvin	432	.262	19	64	274	7	7	0	2.3	.976	H. Wilhelm	57	111	12	4	7	2.10
C	W. Westrum	246	.187	8	27	419	45	7	8	4.8	.985							
C	R. Katt	200	.255	9	33	265	23	8	4	3.6	.973							
OF	D. Rhodes	164	.341	15	50	62	1	1	0	1.7	.984							
UT	B. Hofman	125	.224	8	30	192	32	4	25		.982							

1955 W-80 L-74 Leo Durocher

POS	Player	AB	BA	HR	RBI	PO	A	E	DP	TC/G	FA	Pitcher	G	IP	W	L	SV	ERA
1B	G. Harris	263	.232	12	36	617	50	12	65	9.1	.982	J. Antonelli	38	235	14	16	1	3.33
2B	Terwilliger	257	.257	1	18	212	240	7	70	5.9	.985	J. Hearn	39	227	14	16	0	3.73
SS	A. Dark	475	.282	9	45	213	324	21	70	4.9	.962	R. Gomez	33	185	9	10	1	4.56
3B	H. Thompson	432	.245	17	63	104	262	22	23	3.1	.943	S. Maglie	23	130	9	5	0	3.75
RF	D. Mueller	605	.306	8	83	239	5	6	1	1.7	.976	D. Liddle	33	106	10	4	1	4.23
CF	W. Mays	580	.319	51	127	407	23	8	8	2.9	.982	H. Wilhelm	59	103	4	1	0	3.93
LF	W. Lockman	576	.273	15	49	167	4	3	1	2.1	.983	W. McCall	42	95	6	5	3	3.69
C	R. Katt	326	.215	7	28	482	45	7	7	4.4	.987	R. Monzant	28	95	4	8	0	3.99
2B	D. Williams	247	.251	4	15	139	162	10	39	4.4	.968	M. Grissom	55	89	5	4	8	2.92
UT	B. Hofman	207	.266	10	28	259	59	1	30		.997							
OF	D. Rhodes	187	.305	6	32	68	2	1	0	1.6	.986							
SS	B. Gardner	187	.203	3	17	65	122	12	28	5.2	.940							
30	S. Gordon	144	.243	7	25	57	61	0	6		1.000							

POS	Player	AB	BA	HR	RBI	PO	A	E	DP	TC/G	FA		Pitcher	G	IP	W	L	SV	ERA

1956 W-67 L-87 Billy Rigney

POS	Player	AB	BA	HR	RBI	PO	A	E	DP	TC/G	FA	Pitcher	G	IP	W	L	SV	ERA
1B	B. White	508	.256	22	59	**1256**	111	15	106	**10.0**	.989	J. Antonelli	41	258	20	13	1	2.86
2B	Schoendienst	334	.296	2	14	199	215	3	52	4.9	.993*	R. Gomez	40	196	7	17	0	4.58
SS	D. Spencer	489	.221	14	42	113	169	6	33	4.4	.979	Worthington	28	166	7	14	0	3.97
3B	F. Castleman	385	.226	14	45	90	213	17	10	3.0	.947	J. Hearn	30	129	5	11	1	3.97
RF	D. Mueller	453	.269	5	41	180	4	2	2	1.6	.989	Littlefield	31	97	4	4	2	4.08
CF	W. Mays	578	.296	36	84	415	14	9	6	2.9	.979	J. Margoneri	23	92	6	6	0	3.93
LF	J. Brandt	351	.299	11	47	165	8	2	0	1.8	.989*	H. Wilhelm	64	89	4	9	8	3.83
C	B. Sarni	238	.231	5	23	367	36*	3	9*	5.4	.993	W. McCall	46	77	3	4	7	3.61
OF	D. Rhodes	244	.217	8	59	85	6	4	11	1.4	.958							
SS	A. Dark	206	.252	2	17	89	132	9	27	4.8	.961							
3B	H. Thompson	183	.235	8	29	25	94	12	7	3.0	.908							
OF	W. Lockman	169	.272	1	10	69	3	3	1	1.9	.960							
SS	E. Bressoud	163	.227	0	9	67	125	10	26	4.2	.950							

1957 W-69 L-85 Billy Rigney

POS	Player	AB	BA	HR	RBI	PO	A	E	DP	TC/G	FA	Pitcher	G	IP	W	L	SV	ERA
1B	W. Lockman	456	.248	7	30	981	71	10	94	10.4	.991	R. Gomez	38	238	15	13	0	3.78
2B	D. O'Connell	364	.266	7	28	156	194	7	50	5.3	.980	J. Antonelli	40	212	12	18	0	3.77
SS	D. Spencer	534	.249	11	50	213	342	29	95	5.3	.950	C. Barclay	37	183	9	9	0	3.44
3B	R. Jablonski	305	.289	9	57	44	130	11	15	2.6	.941	Worthington	55	158	8	11	4	4.22
RF	D. Mueller	450	.258	6	37	174	13	2	4	1.6	.989	S. Miller	38	124	7	9	1	3.63
CF	W. Mays	585	.333	35	97	422	14	9	5	3.0	.980	R. Crone	25	121	4	8	1	4.33
LF	H. Sauer	378	.259	26	76	125	4	1	0	1.3	.992	M. Grissom	56	83	4	4	14	2.61
C	V. Thomas	241	.249	6	31	396	31	4	8	4.9	.991							
2B	Schoendienst	254	.307	9	33	141	166	5	41	5.5	.984							
3B	O. Virgil	226	.235	4	24	27	111	11	10	2.4	.926							
1B	G. Harris	225	.240	9	31	502	37	8	53	9.0	.985							
OF	B. Thompson	215	.242	8	38	124	2	1	0	1.8	.992							
OF	D. Rhodes	190	.205	4	19	63	0	0	0	1.4	1.000							
C	R. Katt	165	.230	2	17	238	25	5	4	3.9	.981							

ROSTER 1947–1957

Gordon, Sid, 1947–1949, 1955   OF-IF
Gregg, Hal, 1952   P
Grissom, Marv, 1953–1957   P
Haas, Bert, 1949   IF
Hallett, Jack, 1948   P
Hansen, Andy, 1947–1950   P
Hardy, Red, 1951   P
Harris, Gail, 1955–1957   1B
Harshman, Jack, 1948, 1950   P
Hartung, Clint, 1947–1952   OF
Hausmann, George, 1949   IF
Hearn, Jim, 1950–1956   P
Higbe, Kirby, 1949–1950   P
Hiller, Frank, 1953   P
Hofman, Bobby, 1949, 1952–1957   IF
Howerton, Bill, 1952   OF
Iott, Hooks, 1947   P
Irvin, Monte, 1949–1955   OF
Jablonski, Ray, 1957   IF
Jansen, Larry, 1947–1954   P
Jones, Gordon, 1957   P
Jones, Sheldon, 1947–1951   P
Jorgensen, Spider, 1950–1951   OF-IF
Katt, Ray, 1952–1957   C
Kennedy, Monte, 1947–1953   P
Kerr, Buddy, 1947–1949   IF
Konikowski, Alex, 1948, 1951   P
Koslo, Dave, 1947–1953   P
Kramer, Jack, 1950–1951   P
Lafata, Joe, 1947–1949   OF-IF
Lanier, Max, 1952–1953   P
Layton, Les, 1948   P
Lee, Thornton, 1948   P
Lennon, Bob, 1954   OF
Liddle, Don, 1954–1956   P
Littlefield, Dick, 1956   P
Livingston, Livingston, 1947–1949   C
Lockman, Whitey, 1947–1957   IF-OF
Lohrke, Jack, 1947–1951   IF
Lombardi, Ernie, 1947   C
Lombardo, Lou, 1948   P
Maglie, Sal, 1950–1955   P
Maguire, Jack, 1950–1951   OF
Mangan, Jim, 1956   C
Margoneri, Joe, 1956–1957   P
Marshall, Willard, 1947–1949   OF

Mays, Willie, 1951–1952, 1954–1957   OF
McCall, Windy, 1954–1957   P
McCarthy, Johnny, 1948   FB
McCormick, Mike, 1950   OF
McCormick, Mike Frances, 1956–1957   P
McGowan, Mickey, 1948   P
Miller, Stu, 1957   P
Milne, Pete, 1948–1950   OF
Mize, Johnny, 1946–1949   IF
Monzant, Ray, 1954–1957   P
Mueller, Don, 1948–1957   OF
Mueller, Ray, 1949–1950   C
Newsom, Bobo, 1948   P
Noble, Ray, 1951–1953   C
O'Connell, Danny, 1957   IF
Picone, Mario, 1947, 1952   P
Poat, Ray, 1947–1949   P
Rapp, Earl, 1951   OF
Reyes, Nap, 1950   IF
Rhawn, Bobby, 1947–1949   IF
Rhodes, Dusty, 1952–1957   OF
Ridzik, Steve, 1956–1957   P
Rigney, Bill, 1947–1953   IF
Rodgers, Andre, 1957   IF
Rodin, Eric, 1954   OF
Rufer, Rudy, 1949–1950   IF
Samford, Ron, 1954   IF
Sarni, Bill, 1956   C
Sauer, Hank, 1957   OF
Schenz, Hank, 1951   IF
Schoendienst, Red, 1956–1957   IF
Spencer, Daryl, 1952–1953, 1956–1957   IF
Spencer, George, 1950–1955   P
St. Claire, Ebba, 1954   C
Stanky, Eddie, 1950–1951   IF
Surkont, Max, 1956–1957   P
Taylor, Bill, 1954–1957   OF
Terwilliger, Wayne, 1955–1956   IF
Thomas, Valmy, 1957   C
Thompson, Hank, 1949–1956   OF, IF
Thompson, Junior, 1947   P
Thomson, Bobby, 1947–1953, 1957   OF-IF
Tomasic, Andy, 1949   P
Trinkle, Ken, 1947–1948   P
Virgil, Ozzie, 1956–1957   IF
Voiselle, Bill, 1947   P
Wakefield, Dick, 1952   OF

Warren, Bennie, 1947   C
Weatherly, Roy, 1950   OF
Webb, Red, 1948–1949   P
Westrum, Wes, 1947–1957   C
White, Bill, 1956   IF
White, Fuzz, 1947   OF
Wilhelm, Hoyt, 1952–1956   P
Williams, Davey, 1949,
    1951–1955   IF

Wilson, Artie, 1951   IF
Wilson, Ted, 1952–1953, 1956   OF
Witek, Mickey, 1947   IF
Worthington, Al, 1953–1954,
    1956–1957   P
Wright, Roy, 1956   P
Yvars, Sal, 1947–1953   C

BROOKLYN DODGERS

POS	Player	AB	BA	HR	RBI	PO	A	E	DP	TC/G	FA	Pitcher	G	IP	W	L	SV	ERA
1947 W-94 L-60			Clyde Sukeforth W-1 L-0				Burt Shotton W-93 L-60											
1B	J. Robinson	590	.297	12	48	1323	92	16	**144**	9.5	.989	R. Branca	43	280	21	12	1	2.67
2B	E. Stanky	559	.252	3	53	402	406	12	**123**	5.6	**.985**	J. Hatten	42	225	17	8	0	3.63
SS	P. Reese	476	.284	12	73	266	441	25	99	5.2	.966	V. Lombardi	33	175	12	11	3	2.99
3B	S. Jorgensen	441	.274	5	67	116	235	19	26	2.9	.949	H. Taylor	33	162	10	5	1	3.11
RF	D. Walker	529	.306	9	94	261	9	10	0	1.9	.964	H. Gregg	37	104	4	5	1	5.87
CF	C. Furillo	437	.295	8	88	287	9	7	3	2.5	.977	H. Behrman	40	92	5	3	8	5.48
LF	P. Reiser	388	.309	5	46	240	3	3	0	2.3	.988	C. King	29	88	6	5	0	2.77
C	B. Edwards	471	.295	9	80	**592**	58	11	11	5.2	.983	H. Casey	46	77	10	4	**18**	3.99
OF	G. Hermanski	189	.275	7	39	105	5	2	0	1.7	9.82							
OF	A. Vaughan	126	.325	2	25	56	20	0	3		1.000							
1948 W-84 L-70			Leo Durocher W-36 L-37				Burt Shotton W-48 L-33											
1B	G. Hodges	481	.249	11	70	830	60	13	85	9.4	.986	R. Barney	44	247	15	13	0	3.10
2B	J. Robinson	574	.296	12	85	308	315	13	80	5.5	**.980**	R. Branca	36	216	14	9	1	3.51
SS	P. Reese	566	.274	9	75	**335**	453	31	**93**	**5.5**	.962	J. Hatten	42	209	13	10	0	3.58
3B	B. Cox	237	.249	3	15	51	107	7	7	2.4	.958	P. Roe	34	178	12	8	2	2.63
RF	G. Hermanski	400	.290	15	60	225	13	7	1	2.1	.971	E. Palica	41	125	6	6	3	4.45
CF	C. Furillo	364	.297	4	44	274	13	5	2	2.8	.983	H. Behrman	34	91	5	4	7	4.05
LF	M. Rackley	281	.327	0	15	143	7	8	1	2.1	.949	W. Ramsdell	27	50	4	4	4	5.19
C	R. Campanella	279	.258	9	45	413	45	9	**12**	6.0	.981							
UT	B. Edwards	286	.276	8	54	264	43	12	2		.962							
2B	E. Miksis	221	.213	2	16	122	143	9	19		.967							
OF	D. Whitman	165	.291	0	20	93	3	1	0	2.0	.990							
OF	G. Shuba	161	.267	4	32	87	1	6	1	1.7	.936							
OF	D. Snider	160	.244	5	21	87	5	1	0	2.0	.989							
1B	P. Ward	146	.260	1	21	268	20	3	21	7.7	.990							
3B	T. Brown	145	.241	2	20	43	60	7	7	2.6	.936							
OF	A. Vaughan	123	.244	3	22	47	4	0	0	2.0	1.000							
1949 W-97 L-57			Burt Shotton															
1B	G. Hodges	596	.285	23	115	**1336**	80	7	**142**	9.1	**.995**	D. Newcombe	38	244	17	8	1	3.17
2B	J. Robinson	593	**.342**	16	124	395	421	16	**119**	5.3	.981	P. Roe	30	213	15	6	1	2.79
SS	P. Reese	617	.279	16	73	**316**	454	18	93	5.1	**.977**	J. Hatten	37	187	12	8	2	4.18
3B	B. Cox	390	.233	8	40	104	213	12	28	3.3	.964	R. Branca	34	187	13	5	1	4.39
RF	C. Furillo	549	.322	18	106	286	13	11	2	2.2	.965	J. Banta	48	152	10	6	3	3.37
CF	D. Snider	552	.292	23	92	355	12	6	2	2.6	.984	R. Barney	38	141	9	8	1	4.41
LF	G. Hermanski	224	.299	8	42	140	7	3	1	1.9	.980	E. Palica	49	97	8	9	6	3.62
C	R. Campanella	436	.287	22	82	**684**	55	11	5	**5.9**	.985							
C	B. Edwards	148	.209	8	25	184	13	2	0	4.9	.990							

POS	Player	AB	BA	HR	RBI	PO	A	E	DP	TC/G	FA

1950   W-89 L-65   Burt Shotton

POS	Player	AB	BA	HR	RBI	PO	A	E	DP	TC/G	FA
1B	G. Hodges	561	.283	32	113	1273	100	8	159	9.0	.994
2B	J. Robinson	518	.328	14	81	359	390	11	133	5.3	.986
SS	P. Reese	531	.260	11	52	282	398	26	94	5.3	.963
3B	B. Cox	451	.257	8	44	102	233	15	35	3.3	.957
RF	C. Furillo	620	.305	18	106	246	18	8	2	1.8	.971
CF	D. Snider	620	.321	31	107	378	15	7	1	2.6	.983
LF	G. Hermanski	289	.298	7	34	172	5	2	0	2.3	.989
C	R. Campanella	437	.281	31	89	683	54	11	14	6.1	.985
OF	J. Russell	214	.229	10	32	131	3	1	0	2.5	.993
3B	B. Morgan	199	.226	7	21	33	121	5	15	3.1	.969
OF	T. Brown	86	.291	8	20	31	2	3	0	2.3	.917

Pitcher	G	IP	W	L	SV	ERA
D. Newcombe	40	267	19	11	3	3.70
P. Roe	36	251	19	11	1	3.30
E. Palica	43	201	13	8	1	3.58
R. Branca	43	142	7	9	7	4.69
D. Bankhead	41	129	9	4	3	5.50
C. Erskine	22	103	7	6	1	4.72
B. Podbielan	20	73	5	4	1	5.33
J. Banta	16	41	4	4	2	4.35

1951   W-97 L-60   Chuck Dressen

POS	Player	AB	BA	HR	RBI	PO	A	E	DP	TC/G	FA
1B	G. Hodges	582	.268	40	103	1365	126	12	171	9.5	.992
2B	J. Robinson	548	.338	19	88	390	435	7	137	5.4	.992
SS	P. Reese	616	.286	10	84	292	422	35	106	4.9	.953
3B	B. Cox	455	.279	9	51	140	264	14	26	3.0	.967
RF	C. Furillo	677	.295	16	91	330	24	5	6	2.3	.986
CF	D. Snider	606	.277	29	101	382	12	5	1	2.7	.987
LF	A. Pafko	277	.249	18	58	144	8	1	0	2.0	.993
C	R. Campanella	505	.325	33	108	722	72	11	12	5.8	.986

Pitcher	G	IP	W	L	SV	ERA
D. Newcombe	40	272	20	9	0	3.28
P. Roe	34	258	22	3	0	3.04
R. Branca	42	204	13	12	3	3.26
C. Erskine	46	190	16	12	4	4.46
C. King	48	121	14	7	6	4.15

1952   W-96 L-57   Chuck Dressen

POS	Player	AB	BA	HR	RBI	PO	A	E	DP	TC/G	FA
3B	B. Morgan	191	.236	7	16	45	107	5	10	2.6	.968
1B	G. Hodges	508	.254	32	102	1322	116	11	152	9.5	.992
2B	J. Robinson	510	.308	19	75	353	400	20	113	5.3	.974
SS	P. Reese	559	.272	6	58	282	381	21	89	4.7	.969
3B	B. Cox	455	.259	6	34	100	157	8	26	2.7	.970
RF	C. Furillo	425	.247	8	59	225	12	3	2	1.8	.988
CF	D. Snider	534	.303	21	92	341	13	3	3	2.5	.992
LF	A. Pafko	551	.287	19	85	229	18	3	2	1.8	.988
C	R. Campanella	468	.269	22	97	662	55	4	7	5.9	.994
OF	G. Shuba	256	.305	9	40	116	2	1	0	1.8	.992

Pitcher	G	IP	W	L	SV	ERA
C. Erskine	33	207	14	6	2	2.70
B. Loes	39	187	13	8	1	2.69
B. Wade	37	180	11	9	3	3.60
P. Roe	27	159	11	2	0	3.12
J. Black	56	142	15	4	15	2.15
C. Van Cuyk	23	98	5	6	1	5.16
J. Rutherford	22	97	7	7	2	4.25
C. Labine	25	77	8	4	0	5.14

1953   W-105 L-49   Chuck Dressen

POS	Player	AB	BA	HR	RBI	PO	A	E	DP	TC/G	FA
1B	G. Hodges	520	.302	31	122	1025	99	8	105	8.9	.993
2B	J. Gilliam	605	.278	6	63	332	426	19	102	5.2	.976
SS	P. Reese	524	.271	13	61	265	380	23	83	4.9	.966
3B	B. Cox	327	.291	10	44	86	142	6	20	2.6	.974
RF	C. Furillo	479	.344	21	92	232	11	3	3	1.9	.988
CF	D. Snider	590	.336	42	126	370	7	5	3	2.5	.987
LF	J. Robinson	484	.329	12	95	145	9	3	0	2.1	.981
C	R. Campanella	519	.312	41	142	807	57	10	9	6.2	.989
3S	B. Morgan	196	.260	7	33	71	105	10	19		.946
OF	G. Shuba	169	.254	5	23	59	1	1	1	1.4	.984
1B	W. Belardi	163	.239	11	34	283	23	5	34	8.2	.984

Pitcher	G	IP	W	L	SV	ERA
C. Erskine	39	247	20	6	3	3.54
R. Meyer	34	191	15	5	0	4.56
B. Loes	32	163	14	8	0	4.54
P. Roe	25	157	11	3	0	4.36
B. Milliken	37	118	8	4	2	3.37
J. Podres	33	115	9	4	0	4.43
C. Labine	37	110	11	6	7	2.77
B. Wade	32	90	7	5	3	3.79
J. Hughes	48	86	4	3	9	3.47
J. Black	34	73	6	3	5	5.33

1954   W-92 L-62   Walter Alston

POS	Player	AB	BA	HR	RBI	PO	A	E	DP	TC/G	FA
1B	G. Hodges	579	.304	42	130	1381	132	7	129	9.9	.995
2B	J. Gilliam	607	.282	13	52	340	388	17	99	5.2	.977
SS	P. Reese	554	.309	10	69	270	426	25	74	5.2	.965
3B	D. Hoak	261	.245	7	26	71	139	11	12	2.9	.950
RF	C. Furillo	547	.294	19	96	86	10	9	3		.972
CF	D. Snider	584	.341	40	130	360	8	7	1	2.5	.981
LF	S. Amoros	263	.274	9	34	149	6	2	1	2.2	.987
C	R. Campanella	397	.207	19	51	600	58	7	7	6.0	.989
OF	J. Robinson	386	.311	15	59	153	99	7	6		.973
3B	B. Cox	226	.235	2	17	57	90	6	7	2.6	.961
C	R. Walker	155	.181	5	23	259	19	1	4	5.9	.996

Pitcher	G	IP	W	L	SV	ERA
C. Erskine	38	260	18	15	1	4.15
R. Meyer	36	180	11	5	0	3.99
J. Podres	29	152	11	7	0	4.27
B. Loes	28	148	13	5	0	4.14
D. Newcombe	29	144	9	8	0	4.55
C. Labine	47	108	7	6	5	4.15
J. Hughes	60	87	8	5	24	3.22

1955   W-98 L-55   Walter Alston

POS	Player	AB	BA	HR	RBI	PO	A	E	DP	TC/G	FA
1B	G. Hodges	546	.289	27	102	1274	105	12	126	10.0	.991
2B	J. Gilliam	538	.249	7	40	213	269	16	64	5.0	.968
SS	P. Reese	553	.282	10	61	239	404	23	86	4.7	.965
3B	J. Robinson	317	.256	8	36	74	180	9	18	3.1	.966
RF	C. Furillo	523	.314	26	95	249	10	5	4	1.9	.981
CF	D. Snider	538	.309	42	136	348	9	4	0	2.5	.989
LF	S. Amoros	388	.247	10	51	201	10	6	7	2.0	.972
C	R. Campanella	446	.318	32	107	672	54	6	8	6.0	.992
2S	D. Zimmer	280	.239	15	50	182	199	12	63		.969
3B	D. Hoak	279	.240	5	19	82	183	11	15	3.5	.960
P	D. Newcombe	117	.359	7	23	15	24	4	5	1.3	.907

Pitcher	G	IP	W	L	SV	ERA
D. Newcombe	34	234	20	5	0	3.20
C. Erskine	31	195	11	8	1	3.79
J. Podres	27	159	9	10	0	3.95
C. Labine	60	144	13	5	11	3.24
B. Loes	22	128	10	4	0	3.59
K. Spooner	29	99	8	6	2	3.65
R. Craig	21	91	5	3	2	2.78
E. Roebuck	47	84	5	6	12	4.71
D. Bessent	24	63	8	1	3	2.70

POS	Player	AB	BA	HR	RBI	PO	A	E	DP	TC/G	FA	Pitcher	G	IP	W	L	SV	ERA

1956 W-93 L-61   Walter Alston

POS	Player	AB	BA	HR	RBI	PO	A	E	DP	TC/G	FA	Pitcher	G	IP	W	L	SV	ERA
1B	G. Hodges	550	.265	32	87	1190	103	10	105	9.4	.992	D. Newcombe	38	268	27	7	0	3.06
2B	J. Gilliam	594	.300	6	43	233	326	11	64	5.6	.981	R. Craig	35	199	12	11	1	3.71
SS	P. Reese	572	.257	9	46	263	367	23	79	4.8	.965	S. Maglie	28	191	13	5	0	2.87
3B	R. Jackson	307	.274	8	53	84	184	2	19	3.4	.993	C. Erskine	31	186	13	11	0	4.25
RF	C. Furillo	523	.289	21	83	230	10	4	2	1.7	.984	C. Labine	62	116	10	6	19	3.35
CF	D. Snider	542	.292	43	101	358	11	6	1	2.5	.984	D. Drysdale	25	99	5	5	0	2.64
LF	S. Amoros	292	.260	16	58	123	3	6	0	1.5	.955	E. Roebuck	43	89	5	4	1	3.93
C	R. Campanella	388	.219	20	73	659	49	11	3	5.9	.985	D. Bessent	38	79	4	3	9	2.50
UT	J. Robinson	357	.275	10	43	169	230	9	37		.978							
C	R. Walker	146	.212	3	20	184	20	3	4	4.8	.986							

1957 W-84 L-70   Walter Alston

POS	Player	AB	BA	HR	RBI	PO	A	E	DP	TC/G	FA	Pitcher	G	IP	W	L	SV	ERA
1B	G. Hodges	579	.299	27	98	1317	115	14	115	9.6	.990	D. Drysdale	34	221	17	9	0	2.69
2B	J. Gilliam	617	.250	2	37	407	390	11	90	5.5	.986	D. Newcombe	28	199	11	12	0	3.49
SS	C. Neal	448	.270	12	62	151	298	24	60	4.7	.949	J. Podres	31	196	12	9	3	2.66
3B	P. Reese	330	.224	1	29	51	166	13	5	3.1	.943	D. McDevitt	22	119	7	4	0	3.25
RF	C. Furillo	395	.306	12	66	153	7	2	1	1.5	.988	R. Craig	32	111	6	9	0	4.61
CF	D. Snider	508	.274	40	92	304	6	3	1	2.3	.990	C. Labine	58	105	5	7	17	3.44
LF	G. Cimoli	532	.293	10	57	265	11	6	2	2.0	.979	S. Koufax	34	104	5	4	0	3.88
C	R. Campanella	330	.242	13	62	618	51	5	5	6.7	.993	S. Maglie	19	101	6	6	1	2.93
3S	D. Zimmer	269	.219	6	19	99	170	13	20		.954	E. Roebuck	44	96	8	2	8	2.71
OF	S. Amoros	238	.277	7	26	122	2	2	0	1.9	.984							
C	R. Walker	166	.181	2	23	230	20	2	3	5.0	.992							
OF	E. Valo	161	.273	4	26	57	0	0	0	1.6	1.000							

ROSTER 1947–1957

Abrams, Cal, 1949–1952   P
Amoros, Sandy, 1952–1957   OF
Bankhead, Dan, 1947, 1950–1951   P
Banta, Jack, 1947–1950   P
Barney, Rex, 1947–1950   P
Behrman, Hank, 1947–1948   P
Belardi, Wayne, 1950–1951,
   1953–1954   OF
Bessent, Don, 1955–1957   P
Black, Joe, 1952–1954   P
Borkowski, Bob, 1955   OF
Bragan, Bobby, 1947–1948   C, IF
Branca, Ralph, 1947–1953   P
Bridges, Rocky, 1951–1952   IF
Brown, Tommy, 1947–1951   IF, OF
Campanella, Roy, 1948–1957   C, OF
Casey, Hugh, 1947–1948   P
Chandler, Ed, 1947   P
Cimoli, Gino, 1956–1957   OF
Collum, Jackie, 1957   P
Connors, Chuck, 1949   1B
Cox, Billy, 1948–1954   IF
Craig, Roger, 1955–1957   P
Darnell, Bob, 1954–1956   P
Demeter, Don, 1956–1957   OF
Dockins, George, 1947   P
Drysdale, Don, 1956–1957   P
Edwards, Bruce, 1947–1951   C

Edwards, Hank, 1951   C
Elston, Don, 1957   P
Epperly, Al, 1950   P
Erskine, Carl, 1948–1957   P
Fernandez, Chico, 1956   SS
Furillo, Carl, 1947–1957   OF
Gentile, Jim, 1957   1B
Gilliam, Junior, 1953–1957   IF-OF
Gionfriddo, Al, 1947   OF
Gregg, Hal, 1947   P
Hall, John, 1948   P
Hamrick, Odbert, 1955   OF
Harris, Bill, 1957   P
Hatten, Joe, 1947–1951   P
Haugstad, Phil, 1947–1948, 1951   P
Hermanski, Gene, 1947–1951   OF
Higbe, Kirby, 1947   P
Hoak, Don, 1954–1955   3B
Hodges, Gil, 1947–1957   1B, C, OF
Holmes, Tommy, 1952   OF
Hopp, Johnny, 1949   1B
Howell, Dixie, 1953, 1955   C
Hughes, James R., 1952–1956   P
Jackson, Ransom, 1956–1957   3B
Jorgensen, Johnny, 1947–1950   3B
Kellert, Frank, 1955   OF
King, Clyde, 1947–1948,
   1951–1952   P

Kipp, Fred, 1957   P
Koufax, Sandy, 1955–1957   P
Labine, Clem, 1950–1957   P
Landrum, Joe, 1950, 1952   P
Lasorda, Tom, 1954   P
Lavagetto, Harry, 1947   3B
Lehman, Ken, 1952, 1956   P
Lembo, Steve, 1950, 1952   C
Livingston, Mickey, 1951   C
Loes, Billy, 1950–1955   P
Lombardi, Vic, 1947   P
Lund, Don, 1947–1948   OF
Maglie, Sal, 1956–1957   P
Mallette, Mal, 1950   P
Martin, Morris, 1949   P
Mauro, Carmen, 1953   OF
McCormick, Myron, 1949   OF
McDevitt, Danny, 1957   P
McGlothlin, Pat, 1949–1950   P
Melton, Rube, 1947   P
Meyer, Russ, 1953–1954   P
Mickens, Glenn, 1953   P
Miksis, Eddie, 1947–1951   IF
Miller, Rodney, 1957   IF
Milliken, Bob, 1953–1954   P
Minner, Paul, 1947–1949   P
Mitchell, Dale, 1956   OF
Moore, Ray, 1952–1953   P
Morgan, Bobby, 1950, 1952–1953   IF
Moryn, Walt, 1954–1955   OF
Neal, Charlie, 1956–1957   IF
Negray, Ron, 1952   P
Nelson, Rocky, 1952, 1956   IB
Newcombe, Don, 1949–1957   P
Olmo, Luis, 1947–1951   IF-OF
Pafko, Andy, 1951–1952   OF-IB
Palica, Irv, 1947–1952   P
Pignatano, Joe, 1957   C
Podbielan, Bud, 1949–1952   P
Podres, Johnny, 1953–1957   P
Rackley, Marv, 1947–1949   OF

Ramazzotti, Bob, 1948–1949   IF
Ramsdell, Willard, 1947–1948, 1950   P
Reese, Harold, 1947–1957   SS
Reiser, Pete, 1947–1948   IF, OF
Robinson, Jackie, 1947–1956   IF
Roe, Preacher, 1948–1954   P
Roebuck, Ed, 1955–1957   P
Rojek, Stan, 1947   IF
Romano, Jim, 1950   P
Roseboro, John, 1957   C
Russell, Jim, 1950–1951   OF
Rutherford, John, 1952   P
Schmitz, Johnny, 1951–1952   P
Schultz, Howie, 1947   IB
Sexauer, Elmer, 1948   P
Shuba, George, 1948–1955   OF
Sloat, Dwain, 1948   P
Snider, Edwin "Duke," 1947–1957   OF
Spooner, Karl, 1954–1955   P
Stanky, Eddie, 1947   2B
Stevens, Ed, 1947   IB
Tatum, Tom, 1947   OF
Taylor, Harry, 1947   P
Templeton, Chuck, 1955–1956   P
Terwilliger, Wayne, 1951   IF
Thompson, Charles, 1954   C
Thompson, Don, 1951–1954   OF
Valdes, Rene, 1957   P
Valo, Elmer, 1957   OF
Van Cuyk, Chris, 1950–1952   P
Van Cuyk, John, 1947–1949   P
Vaughan, Floyd, 1947–1948   IF
Wade, Ben, 1952–1954   P
Walker, Dixie, 1947   OF
Walker, Rube, 1951–1957   C
Ward, Preston, 1948   IB
Whitman, Dick, 1947–1949   OF
Williams, Dick, 1951–1954   IF-OF
Wojey, Pete, 1954   P
Zimmer, Don, 1954–1957   IF

NEW YORK YANKEES

POS	Player	AB	BA	HR	RBI	PO	A	E	DP	TC/G	FA	Pitcher	G	IP	W	L	SV	ERA
1947	W-97 L-57		Bucky Harris															
1B	G. McQuinn	517	.304	13	80	1198	93	8	120	9.1	.994	A. Reynolds	34	242	19	8	2	3.20
2B	S. Stirnweiss	571	.256	5	41	337	402	13	107	5.1	.983	S. Shea	27	179	14	5	1	3.07
SS	P. Rizzuto	549	.273	2	60	340	450	25	111	5.4	.969	B. Bevens	28	165	7	13	0	3.82
3B	B. Johnson	494	.285	10	95	136	204	17	12	2.7	.952	J. Page	56	141	14	8	17	2.48
RF	T. Henrich	550	.287	16	98	278	13	5	2	2.2	.983	S. Chandler	17	128	9	5	0	2.46
CF	J. DiMaggio	534	.315	20	97	316	2	1	0	2.3	.997	B. Newsom	17	116	7	5	0	2.80
LF	J. Lindell	476	.275	11	67	308	6	7	1	2.7	.978	V. Raschi	15	105	7	2	0	3.87
C	A. Robinson	252	.270	5	36	346	38	1	3	5.2	.997	K. Drews	30	92	6	6	1	4.91
CO	Y. Berra	293	.280	11	54	307	18	9	5		.973							
OF	C. Keller	151	.238	13	36	85	2	3	0	2.1	.967							
1948	W-94 L-60		Bucky Harris															
1B	G. McQuinn	302	.248	11	41	693	48	5	79	8.3	.993	A. Reynolds	39	236	16	7	3	3.77
2B	S. Stirnweiss	515	.252	3	32	346	364	5	103	5.1	.993	E. Lopat	33	227	17	11	0	3.65
SS	P. Rizzuto	464	.252	6	50	259	348	17	85	4.9	.973	V. Raschi	36	223	19	8	1	3.84
3B	B. Johnson	446	.294	12	64	147	213	20	25	3.2	.947	S. Shea	28	156	9	10	1	3.41
RF	T. Henrich	588	.308	25	100	216	8	5	4	2.2	.978	T. Byrne	31	134	8	5	2	3.30
CF	J. DiMaggio	594	.320	39	155	441	8	13	1	3.0	.972	J. Page	55	108	7	8	16	4.26
LF	J. Lindell	309	.317	13	55	165	7	1	1	2.2	.994							
C	G. Niarhos	228	.268	0	19	376	33	4	7	5.0	.990							
CO	Y. Berra	469	.305	14	98	390	40	9	7		.979							
UT	B. Brown	363	.300	3	48	130	173	18	33		.944							
OF	C. Keller	247	.267	6	44	126	1	3	0	2.0	.977							
1949	W-97 L-57		Casey Stengel															
1B	T. Henrich	411	.287	24	85	445	28	2	64	9.1	.996	V. Raschi	38	275	21	10	0	3.34
2B	J. Coleman	447	.275	2	42	298	315	12	102	5.1	.981	E. Lopat	31	215	15	10	1	3.26
SS	P. Rizzuto	614	.275	5	64	329	440	23	118	5.2	.971	A. Reynolds	35	214	17	6	1	4.00
3B	B. Brown	343	.283	6	61	84	158	13	17	3.0	.949	T. Byrne	32	196	15	7	0	3.72
RF	H. Bauer	301	.272	10	45	156	11	4	3	1.8	.977	J. Page	60	135	13	8	27	2.59
CF	C. Mapes	304	.247	7	38	228	14	6	4	2.3	.976	F. Sanford	29	95	7	3	0	3.87
LF	G. Woodling	296	.270	5	44	163	5	3	1	1.7	.982							
C	Y.Berra	415	.277	20	91	544	60	7	18	5.6	.989							
3B	B. Johnson	329	.249	8	56	77	136	11	16	2.8	.951							
OF	J. DiMaggio	272	.346	14	67	195	1	3	0	2.6	.985							
OF	J. Lindell	211	.242	6	27	114	4	2	1	1.8	.983							
1B	D. Kryhoski	177	.294	1	27	363	31	7	39	7.9	.983							
2B	S. Stirnweiss	157	.261	0	11	121	106	6	34	4.6	.974							

POS	Player	AB	BA	HR	RBI	PO	A	E	DP	TC/G	FA	Pitcher	G	IP	W	L	SV	ERA

1950   W-98 L-56   Casey Stengel

POS	Player	AB	BA	HR	RBI	PO	A	E	DP	TC/G	FA	Pitcher	G	IP	W	L	SV	ERA
1B	J. Collins	205	.234	8	28	480	36	7	62	5.3	.987	V. Raschi	33	257	21	8	1	4.00
2B	J. Coleman	522	.287	6	69	384	384	18	137	5.2	.977	A. Reynolds	35	241	16	12	2	3.74
SS	P. Rizzuto	617	.324	7	66	301	452	14	123	4.9	.982	E. Lopat	35	236	18	8	1	3.47
3B	B. Johnson	327	.260	6	40	82	169	11	20	2.6	.958	T. Byrne	31	203	15	9	0	4.74
RF	H. Bauer	415	.320	13	70	228	8	3	3	2.2	.987	F. Sanford	26	113	5	4	0	4.55
CF	J. DiMaggio	525	.301	32	122	363	9	9	1	2.8	.976	W. Ford	20	112	9	1	1	2.81
LF	G. Woodling	449	.283	6	60	263	16	2	3	2.4	.993	T. Ferrick	30	57	8	4	9	3.65
C	Y. Berra	597	.322	28	124	777	64	13	16	5.8	.985	J. Page	37	55	3	7	13	5.04
OF	C. Mapes	356	.247	12	61	183	8	10	4	2.0	.950							
3B	B. Brown	277	.267	4	37	63	140	9	13	2.6	.958							
1B	J. Mize	274	.277	25	72	490	31	2	73	7.3	.996							
1B	T. Henrich	151	.272	6	34	224	7	3	23	6.9	.987							

1951   W-98 L-56   Casey Stengel

POS	Player	AB	BA	HR	RBI	PO	A	E	DP	TC/G	FA	Pitcher	G	IP	W	L	SV	ERA
1B	J. Collins	262	.286	9	48	556	56	8	65	5.4	.987	V. Raschi	35	258	21	10	0	3.27
2B	J. Coleman	362	.249	3	43	245	268	17	84	5.2	.968	E. Lopat	31	235	21	9	0	2.91
SS	P. Rizzuto	540	.274	2	43	317	407	24	113	5.2	.968	A. Reynolds	40	221	17	8	7	3.05
3B	B. Brown	313	.268	6	51	80	151	11	14	2.7	.955	T. Morgan	27	125	9	3	2	3.68
RF	H. Bauer	348	.296	10	54	188	7	2	1	1.8	.990	S. Shea	25	96	5	5	0	4.33
CF	J. DiMaggio	415	.263	12	71	288	11	3	3	2.7	.990	J. Ostrowski	34	95	6	4	5	3.49
LF	G. Woodling	420	.281	15	71	265	5	2	0	2.3	.993	B. Kuzava	23	82	8	4	5	2.40
C	Y. Berra	547	.294	27	88	693	82	13	25	5.6	.984							
32	G. McDougald	402	.306	14	63	174	249	14	46		.968							
OF	M. Mantle	341	.267	13	65	135	4	6	1	1.7	.959							
1B	J. Mize	332	.259	10	49	632	44	4	86	7.3	.994							
OF	J. Jensen	168	.298	8	25	106	6	3	1	2.4	.974							

1952   W-95 L-59   Casey Stengel

POS	Player	AB	BA	HR	RBI	PO	A	E	DP	TC/G	FA	Pitcher	G	IP	W	L	SV	ERA
1B	J. Collins	428	.280	18	59	1047	73	11	123	9.5	.990	A. Reynolds	35	244	20	8	6	2.06
2B	B. Martin	363	.267	3	33	244	323	9	92	5.4	.984	V. Raschi	31	233	16	6	0	2.78
SS	P. Rizzuto	578	.254	2	43	308	458	19	116	5.2	.976	E. Lopat	20	149	10	5	0	2.53
3B	G. McDougald	555	.263	11	78	124	273	13	38	3.5	.968	J. Sain	35	148	11	6	7	3.46
RF	H. Bauer	553	.293	17	74	233	16	4	2	1.8	.984	B. Kuzava	28	133	8	8	3	3.45
CF	M. Mantle	549	.311	23	87	347	15	12	5	2.7	.968	T. Morgan	16	94	5	4	2	3.07
LF	G. Woodling	408	.309	12	63	241	12	1	4	2.2	.996	B. Miller	21	88	4	6	0	3.48
C	Y. Berra	534	.273	30	98	700	73	6	10	5.6	.992	B. Hogue	27	47	3	5	4	5.32
OF	I. Noren	272	.235	5	21	95	3	0	1	1.6	1.000							
1B	J. Mize	137	.263	4	28	218	18	3	32	8.9	.987							

1953   W-99 L-52   Casey Stengel

POS	Player	AB	BA	HR	RBI	PO	A	E	DP	TC/G	FA	Pitcher	G	IP	W	L	SV	ERA
1B	J. Collins	387	.269	17	44	826	65	10	100	8.0	.989	W. Ford	32	207	18	6	0	3.00
2B	B. Martin	587	.257	15	75	376	390	12	121	5.3	.985	J. Sain	40	189	14	7	9	3.00
SS	P. Rizzuto	413	.271	2	54	214	409	24	100	4.9	.963	V. Raschi	28	181	13	6	1	3.33
3B	G. McDougald	541	.285	10	83	147	299	22	36	3.4	.953	E. Lopat	25	178	16	4	0	2.42
RF	H. Bauer	437	.304	10	57	230	13	2	3	1.9	.992	A. Reynolds	41	145	13	7	13	3.41
CF	M. Mantle	461	.295	21	92	322	10	6	2	2.8	.982	J. McDonald	27	130	9	7	0	3.82
LF	G. Woodling	395	.306	10	58	240	6	1	2	2.1	.996	B. Kuzava	33	92	6	5	4	3.31
C	Y. Berra	503	.296	27	108	566	64	9	9	4.8	.986	T. Gorman	40	77	4	5	6	3.39
OF	I. Noren	345	.267	6	46	208	11	2	1	2.3	.991							
1B	D. Bollweg	155	.297	6	24	323	15	6	37	8.0	.983							
1B	J. Mize	104	.250	4	27	113	7	0	19	8.0	1.000							

1954   W-103 L-51   Casey Stengel

POS	Player	AB	BA	HR	RBI	PO	A	E	DP	TC/G	FA	Pitcher	G	IP	W	L	SV	ERA
1B	J. Collins	343	.271	12	46	759	60	7	105	7.1	.992	W. Ford	34	211	16	8	1	2.82
2B	G. McDougald	394	.259	12	48	224	233	5	84	5.0	.989	B. Grim	37	199	20	6	0	3.26
SS	P. Rizzuto	307	.195	2	15	184	294	16	84	3.9	.968	E. Lopat	26	170	12	4	0	3.55
3B	A. Carey	411	.302	8	65	154	283	15	32	3.8	.967	A. Reynolds	36	157	13	4	7	3.32
RF	H. Bauer	377	.294	12	54	179	6	2	1	1.7	.989	T. Morgan	32	143	11	5	1	3.34
CF	M. Mantle	543	.300	27	102	327	20	9	5	2.5	.975	H. Byrd	25	132	9	7	0	2.99
LF	I. Noren	426	.319	12	66	242	9	5	2	2.2	.980	J. Sain	45	77	6	6	22	3.16
C	Y. Berra	584	.307	22	125	717	63	8	14	5.3	.990							
OF	G. Woodling	304	.250	3	40	164	5	3	1	1.9	.983							
2B	J. Coleman	300	.217	3	21	183	198	9	62	4.9	.977							
1B	B. Skowron	215	.340	7	41	395	28	6	48	7.0	.986							
1B	E. Robinson	142	.261	3	27	227	19	5	21	8.7	.980							

POS	Player	AB	BA	HR	RBI	PO	A	E	DP	TC/G	FA	Pitcher	G	IP	W	L	SV	ERA

1955 W-96 L-58   Casey Stengel

POS	Player	AB	BA	HR	RBI	PO	A	E	DP	TC/G	FA	Pitcher	G	IP	W	L	SV	ERA
1B	B. Skowron	288	.319	12	61	517	37	6	63	7.6	.989	W. Ford	39	254	18	7	2	2.63
2B	G. McDougald	533	.285	13	53	352	348	11	119	5.6	.985	B. Turley	36	247	17	13	1	3.06
SS	B. Hunter	255	.277	3	20	115	249	16	60	3.9	.958	T. Byrne	27	160	16	5	2	3.15
3B	A. Carey	510	.257	7	47	154	301	22	37	3.5	.954	J. Kucks	29	127	8	7	0	3.41
RF	H. Bauer	492	.278	20	53	248	13	5	3	2.0	.981	D. Larsen	19	97	9	2	2	3.06
CF	M. Mantle	517	.306	37	99	372	11	2	2	2.7	.995	B. Grim	26	92	7	5	4	4.19
LF	I. Noren	371	.253	8	59	238	9	5	0	2.0	.980	E. Lopat	16	87	4	8	0	3.74
C	Y. Berra	541	.272	27	108	721	54	13	10	5.4	.984	J. Konstanty	45	74	7	2	11	2.32
OF	E. Howard	279	.290	10	43	124	10	3	1	1.8	.978	T. Morgan	40	72	7	3	10	3.25
1B	J. Collins	278	.234	13	45	395	42	1	63	6.0	.998							
1B	E. Robinson	173	.208	16	42	390	20	2	35	9.0	.995							
OF	B. Cerv	85	.341	3	22	25	1	0	0	1.3	1.000							

1956 W-97 L-57   Casey Stengel

POS	Player	AB	BA	HR	RBI	PO	A	E	DP	TC/G	FA	Pitcher	G	IP	W	L	SV	ERA
1B	B. Skowron	464	.308	23	90	968	80	7	138	8.8	.993	W. Ford	31	226	19	6	1	2.47
2B	B. Martin	458	.264	9	49	241	260	10	84	4.9	.980	J. Kucks	34	224	18	9	0	3.85
SS	G. McDougald	438	.311	13	56	177	273	14	77	5.0	.970	D. Larsen	38	180	11	5	1	3.26
3B	A. Carey	422	.237	7	50	114	265	21	26	3.1	.948	T. Sturdivant	32	158	16	8	5	3.30
RF	H. Bauer	539	.241	26	84	242	10	8	2	1.8	.969	B. Turley	27	132	8	4	1	5.05
CF	M. Mantle	533	.353	52	130	370	10	4	3	2.7	.990	T. Byrne	37	110	7	3	6	3.36
LF	E. Howard	290	.262	5	34	97	2	1	0	1.5	.990	R. Coleman	28	88	3	5	2	3.67
C	Y. Berra	521	.298	30	105	732	55	11	15	5.9	.986	B. Grim	26	75	6	1	5	2.77
01	J. Collins	262	.225	7	43	346	32	1	37		.997	T. Morgan	41	71	6	7	11	4.16
UT	J. Coleman	183	.257	0	18	138	152	9	46		.970							
OF	N. Siebern	162	.204	4	21	100	1	3	0	2.0	.971							
OF	B. Cerv	115	.304	3	25	59	4	1	2	1.5	.984							

1957 W-98 L-56   Casey Stengel

POS	Player	AB	BA	HR	RBI	PO	A	E	DP	TC/G	FA	Pitcher	G	IP	W	L	SV	ERA
1B	B. Skowron	457	.304	17	88	1026	86	9	116	9.7	.992	T. Sturdivant	28	202	16	6	0	2.54
2B	B. Richardson	305	.256	0	19	206	223	9	60	4.7	.979	J. Kucks	37	179	8	10	2	3.56
SS	G. McDougald	539	.289	13	62	247	391	16	104	5.4	.976	B. Turley	32	176	13	6	3	2.71
3B	A. Carey	247	.255	6	33	66	147	5	9	2.7	.977	B. Shantz	30	173	11	5	5	2.45
RF	H. Bauer	479	.259	18	65	200	7	3	1	1.6	.986	D. Larsen	27	140	10	4	0	3.74
CF	M. Mantle	474	.365	34	94	324	6	7	1	2.4	.979	W. Ford	24	129	11	5	0	2.57
LF	E. Slaughter	209	.254	5	34	97	2	0	0	1.5	1.000	A. Ditmar	46	127	8	3	6	3.25
C	Y. Berra	482	.251	24	82	704	61	4	12	6.4	.995	T. Byrne	30	85	4	6	2	4.36
UT	T. Kubek	431	.297	3	39	189	183	20	33		.949	B. Grim	46	72	12	8	19	2.63
OC	E. Howard	356	.253	8	44	246	16	6	4		.978							
01	H. Simpson	224	.250	7	39	198	13	3	19		.986							
23	J. Coleman	157	.268	2	12	89	115	7	33		.967							

ROSTER 1947–1957

Ardizoia, Rugger, 1947   P
Babe, Loren, 1952–1953   IF
Bauer, Hank, 1948–1957   OF
Bella, Zeke, 1957   OF
Berberet, Lou, 1954–1955   P
Berra, Yogi, 1947–1957   C
Bevens, Bill, 1947   P
Blackwell, Ewell, 1952–1953   P
Blanchard, Johnny, 1955   C
Bollweg, Don, 1953   IF
Branca, Ralph, 1954   P
Brideweser, Jim, 1951–1953   IF
Brown, Bobby, 1947–1952,
    1954   IF
Burdette, Lew, 1950   P

Buxton, Ralph, 1949   P
Byrd, Harry, 1954   P
Byrne, Tommy, 1947–1951,
    1954–1957   P
Carroll, Tommy, 1955–1956   IF
Casey, Hugh, 1949   P
Cerv, Bob 1951–1956   OF
Cicotte, Al, 1957   P
Clark, Allie, 1947   C
Coates, Jim, 1956   P
Coleman, Jerry, 1949–1957   IF
Coleman, Rip, 1955–1956   P
Collins, Joe, 1948–1957   IF
Colman, Frank, 1947   P
Courtney, Clint, 1951   C

Del Greco, Bobby, 1957   OF
Delsing, Jim, 1949–1950   OF
DiMaggio, Joe, 1947–1951   OF
Ditmar, Art, 1957   P
Dixon, Sonny, 1956   P
Drews, Karl, 1947–1948   P
Embree, Red, 1948   P
Ferrick, Tom, 1950–1951   P
Ford, Whitey, 1950, 1953–1957   P
Frey, Lonny, 1947–1948   IF
Gorman, Tom, 1952–1954   P
Gray, Ted, 1955   P
Grim, Bob, 1954–1957   P
Gumpert, Randy, 1947–1948   P
Held, Woodie, 1954   IF
Henrich, Tommy, 1947–1950   OF
Hiller, Frank, 1948–1949   P
Hogue, Bobby, 1951–1952   P
Hood, Wally, 1949   OF
Hopp, Johnny, 1950–1952   IF
Houk, Ralph, 1947–1954   C
Howard, Elston, 1955–1957   C
Hunter, Billy, 1955–1956   IF
Jensen, Jackie, 1950–1952   OF
Johnson, Billy, 1947–1951   IF
Johnson, Darrell, 1957   C
Johnson, Don, 1947   P
Keller, Charlie, 1947–1949,
    1952   OF
Konstanty, Jim, 1954–1956   P
Kraly, Steve, 1953   P
Kramer, Jack, 1951   P
Kryhoski, Dick, 1949   IF
Kubek, Tony, 1957   IF-OF
Kucks, Johnny, 1955–1957   P
Kuzava, Bob, 1951–1954   P
Larsen, Don, 1955–1957   P
Leja, Frank, 1954–1955   IF
Lindell, Johnny, 1947–1950   OF
Lollar, Sherman, 1947–1948   C
Lopat, Ed, 1948–1955   P
Lucadello, Johnny, 1947   IF
Lumpe, Jerry, 1956–1957   IF
Lyons, Al, 1947   P
Mack, Ray, 1947   IF
Madison, Dave, 1950   P
Maglie, Sal, 1957   P
Mantle, Mickey, 1951–1957   OF
Mapes, Cliff, 1948–1951   OF
Marshall, Cuddles, 1948–1949   P
Martin, Billy, 1950–1953,
    1955–1957   IF

McDermott, Mickey, 1956   P
McDonald, Jim, 1952–1954   P
McDougald, Gil, 1951–1957   IF
McQuinn, George, 1947–1948   IF
Miller, Bill, 1952–1954   P
Miranda, Willie, 1953–1954   IF
Mize, Johnny, 1949–1953   IF
Mole, Fenton, 1949   IF
Morgan, Tom, 1951–1952,
    1954–1956   P
Muncrief, Bob, 1951   P
Nevel, Ernie, 1950–1951   P
Newsom, Bobo, 1947   P
Niarhos, Gus, 1948–1950   C
Noren, Irv, 1952–1956   OF
Ostrowski, Joe, 1950–1952   P
Overmire, Stubby, 1951   P
Page, Joe, 1947–1950   P
Phillips, Jack, 1947–1949   IF
Pillette, Duane, 1949–1950   P
Porterfield, Bob, 1948–1951   P
Queen, Mel, 1947   P
Raschi, Vic, 1947–1953   P
Renna, Bill, 1953   OF
Reynolds, Allie, 1947–1954   P
Richardson, Bobby, 1955–1957   IF
Rizzuto, Phil, 1947–1956   IF
Robinson, Aaron, 1947   C
Robinson, Eddie, 1954–1956   IF
Sanford, Fred, 1949–1951   P
Scarborough, Ray, 1952–1953   P
Schaeffer, Harry, 1952   P
Schallock, Art, 1951–1955   P
Schmitz, Johnny, 1952–1953   P
Schult, Art, 1953   OF
Segrist, Kal, 1952   IF
Sepkowski, Ted, 1947   IF
Shantz, Bobby, 1957   P
Shea, Spec, 1947–1949, 1951   P
Siebern, Norm, 1956   OF
Silvera, Charlie, 1948–1956   C
Silvestri, Ken, 1947   C
Simpson, Harry, 1957   OF
Skizas, Lou, 1956   OF
Skowron, Bill, 1954–1957   IF
Slaughter, Enos, 1954–1957   OF
Staley, Gerry, 1955–1956   P
Starr, Dick, 1947–1948   P
Stewart, Bud, 1948   OF
Stirnweiss, Snuffy, 1947–1950   IF
Stuart, Martin, 1954   P
Sturdivant, Tom, 1955–1957   P

Terry, Ralph, 1956–1957   P
Tettelbach, Dick, 1955   OF
Throneberry, Marv, 1955   IF
Triandos, Gus, 1953–1954   C
Turley, Bob, 1955–1957   P
Verdi, Frank, 1953   IF
Wakefield, Dick, 1950   OF

Wiesler, Bob, 1951, 1954–1955   P
Wight, Bill, 1947   P
Wilson, Archie, 1951–1952   OF
Wilson, Ted, 1956   OF
Witek, Mickey, 1949   IF
Woodling, Gene, 1949–1954   OF
Workman, Hank, 1950   IF

MISCELLANEOUS STATISTICS

STANDINGS

YEAR	W–L	PCT	POS	W–L	PCT	POS	W–L	PCT	POS
	Dodgers			Giants			Yankees		
1947	94–60	.610	1	81–73	.526	4	97–57	.630	1
1948	84–70	.545	3	78–76	.506	5	94–60	.610	3
1949	97–57	.630	1	73–81	.474	5	97–57	.636	1
1950	89–65	.578	2	86–68	.558	3	98–56	.636	1
1951	97–60	.618	2	98–59	.624	1	98–56	.636	1
1952	96–57	.627	1	92–62	.597	2	95–59	.617	1
1953	105–49	.682	1	70–84	.455	5	99–52	.656	1
1954	92–62	.597	2	97–57	.630	1	103–51	.669	2
1955	98–55	.641	1	80–74	.519	3	96–58	.623	1
1956	93–61	.604	1	67–87	.435	6	97–57	.630	1
1957	84–70	.545	3	69–85	.448	6	98–56	.636	1

INDIVIDUAL AWARDS

Batting Titles

1949 Jackie Robinson (Dodgers) .342
1953 Carl Furillo (Dodgers) .344
1954 Willie Mays (Giants) .345
1956 Mickey Mantle (Yankees) .353

League Home Run Leaders

1947 Johnny Mize* (Giants) 51
1948 Johnny Mize* (Giants) 40
1948 Joe DiMaggio (Yankees) 39
1955 Willie Mays (Giants) 51
1955 Mickey Mantle (Yankees) 37
1956 Duke Snider (Dodgers) 43
1956 Mickey Mantle (Yankees) 52

*tied with Ralph Kiner for title

Runs Batted In

1947 Johnny Mize (Giants) 138
1948 Joe DiMaggio (Yankees) 155
1951 Monte Irvin (Giants) 121
1953 Roy Campanella (Dodgers) 142
1955 Duke Snider (Dodgers) 136
1956 Mickey Mantle (Yankees) 130

Stolen Bases

1947 Jackie Robinson 29
1949 Jackie Robinson 37
1952 Pee Wee Reese 30
1956 Willie Mays 40
1957 Willie Mays 38

Most Valuable Player

1947 Joe DiMaggio (Yankees)
1949 Jackie Robinson (Dodgers)
1950 Phil Rizzuto (Yankees)
1951 Roy Campanella (Dodgers)
1951 Yogi Berra (Yankees)
1953 Roy Campanella (Dodgers)
1954 Willie Mays (Giants)
1954 Yogi Berra (Yankees)
1955 Roy Campanella (Dodgers)
1955 Yogi Berra (Yankees)
1956 Don Newcombe (Dodgers)

1956 Mickey Mantle (Yankees)
1957 Mickey Mantle (Yankees)

Rookie of the Year

1947 Jackie Robinson (Dodgers)
1949 Don Newcombe (Dodgers)
1951 Gil McDougald (Yankees)
1951 Willie Mays (Giants)
1952 Joe Black (Dodgers)
1953 Junior Gilliam (Dodgers)
1954 Bob Grim (Yankees)
1957 Tony Kubek (Yankees)

PITCHERS: WON-LOST PERCENTAGE

Giants and Dodgers

1947 Larry Jansen (Giants)	21–5	.808
1949 Preacher Roe (Dodgers)	15–6	.714
1950 Sal Maglie (Giants)	18–4	.818
1951 Preacher Roe (Dodgers)	22–3	.880
1952 Hoyt Wilhelm (Giants)	15–3	.833
1953 Carl Erskine (Dodgers)	20–6	.769
1954 Johnny Antonelli (Giants)	21–7	.750
1955 Don Newcombe (Dodgers)	20–5	.800
1956 Don Newcombe (Dodgers)	20–7	.794

Yankees

1947 Allie Reynolds	19–8	.704
1950 Vic Raschi	21–8	.724
1953 Ed Lopat	16–4	.800
1955 Tommy Byrne	16–5	.762
1956 Whitey Ford	19–6	.760
1957 Tom Sturdivant*	16–6	.727

*tied

EARNED RUN AVERAGE

Dodgers and Giants

1949 Dave Koslo (Giants)	2.50
1950 Jim Hearn (Giants)	2.49
1952 Hoyt Wilhelm (Giants)	2.43
1954 Johnny Antonelli (Giants)	2.29
1957 Johnny Podres (Dodgers)	2.66

Yankees

1947 Spud Chandler	2.46
1952 Allie Reynolds	2.07
1953 Ed Lopat	2.43
1956 Whitey Ford	2.47

SAVES

Dodgers and Giants

1947 Hugh Casey (Dodgers)	18
1954 Jim Hughes (Dodgers)	24
1956 Clem Labine (Dodgers)	19
1957 Clem Labine (Dodgers)	17

Yankees

1947 Hugh Casey	17
1949 Joe Page	27
1954 Johnny Sain	22
1957 Bob Grim	19

NO-HITTERS

September 9, 1948 Rex Barney (Dodgers) defeated New York Giants, 2–0.

July 12, 1951 Allie Reynolds (Yankees) defeated Cleveland Indians, 1–0.

September 28, 1951 Allie Reynolds (Yankees) defeated Boston Red Sox, 8–0.

June 19, 1952 Carl Erskine (Dodgers) defeated Chicago Cubs, 5–0.

May 12, 1956 Carl Erskine (Dodgers) defeated New York Giants 3–0.

September 25, 1956 Sal Maglie (Dodgers) defeated Philadelphia Phillies, 5–0.

ATTENDANCE

	Dodgers	Giants	Yankees		Dodgers	Giants	Yankees
1947	1,807,596	1,599,784	2,200,369	1953	1,163,419	811,519	1,538,007
1948	1,398,967	1,459,269	2,373,901	1954	1,020,531	1,155,067	1,475,171
1949	1,633,747	1,218,446	2,283,676	1955	1,033,589	824,112	1,490,138
1950	1,185,099	1,009,951	2,081,375	1956	1,213,562	629,267	1,491,594
1951	1,282,628	1,059,539	1,950,107	1957	1,026,158	653,903	1,497,134
1952	1,088,704	984,940	1,629,665